ILLUSTRATED SCIENCE ENCYCLOPEDIA
GREAT INVENTIONS
THAT SHAPED THE WORLD

ILLUSTRATED SCIENCE ENCYCLOPEDIA

GREAT INVENTIONS
THAT SHAPED THE WORLD

All about the amazing scientific discoveries that shaped our world

AUTHORS
STEPHEN BENNINGTON • PETER HARRISON • AL MORRISON • CHRIS OXLADE

CONSULTANTS
PAUL FISHER • JOHN FREEMAN • PETER MELLETT • GRAHAM PEACOCK

LORENZ BOOKS

CONTENTS

INTRODUCTION

Gadgets and machines are so much a part of our lives that we do not think about how they came to be. How we live – what we wear, eat and drink, how we work, travel and enjoy ourselves – has been shaped by discoveries and inventions made throughout history.

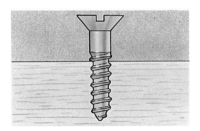

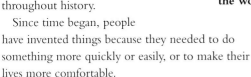

The simple addition of a sloping ramp to a nail created the wood screw.

Since time began, people have invented things because they needed to do something more quickly or easily, or to make their lives more comfortable.

The ancient Egyptians, for example, needed to join parts of their coffins together. They invented metal nails to do the job. The wood screw that joins wood neatly and efficiently was introduced in the 1760s. It added another early invention, the ramp (sloping surface) to the nail idea, to provide the grooved holding power.

Building on the basics

Many inventions are improvements or modifications of what has gone before. Six thousand years ago, the ancient Egyptians and Assyrians worked out that pushing down on a lever helped them to shift the massive blocks of stone needed to build their mighty pyramids and temples. Once the principle had been established, it was adopted and adapted to all sorts of situations. Balancing scales, nutcrackers and pliers are all based on the levering principle. The wheel was modified into its toothed version to make gears, which paved the way for the moving mechanisms of windmills, clocks and watches, and the gear box of a car.

Complex machines such as aircraft or motor vehicles are made up of many simple machines, all working together. They are the result of thousands of years of discoveries of raw materials such as metal ores, of scientific understanding and knowledge, and development of practical inventions.

When someone finds out about a material or substance that exists, such as metal or petroleum, they have made a discovery. Inventions are newly created manmade methods and devices that enable natural resources like this to be used. Solar panels, for example, were devised to harness the power of the sun, and giant spinning turbines convert the energy generated by heat or fast-moving water into a form of electric power that can be used in our homes. Some inventions have

A man's strength is increased by the giant wheels of a treadmill to keep machinery going.

gone through many stages of development to become highly specialized pieces of equipment. The modern camera is an example. It was developed from various discoveries and inventions throughout history, which were, in turn, the launching pad for many other inventions. In a camera, wheels, gears and glass lenses work together to beam light on to a light-sensitive

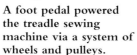

A foot pedal powered the treadle sewing machine via a system of wheels and pulleys.

surface and so record an image. The magnifying and reflective qualities of glass were discovered more than 2,000 years ago. In the 1600s, experiments with lenses led to the development of the telescope and microscope. In the 1700s, hand-painted glass slides were slotted into a magic lantern, and a candle set behind the lens to project the painted image on to a plain surface. The camera as we know it today developed from experiments such as this. Other lines of invention from the same starting point were movies and animation (cartoons). Today, video and computerized photography are further variations on the camera theme.

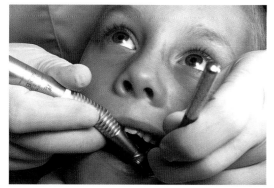

Pneumatic power is added to a simple drill to enable it to cut through enamel and bone.

Global impact

Some inventions affect only the small number of people who may use them. Others revolutionize the lives of us all. The wheel was one of these. The computer is another. It is the ultimate basic machine, one that can be adapted and programmed for the needs of individual users. And like the wheel or the lever, the ubiquitous microchip can be a part of or used to control practically any other machine or process you can think of.

It may seem as if there is nothing left to invent, but it seems to be a basic human instinct. Perhaps the challenge now is to use our knowledge to safeguard the future of our planet. We have learnt to harness nuclear power, but have yet to find a safe way of storing waste from it. Many inventions, such as electrical gadgets and road vehicles, create pollution that threatens the health of our planet. Scientists are learning to produce failsafe, genetically modified crops that could provide food enough for the world's constantly growing population. But they might destroy the balance of the natural world forever.

In 30 years, computers have shrunk from room-sized models to ones that fit on your lap.

The way we live now has been shaped by the inventions of the past. We now have the knowledge to choose the directions of the future. Whichever choices and inventions prevail, they are going to have just as much effect on how our children live as the technological revolutions of the past.

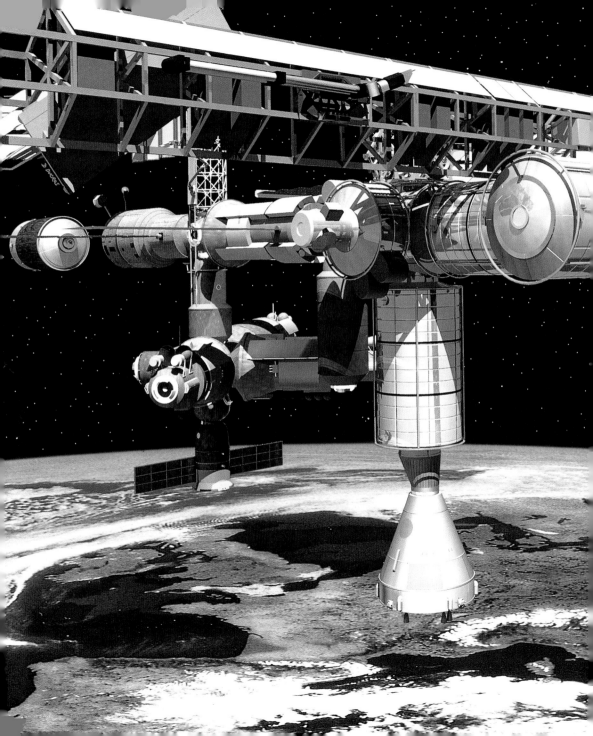

PART ONE

INVENTIONS AND DISCOVERIES

Civilization and the way we live today come from the human being's seemingly endless desire to create something new. The mortar that held Roman buildings together and the computerized medical technology that can make pictures of the human brain are examples of how inventors have worked hand-in-hand with discovery to find new ways to enrich people's lives. Invention is about constant improvement. Beside the Hubble space telescope, Galileo's telescope seems little more than a small, hollow tube, yet without that tube, the space telescope would have been impossible.

AUTHOR
Peter Harrison
CONSULTANT
Peter Mellett

SHAPING OUR WORLD

ANY things you do, from reading this book to flying abroad on holiday, would be impossible without the work of inventors. Without Johannes Gutenberg who, in the mid-1400s invented the first printing press in Europe, this book could not have been printed. In 1903, the brothers Orville and Wilbur Wright were the first people to build and fly an aeroplane successfully. The aeroplane that takes you on holiday could not have been built without their pioneering work.

Human beings have been inventing things for thousands of years. The wooden wheel was first used as a means of transport 5,500 years ago. Inventors have also improved upon existing inventions, to shape the world we live in today. Nowadays trains and cars travel on wheels made of metal and rubber at speeds of up to about 200kph. This book is about how inventions have formed today's world.

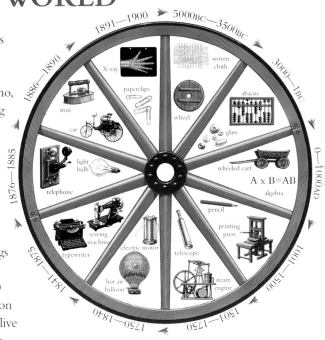

Moving on

In this wheel are some of the objects invented from 4000BC to AD1900 that have fundamentally changed our lives. Follow the arrowheads to see the progression of invention through the ages.

Clean and dry

In the past, people washed clothes by putting them in a tub of hot water and rubbing them with soap. William Sillars invented the first machine for washing clothes in 1890. By turning the big wheel on the lid of the tub, a person could turn the long pegs on the underside of the lid. The moving pegs swirled the clothes around in the tub and so washed out the dirt. The first electric washing machine that washes and spins in a tub, was invented in 1901 by Alva J. Fisher.

modern washing machine

1890 washing machine

Flyer 1

Boeing 747

416 passengers on board

jet engines

tail fin

Big Brother

The Wright Brothers' first aeroplane, *Flyer 1*, was only 6.4m long. A modern *Boeing 747* is over 10 times bigger, and is almost 71m long. Only one person could fly on *Flyer 1*, while a *Boeing 747-400* can carry 416 passengers. Most modern passenger aircraft, such as the *Boeing*, are powered by jet engines. The jet engine was invented by Sir Frank Whittle in 1930.

It's good to talk

People can make telephone calls from wherever they want using a modern cellular phone such as the one seen here (*right*). The first telephone was invented by Alexander Graham Bell in 1876. He is seen in this engraving. He is testing the first telephone line to run between New York and Chicago, United States, in 1892. Bell's telephone sent voice messages along wires. To make a call, the user's phone had to be connected to a telephone wire. Cellular phones use radio waves and do not need wires.

MAKING LIFE EASIER

WITHOUT the development of bricks and mortar, it would not be possible to build the houses we live in today. People in modern houses, schools, offices and factories can turn on lights and heaters at the flick of a switch, turn taps for water, and look out through windows. In the 1700s and before, people had to fetch water from wells. Today water comes into buildings in pipes under the ground. Before there were electric lights, people used to light candles or lamps burning olive or whale oil.

The wires and pipes that supply electricity, water and gas to buildings today were invented in the 1800s. Many different people took part in their invention. The first electric power station was built in New York in 1884, based on the ideas of Thomas Edison. In the early 1800s, William Murdock, a British inventor, was the first person to set up a factory that produced gas for lighting streets and buildings. In the 1800s too, many people in cities were affected by diseases, such as cholera, that were caused by poor hygiene. Sewer pipes were built to carry drain water away from cities to treatment plants.

Straight and narrow
People used bricks to build gateways such as this 5,000 years ago in the part of the Middle East now called Iraq. These bricks made strong walls that could stand for many years.

Built to last
Gates in the German city of Trier (Trèves) were built almost 2,000 years ago. The mortar (cement) that holds the stones in the gates together was invented by the Romans, who then ruled all of France and parts of Germany. The long-lasting strength of mortar is an important reason why so many ancient Roman buildings have survived to this day.

Onwards and upwards
People are lifting blocks of stone on a winch, standing on scaffolding and cutting stone at the top of the tower in this illustration from the 1400s. Winches and scaffolding made it easier to lift heavy weights and keep stone in place.

Dangerous metal

Lead was used for centuries to make the pipes through which water flowed from reservoirs to houses and public buildings such as baths. Lead dissolves in water and harms the health of the people who drink it. Since the 1950s, plastic water pipes have been used as a safer alternative.

Letting in light

Roman glass tiles, such as this one, were made 2,000 years ago. Ways to make sheets of clear glass for windows were not found until the 1200s. In the 1800s, the British scientist, Michael Faraday, invented ways of making really large panes of glass.

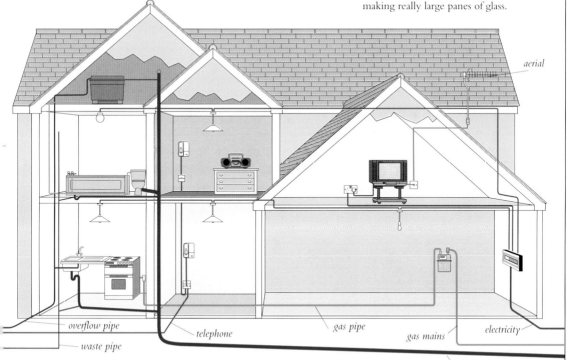

aerial

overflow pipe

telephone

gas pipe

gas mains

electricity

waste pipe

The modern home

A cross-section of a modern house shows some of the amenities that make our lives comfortable. Electricity and telephone wires often run underground but can be carried on poles and pylons from power stations.

water mains

BUILDING FOR STRENGTH

A PLATFORM bridge was one of the earliest human inventions, and was probably first used tens of thousands of years ago. People laid a tree trunk or a single slab of stone across narrow rivers or steep gullies to make travelling across easier. Many modern platform bridges are hollow and made of steel. The model here shows how thin folded sheets make a strong, hollow platform. If you stand on a simple platform bridge, the downward force of your weight makes it sag in the middle. Too much weight can snap a flat wooden plank or crack a stone slab.

Arch bridges, however, as the second project shows, are not flat and they do not sag when loaded. They curve up and over the gap that they span. The Romans were among the first to build arch bridges from many separate stone blocks more than 2,000 years ago. The shape of the bridge holds the stone blocks together. Pushing down on the centre of the bridge creates forces which push outwards so that the load is borne by the supports at either side.

A strong bridge
The Rainhill Bridge spanned the Liverpool and Manchester railway in 1832. It was made by fitting stone blocks around a wooden scaffold. The bridge could support itself when workers hammered the keystone at the very top into place.

MAKE A PLATFORM

You will need: *scissors, stiff card, ruler, pen, 2 boards 20x20cm, modelling clay.*

Your platform is stronger than a platform bridge because it is supported on four sides. Without this support it would sag in the middle.

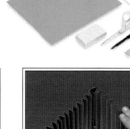

1 Cut out four strips of card 40x10cm. With a ruler and pen, draw lines 1cm apart across each card. Fold each card back and forth across the lines to form zigzag pleats.

2 Lay one board flat on the table. Stand a piece of pleated card upright along the board's edges. Repeat for the other three sides. Use modelling clay to secure each corner.

3 When all sides of the platform are in place, lay the second board on top. Push downwards with your hand. Pleating the card has made the platform very strong.

MAKE AN ARCH

You will need: 2 house-bricks, ruler, sand, 6 wooden toy building blocks, builder's plaster, water, plastic spoon, plastic knife.

1 Although it is not shown in this picture, it would be a good idea to cover the table with newspaper first of all. Place the two bricks on the table. They should be about 20cm apart.

2 Pile up sand between the bricks and smooth it with your hands to make a curved mound. Place the wooden blocks side by side across the sand. The bricks should touch the outer blocks.

Like stone blocks in real bridges, the wooden toy blocks make a remarkably strong curve.

3 Notice that the inner blocks touch each other and have V-shaped gaps between them. Mix the plaster with water until it forms a stiff paste. Use the knife to fill the gaps between the blocks with paste.

4 Make sure you have filled each space where the arch meets the bricks. Wait for the plaster to dry. Once dry, remove the sand from underneath the arch.

5 Push down on the arch and feel how firm it is. The weight that you are putting on the bridge is supported by the two bricks at the side. This bridge is stronger than the platform bridge and does not sag in the middle.

HOME IMPROVEMENTS

EARLY humans lived in caves or shelters made from stones, wood or earth. They first discovered how to start a fire by rubbing sticks together. Fire provided them with warmth and a way to cook. The earliest houses with permanent walls, roofs and windows were built in villages such as Catal Hüyük in southern Turkey around 8,000 years ago. People there washed with hot water, had fireplaces in the middle of rooms and slept on shelves built against the walls of the houses.

Furniture, such as beds, chairs and tables, was first made by the ancient Egyptians. The ancient Romans built huge public baths and even had central heating 2,000 years ago. The basic design of homes has not changed very much since then. However, houses in Europe did not have chimneys until the 1200s and glass windows were unusual until the 1400s. It was not until the 1800s that many houses were built with indoor plumbing, and electric wiring was not built into the walls of houses until the 1900s.

Let there be light
This ancient Greek lamp is similar to those people used all over the world for thousands of years to light their homes. Lamps such as this burn olive oil. The flame they give is smoky and not very bright. Candles were also used for lighting in homes as early as 5000BC.

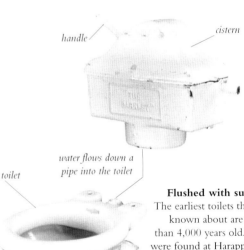

handle / cistern

toilet

water flows down a pipe into the toilet

Flushed with success
The earliest toilets that are known about are more than 4,000 years old. They were found at Harappa and Mohenjo-Daro in Pakistan. Joseph Bramah, who invented the lock, invented the first flush toilet in 1778. This glazed ceramic (pottery) toilet was manufactured in 1850. It used water kept in a cistern (small water tank) above the toilet seat.

Finding the key
Homes need strong locks to keep valuables safe inside. The lock shown in this picture was invented by Joseph Bramah in 1787. It was the safest lock ever invented at the time. He boasted that he would give a reward to anyone who could pick the lock (unlock it without a key). It was 67 years before anyone succeeded.

1910 vacuum cleaner

1993 vacuum cleaner

Crisp creases

For over 2,000 years, people have heated flattened pieces of iron to press on to clothes to smooth out wrinkles. In the past, people heated the iron on a fire or on a stove. In the late 1800s, inventors found a way to heat an iron using electricity. This electric iron was first produced in 1903.

Dust buster

Keeping homes clean has always been a concern. Prehistoric people threw their rubbish on to heaps at the edges of villages. In the 1900s, ways of using a vacuum (airless space) to suck in dirt were invented. This early vacuum cleaner, called the Daisy, was first made in 1910. It worked by using a bellows (pump for sucking out air). Modern vacuum cleaners, such as the 1993 Hoover, use power from an electric motor to suck dirt into a bag.

FACT BOX

• People living about 4,500 years ago in the cities of Harappa and Mohenjo-Daro in Pakistan had proper bathrooms in their public buildings. The well-planned cities were built with running water and drains under the streets.

• The oldest known type of lock, called a pin tumbler, is at least 4,000 years old. The oldest example was discovered in Nineveh, Iraq. Locks of this kind were used by the ancient Egyptians and are still used today in some parts of the world.

• Before people in cities had plumbing, they collected waste water in bowls and threw it out of the window into the street. Sometimes the muck fell on other people's heads.

WEAVING

Secret silk
For centuries, weaving silk was a secret known only to the people of China. They learned how to create fine, richly coloured cloth of the kind seen in this banner. It was buried 2,000 years ago.

ALMOST every kind of cloth is made by weaving. Threads made out of plant material such as cotton, or animal fleece such as wool, are woven on a loom. The oldest pieces of cloth known were found in Switzerland and are estimated to be about 7,000 years old. Before people invented ways to make cloth, they wore the skins of the animals they hunted, to keep warm and dry.

The cotton plant grew plentifully in Egypt and India 5,000 years ago. People there invented ways to weave it into clothing. In other parts of the world clothes were made from the wool of sheep or goats. The flax plant was also used to make cloth called linen. In China silk was woven as long as 4,500 years ago. In the 1700s, several inventions made it much easier to spin and weave both cotton and wool thread. These inventions allowed cloth to be made in much larger quantities than ever before. In the 1900s, artificial fibres such as nylon were invented that allowed new kinds of cloth to be made.

1300s spinning wheel

Fine thread
Silk is made from the thread that forms the cocoon (covering) spun around themselves by silk moth caterpillars. The cocoons are gathered and washed, and then the thread is unwound. The threads are plaited together to make strong thread for weaving. This Chinese painting from 500 years ago shows women spinning silk thread.

Spin me a yarn
The plant fibres or animal hair from which most cloth is made have to be spun together to make them strong. This is called yarn. In the 1300s, people in Europe first began to use spinning wheels such as this to spin thread. Experts believe wheels like this were first invented in India about 4,000 years ago.

*1769
Arkwright
spinning
machine*

Fast and furious

In the 1700s machines were invented that made it possible to weave cloth far more quickly than before. This meant that thread had to be spun more quickly. In 1769, Richard Arkwright invented a spinning machine that used horse power to turn pulleys and rollers. It spun thread much more quickly than on a spinning wheel.

Power weaving

A factory is fitted with some of the first large-scale weaving machines. Large weaving machines powered by steam engines were invented in the 1800s. These machines produced much more cloth than was possible using older ways of weaving. However, the people who looked after the machines in factories like this had to work very long hours in conditions that were often dangerous.

Stretch and bend

Clothes made from wool or plant fibres could be stiff and heavy to wear. Modern clothes made from synthetic fibres are designed to be more comfortable. The clothes this woman is wearing for exercising are made from Lycra, invented in 1953. It is very flexible and ideal to wear when you need to be able to bend.

Lycra

Smooth and shiny

This boy is wearing a raincoat made from polyvinyl chloride (PVC), a kind of plastic invented in 1913. New ways of making material were invented in the 1900s. New kinds of thread called synthetic (artificial) fibre were made from chemicals, not from plants and animal wool. The materials had names such as nylon and polyester.

CLEVER COOKS

PEOPLE cook food, especially meat, because it kills any germs, which makes it safer to eat. Until about 8,000 years ago the only way to cook meat was by roasting. People pushed a spit (metal rod) through an animal's body and held it over a fire while they turned the meat to cook it all over. The Chinese learned 3,000 years ago how to cook many different kinds of food using the Chinese *wok* (a metal cooking bowl). The ancient Egyptians knew how to bake bread in an oven 5,000 years ago. By the time of the ancient Greeks, people cooked using ovens, saucepans and frying pans. Not surprisingly, the first ever cookery book was written 2,300 years ago by the ancient Greek, Archestratus. Cooking methods changed very little for the next 2,000 years.

Ways of preserving food by freezing were invented in the 1800s and have changed the way people eat. Foods that had only been available in certain seasons could then be eaten all year round. Nowadays people can buy food cooked in advance and heat it up in a few minutes in a microwave oven.

Open-air eating
The Dutch artist Pieter Brueghel the Younger painted village people eating together in the 1500s. The huge cooking pot in the background of the painting were used to cook thick soups or stews over open fires.

1921 electric kettle

heat-proof handle

spout

electric element

socket

Mass catering
In medieval Europe many people lived together in monasteries or castles. Cooking was done in huge kitchens such as this. Large fireplaces made it easier to feed many people quickly. These kitchens continued to be used up until the 1800s, as shown in this drawing of 1816.

Quick cuppa
Tea was first mixed with boiling water as a drink in China 2,000 years ago. It became popular in Europe in the 1600s and is now drunk all over the world. Boiling water in a kettle became much faster in the 1900s when electric kettles like this one were invented.

Long-lasting soup

People have known ways of preserving food (keeping it edible over time) for thousands of years. Meat and fish were salted or dried. Fruit and vegetables were stored in the dark or cooked and then sealed in bottles. In the early 1800s, the Frenchman Nicolas Appert found a new way of keeping food fresh. He sealed it into steel cans, as the men in this factory in the mid-1800s are doing.

Frosty food

Freezing keeps food fresh for a long time. Ice cut out from huge blocks was used in Roman times to keep food fresh, but melted quickly. A number of inventors in the 1800s found ways of using air and liquids to flow round a box and keep it cold indefinitely. Electricity was used in the first refrigerator in 1934.

1934 refrigerator

Ready in a flash

Microwave ovens cook food faster than any ordinary cooker. Scientists invented this way of using radio waves to heat food in the 1940s. By the 1950s, the first microwave ovens were being sold.

Instant oven

Before the invention of gas cookers, ovens had to be fuelled with wood or coal each morning which meant a lot of hard work. In the 1800s inventors discovered how to make gas from coal and store it safely so that it could be fed through pipes to people's houses. Modern gas cookers like this one are linked up to gas pipes. The owner just turns a valve and gas flows into the cooker where it is lit to provide instant heat for cooking.

YEAST FACTORY

Foaming fermenting whisky!
When yeast is mixed with sugar it creates lots of tiny bubbles. This is called fermentation. When yeast and sugar are mixed together it creates alcohol.

YEAST is a type of fungus that lives on the skins of many fruits. People all over the world have used it for thousands of years for brewing beer and baking bread. Just a spoonful of yeast contains millions of separate single-celled (very simple) organisms. They work like tiny chemical factories, taking in sugar and giving out alcohol and carbon dioxide gas. While they feed, the yeast cells grow larger and then reproduce by splitting in half. Yeast turns grape juice into alcoholic wine and makes beer from mixtures of grain and water. When added to uncooked dough, yeast produces gas bubbles that make the bread light and soft. Brewing and baking are important modern industries that depend on yeast working quickly.

This project consists of four separate experiments. By comparing the results you can discover the best conditions for yeast to grow. Yeast grows best in wet places. Removing the water makes yeast cells dry out and hibernate (sleep). Add water to powdery dried yeast even after many years and it becomes active again.

FINDING THE BEST CONDITIONS

You will need: *measuring jug, water, kettle, sticky coloured labels, 4 small jam jars, teaspoon, dried yeast granules, sugar, scissors, clear film, rubber bands, 2 heatproof bowls, ice cubes.*

1 Half fill a kettle with water. Ask an adult to boil it for you and then put it aside to cool. Boiling the water kills all living organisms that might stop the yeast growing.

2 Label the glass jars one to four. Put a level teaspoonful of dried yeast into each jar as shown here. Then put the same amount of sugar into each jar.

3 Pour 150ml of water into each of the first three jars. Stir the mixture to dissolve the sugar. Do not pour water into the fourth jar. Put this jar away in a warm place.

4 Cut out pieces of clear film about twice a jar's width. Stretch one across the neck of each jar and secure it with a rubber band. Put the first jar in a warm place.

5 Place the second jar in a glass bowl. Put ice cubes and cold water in the bowl. This mixture will keep the jar's temperature close to freezing.

6 Place the third jar in another glass bowl. Pour in hot water that is almost too hot to touch. Take care not to use boiling water or the jar may crack.

7 Regularly check all four jars over the next two hours. As the ice cubes melt, add more to keep the temperature low. Add more hot water to keep the third jar hot.

high temperature   warm temperature   cold temperature   dry jar

8 In the jar that was kept hot, the yeast is a cloudy layer at the bottom, killed by the heat. The yeast in the jar that was kept warm has fed on the water and sugar, and its gas is pushing up the clear film. The jar that was kept cold has only a little froth on the surface because the cold has slowed down the yeast. In the dry jar, there are no signs of activity, although the yeast is mixed with the sugar.

Discoveries in the lab

Alexander Fleming, a Scottish scientist, identified the properties of the Penicillium mould. Chemists working in laboratories try to invent new substances such as plastics, drugs and dyes. They carry out experiments to see what happens when different chemicals and other substances are mixed together. Most of the apparatus (equipment) is made from glass so that the chemists can see what is inside.

STAYING WELL

early stethoscopes

Hᴜᴍᴀɴ beings have been seeking new ways to cure illness and look after the sick for thousands of years. Today there are many drugs, machines and tools that doctors and nurses can use to fight disease. Yet in some ways little has changed. In ancient Egypt 4,500 years ago, a doctor would use compression (pressure) to stop someone bleeding. A modern doctor would do exactly the same thing. In China 2,000 years ago, doctors knew a great deal about the human body. They also practised a healing technique called acupuncture (inserting needles into parts of the body), which is still used all over the world.

By the 1500s Chinese doctors knew about some of the drugs that we use today. Medicine in the United States and Europe began to develop quickly in the 1800s. Ways were invented to stop germs infecting people and to anaesthetize (make unconscious) patients in surgery. In the 1920s, the British doctor Alexander Fleming discovered, by chance, the first antibiotics (drugs that kill germs). Many more antibiotics have been invented since then which treat different kinds of diseases.

Sounds under the skin

The French doctor René Laënnec invented a hollow tube in the early 1800s that allowed him to hear the sounds inside a patient's chest and heart. It was called a stethoscope. Four different kinds can be seen in this photograph. A doctor can find out whether there is illness in a patient's lungs and heart by listening through a stethoscope.

FACT BOX

• The great Indian physician (doctor) Susruta, first discovered that mosquitoes spread malaria and that rats spread plague 1,500 years ago.

• Doctor Willem Kolff invented the first artificial kidney machine in 1943. Like a kidney, the machine removes poisons from a person's bloodstream. People whose kidneys are too damaged to work use this machine.

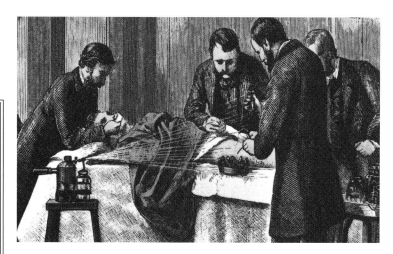

Keeping clean

Surgeons began to use carbolic sprays of the kind shown in this engraving whenever they operated on a patient. Far more people survived surgery because of this. Before the 1800s, many people died after surgery (cutting a body open) because germs infected open wounds. The British surgeon, Joseph Lister, invented a way of preventing this. He washed the wounds in carbolic acid, a chemical that kills germs.

ether inhaler

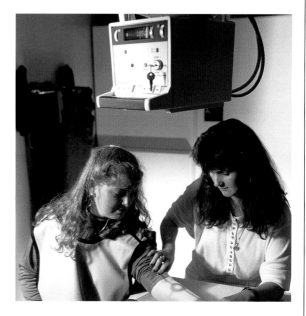

It's a knockout

When surgeons cut people open they are able to give them an anaesthetic (drug that puts people to sleep) to stop them feeling pain. The first modern anaesthetic was discovered in the USA by a dentist, William Morton. In 1846 he used the chemical called ether to stop a patient feeling pain from surgery. Ether inhalers, like the one shown here, were invented to allow patients to breathe in ether before and during an operation.

See-through machine

A radiographer (X-ray specialist) uses an X-ray machine to photograph bones inside a patient's arm. Radiation (radio waves that pass through the air) from the machine passes through the patient and strikes a piece of film leaving a picture of her bones. The German scientist Wilhelm Konrad von Röntgen discovered this special radiation by accident in 1895.

Just a pinprick

Many drugs are given by injecting them into a person's vein or muscle using a hypodermic syringe. Usable syringes were invented in the 1600s but they carried germs. In 1869 the French scientist Luer invented the first all-glass syringe. This was easier to keep germ-free. Disposable syringes became available in the 1970s.

Beating heart

Modern electrocardiographs (ECGs) such as this one can be used in hospitals everywhere to check patients' heartbeats and warn of heart disease. The Dutch scientist Willem Einthoven invented a way of recording the beating of people's hearts as a line on a piece of paper in 1901. However, his machine was very large and heavy. He was awarded the Nobel Prize for his achievement in 1924.

POWER TO THE PEOPLE

D ISCOVERING how to make electricity was one of the most important steps human beings made in using energy for heat, light and many other purposes. Before this discovery, people relied on coal and wood for heat and muscle power for most other work. The ancient Greeks knew that rubbing amber with cloth produces static electricity but they did not know why. From the 1700s, many scientists in Europe and the United States tried to understand how electricity works and how to generate it. It was not until the 1800s that real progress was made. In 1829 Joseph Henry in the USA invented the first true electric motor, a machine that could use electricity to turn moving parts such as wheels and belts. In the 1870s and 1880s in Britain, Sir William Siemens built the first electric railway and the first electric turbines (machines that make electricity by using water force). The age of electricity began in earnest in 1884. The first electric power station, designed by Thomas Edison, was built in New York. In the modern world electricity is used everywhere.

All charged up
The Italian scientist Alessandro Volta shows his invention to the Emperor Napoleon. He invented an electirc battery and named it after himself. He used discs of copper and zinc piled above each other separated by cardboard discs soaked in salt water. When joined together, they produce an electric current.

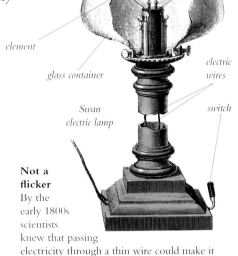

element

glass container

electric wires

Swan electric lamp

switch

Not a flicker
By the early 1800s scientists knew that passing electricity through a thin wire could make it heat up and give out light. But it took until the 1870s for Sir Joseph Swan and Thomas Edison to invent light bulbs that would light an ordinary room without quickly burning out. By the 1880s, the Swan electric lamp was being sold commercially (in shops).

A.

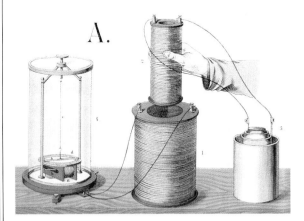

Magnetic power
In 1831 Michael Faraday showed that a magnetic field could produce electricity. Since the 1700s, scientists had experimented to find out if this was possible. Faraday's device produced electricity using changes in the magnetic force of an iron wire. His discovery made it possible to build all later electric generators.

Six-bar sizzler

Electric fires make it very easy for us to warm up when it is cold. The first electric fires were invented in the late 1800s. This fire from the 1900s works in the same way as electric fires of today. Electricity warms up the wire which is coiled around the bars of the fire, to create heat.

1913 Belling electric fire

Bright as day

Electric power enabled work that needed good light, such as making detailed drawings, to be done at night. Before the electric light bulb was invented, people depended on candles, oil lamps and gas lights. They were inconvenient to use. The clear, steady light of electric light bulbs made work easier.

Razzle dazzle

Big cities are full of neon advertisements such as the flashing lights in Piccadilly Circus, London. In 1910, the French chemist George Claude sealed neon gas into a thin glass tube. He discovered that electricity made the gas give out a bright reddish-orange light. Soon after, ways were invented of using this brightly coloured light on the front of buildings to advertise goods.

Power from the atom

A nuclear power station contains nuclear reactors that release energy which generates electricity. The potential of nuclear power was realized with the development of the atomic bomb in World War 2. Making electricity from nuclear power is more expensive than using coal. The radiation from the nuclear waste is also very dangerous.

CREATING ENERGY

ENERGY is needed to do work. Electrical power, steam power, and even horse power are all forms of energy. The two projects described here explore different ways in which energy can do work to make something move. The development of the steam engine and the electric motor in the 1800s provided completely new sources of energy. They used that energy to power ships and railway engines, for example, and to light homes and streets.

The turbine project shows you how the energy of water pouring out of a bottle makes the bottle spin round and round. It is that kind of energy on a much bigger scale that turns turbines in power stations, so generating electricity. The electric motor project shows you how power from an electric battery can turn a cotton reel round and round. Electric motors are used in many household appliances such as vacuum cleaners and washing machines.

Reservoir power
This hydro-electric power station uses falling water to drive turbines that spin generators. The dam is built across a valley and stores water that comes from streams and rivers. Turbines and generators are inside the dam wall.

MAKE A TURBINE

You will need: scissors, plastic drinks bottle, pencil, 2 wide drinking straws, plastic sticky tape, thin string, water.

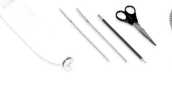

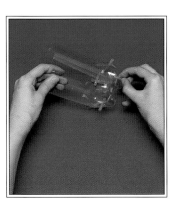

1 Cut off the bottle's top. Use the pencil to poke holes around its base. Cut the straws and push them through the holes. Use sticky tape to hold the straws to the bottle.

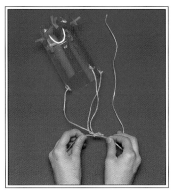

2 Poke three holes around the top of the bottle. Tie three equal lengths of string through the holes and join them to one long piece of string.

3 Hold your turbine over a tray or outdoors so the water will not make a mess. Fill the bottle with water. It squirts out through the straws, causing the bottle to spin.

PROJECT

MAKE AN ELECTRIC MOTOR

You will need: bradawl, ruler, plastic modelling board 5mm thick, (blue) base 15x10cm, 2 (red) end supports 5x5cm, 2 (yellow) coil supports, 6x5cm, 2 (white) coil support spacers 4x1cm, 2 (green) magnet supports 3cm high, glue suitable for sticking plastic, scissors, thin drinking straw, copper wire, aluminium kitchen foil, cotton reel, thin sticky tape, knitting needle 15cm long, 2 powerful bar magnets, 4 paper clips, 2 flexible connecting wires 20cm long, thick plastic sticky tape, 6 volt battery.

1 Use the bradawl to make a hole 1cm from the top of each of the two end supports. Glue them to the base board, 1cm inwards from the shorter edges.

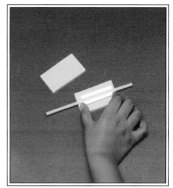

2 Cut a length of straw 12cm. Glue the straw to one coil support. Fix the two coil support spacers either side of the straw. Glue the second support over the top.

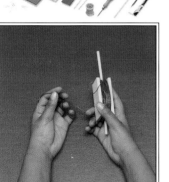

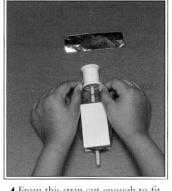

3 Strip 2cm of insulation from one end of the wire and 3cm from the other. Wind the wire tight between the coil supports. Slide the reel on to the straw. Cut a strip of foil the width of the reel.

4 From this strip cut enough to fit three-quarters of the way around the reel. Cut it in half. Put the ends of the wire, which must not touch, against the reel. Tape a piece of foil over each wire so the wire is under the foil's centre.

6 Unbend two paper clips to make hooks. Join one end of each to a connecting wire and fix to the base with thick tape. Using paper clips, join the ends of the wires to the battery. The coil should start spinning round.

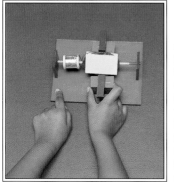

5 Stick the reel to the straw. Hold it between the end plates. Slide the knitting needle through the hole in each end plate. Secure the coil support with wooden blocks. Place the magnets on the supports so that the coil and reel spin freely.

KEEPING IN TOUCH

In the modern world, printed information is found in books, magazines, newspapers and downloaded from computers. None of these would exist without writing and alphabets or without the printing press. The first alphabets were invented between 5,000 and 3,500 years ago in the Middle East, India and the Mediterranean. The letters that make up the words in this book belong to the alphabet invented by the ancient Romans 2,500 years ago. The Romans borrowed and altered the ancient Greeks' alphabet.

Before they knew how to make paper, people in Europe wrote on wax tablets or sheets of parchment (animal skins) or carved words in stone and wood. The Chinese invented papermaking almost 2,000 years ago. The Arabs introduced paper to Europe in the 1100s. The Chinese also invented printing on paper about 1,000 years ago but Johannes Gutenberg invented both movable type (cut-out letters) and the printing press in the mid-1400s. Today, the most popular forms of communication are the telephone, e-mail and the Internet.

Written in stone
The ancient Egyptians had no alphabet. They used written signs called hieroglyphs such as these carved on stone, which illustrate people, animals and gods.

Leaves of skin
Before printing, books in Europe were written by hand. They were often richly decorated. Pictures and writing were made with brushes and pens on parchment.

printing press

printed sheets

ink pad

Read all about it
Johannes Gutenberg examines a page from the printing press that he invented. On the table is a pad for putting ink on the type. The type was made up into words and put under the press. The words were inked, a sheet of paper placed on top of them and the press squeezed down heavily.

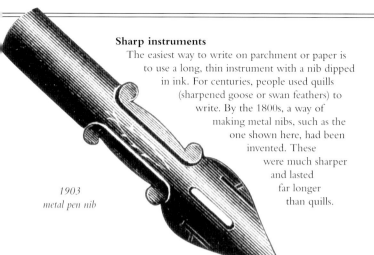

Sharp instruments

The easiest way to write on parchment or paper is to use a long, thin instrument with a nib dipped in ink. For centuries, people used quills (sharpened goose or swan feathers) to write. By the 1800s, a way of making metal nibs, such as the one shown here, had been invented. These were much sharper and lasted far longer than quills.

1903 metal pen nib

FACT BOX

• The oldest alphabet known was found in the ruins of the ancient city of Ugarit in what is now Syria. Tablets found there have an alphabet of 30 characters. The Roman alphabet, used in this book, has 26 characters.

• Before paper was available, people in India and South-east Asia wrote on the leaves of palm trees. These are long and narrow, and must be cleaned before they can be written on. Palm leaves decay easily because of damp, so little of the writing or the leaves has been preserved.

1924 telephone

Neat letters

Documents written on typewriters are easier to read than handwritten ones because the letter shapes do not change and the lines are evenly spaced. Christopher Sholes, the man who invented the first typewriter, was a printer who wanted to find a way to use type for writing rather than printing multiple copies. Sholes's daughter is shown here in 1872 using one of her father's experimental typewriters.

Long distance calls

The invention of the telephone by Alexander Graham Bell in 1876 opened up a new means of communication to people all over the world. Instead of writing to each other, they could simply pick up a telephone and talk. In the 1960s, telecommunication satellites were launched into orbit above the earth, making it easier and much cheaper to talk to people in other countries, often thousands of miles away.

ON THE WIRE

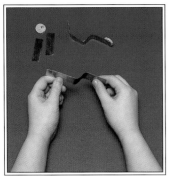

1 Cut 2cm from the end of each copper strip. Bend the longer strips to the shape shown here. Glue a circle of cork to one end.

UNTIL about 200 years ago, the best way to send a message was to write a letter and give it to a rider on a fast horse. In 1838 the American, Samuel Morse, invented an electric telegraph that could send messages over a wire. Morse installed the first telegraph line between Washington and Baltimore in 1844. The first telegraph cable to span the Atlantic Ocean was laid in 1866. Some people have called the telegraph the Victorian Internet. Morse also invented a special code to use with his telegraph. The code is just like an alphabet, but instead of symbols there are long and short bursts of electricity that make blips of sound.

You can make your own telegraph and use it to communicate with a friend. There are two symbols used in telegraph communication, a dot (.) and a dash (-). Each letter of the alphabet is represented by a different group of dots and dashes.

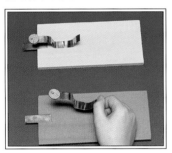

2 Use a drawing pin to fix one 2cm copper strip to each baseboard. Fix one copper strip with the cork to each of the baseboards. Position the cork just over the edge of the board.

MAKE A TELEGRAPH

You will need: scissors, 2 flexible copper strips 10x10cm, strong glue, 2 cork circles, 4 drawing pins, 2 pieces of fibreboard 16x8cm, screwdriver, 2 bulb holders with screws to fix, 2 bulbs, 2 batteries with holders, 2 paper clips, plastic-covered wire.

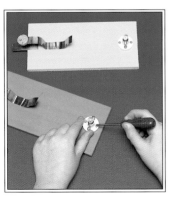

3 Fix each bulb holder to the opposite end of the baseboard. Using a screwdriver, turn the screws clockwise to make them bite into the baseboard.

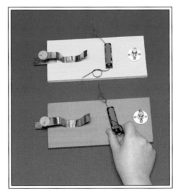

4 Glue a battery holder to each baseboard. Position it midway between the rear of the copper strip and the bulb holder. Remove 1cm of insulation from each of the wires.

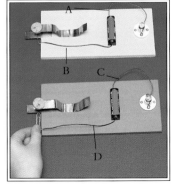

5 Attach the red wires (A and C) to the bulb screws as shown here. Attach the black wires (B and D) to the 2cm copper strip with a paper clip.

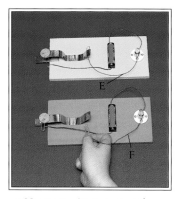

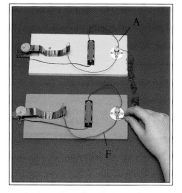

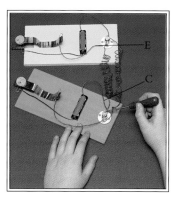

6 Use more wire to connect the rear end of each copper strip to one side of each bulb holder (wires E and F). Tighten the terminals on the holders to make a good connection.

7 Using a length of wire at least a metre long connect wire A to wire F. Make sure the wires are tightly connected.

8 With an equal length of wire connect wire C to wire E as shown here. Again, make sure the wires are tightly conected.

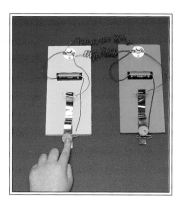

9 The telegraphs are now connected. Press one of the corks down to test whether your telegraph works. Both lights should light up.

10 To make a dash with your telegraph hold down the cork for half a second and to make a dot hold the cork down for a quarter of a second. Now you can try sending messages to a friend. Remember that your partner will have to look up each letter, so leave gaps when sending letters.

Slow talking

A telegraphist of the 1880s could send and receive about 80 letters of the alphabet each minute, which would be about 12 to 15 words a minute. You speak at the rate of about 200 to 300 words a minute.

WARNING!

Please take care when using electrical equipment. Always have an adult present.

WORLD OF SOUND

PEOPLE communicate by sound when they talk to one another, but if they are too far apart, they cannot hear each other. The discovery in the 1800s that it is possible to send sounds over long distances changed people's lives. It allowed them to speak to one another even though they were hundreds of miles apart. Sound can be carried long distances in two ways, along wires or through the air. When Alexander Graham Bell invented the first telephone in 1876, he used wires to send sound. Telephones continued to use wires for many years. In the late 1800s, the Italian Guglielmo Marconi invented a device that sent sounds through the air. It was called radio. Today people all over the world communicate by radio. In the 1800s, machines were also invented that allowed people to store sound so that it could be played back after it had been recorded. The first sound recorder, invented by Thomas Edison in 1877, was called a phonograph. In the mid–1900s, ways were invented to record sound on to tape and plastic compact discs (CDs).

Radio genius
Guglielmo Marconi uses the radio equipment he invented. In 1901 he travelled to Newfoundland in Canada and there received the first transatlantic radio message. This proved that messages could be sent by radio over distances as great as the 4,800km between Europe and America.

Sound bites
On early phonographs such as this 1903 machine the sound was recorded on to a wax-coated cylinder. Each cylinder could only play for three to four minutes. In spite of this, phonographs became very popular.

radio waves

aerial

aerial

radio station

radio

Carried on the air
Sounds such as the human voice are turned into electricity inside a microphone. The electric signal is then transmitted by an aerial as radio waves through the air. These waves travel to an aerial that passes the signal to a radio. The radio can be tuned to turn the signal back into sounds that people can hear.

Sound decorating

By the 1920s radios and speakers such as this were being made for use in the home. The radio, which was finished in a black textured metal case, was orginally designed for use on polar expeditions. The speaker however, was designed to be as beautiful as a piece of furniture.

The Golden Age

By the 1930s, radio had become an entertainment medium (a way of communicating) that broadcast news and music all over the world. People often called the radio the "wireless" because it was not joined to the transmitting station by wires. Millions listened in on radio sets, like the one shown here, to national radio networks such as the BBC in the UK and NBC in the USA.

Dramatically vivid discs

This DVD (Digital Video Disc) player offers a richness of sound and clarity of picture not previously available in other machines. Like a CD (compact disc) player, it uses a laser to scan across the surface of a plastic disc. The digitally recorded sounds on the disc are then fed into earphones through which the user listens.

Cool sounds

This type of radio became very popular in the 1950s. It used transistors, which are tiny electronic components that amplify (strengthen) weak radio signals. Transistor radios were also quite small and therefore portable. The transistor was invented in 1948 and is now used in many electronic devices.

LISTEN TO THIS

Play it again, Sam!
You can play deep notes or low notes on a bass guitar. The sound waves vibrate slowly with a frequency, as low as 50 times each second, high notes vibrate much more rapidly.

S OUND is energy that moves back and forth through the air as vibrations. These vibrations spread outwards as waves, like the ripples caused by a stone dropped into a still lake. Inventors have created ways to communicate by chanelling these sounds.

In the first part of this project, you can see how sound waves can be made to travel in a particular direction. Channelling the sound inside a tube concentrates the waves in the direction of the tube. By channelling sound towards a candle, you can use the energy to blow out the flame. The second part of this project shows how sound is a form of energy. Loud sounds carry large amounts of energy. Scientists say that loud sounds have large amplitudes (variation of range). The last part investigates pitch (range of sounds). Low sounds consist of a small number of vibrations every second. Musicians say low sounds have low pitch but scientists say they have low frequency. You can make a set of panpipes and see how pitch depends on the length of each pipe.

HOW SOUND TRAVELS

You will need: clear film, tube of card, elastic band, candle, matches.

1 Stretch the clear film tightly over the end of the tube. Use the elastic band to fasten it in place. You could also use a flat piece of rubber cut from a balloon.

2 Ask an adult to light the candle. Point the tube at the candle, with the open end 10cm from the flame. Give the clear film a sharp tap with the flat of your hand.

3 You hear the sound coming out of the tube. It consists of pressure waves in the air. The tube concentrates the sound waves towards the candle flame and puts it out.

SOUND WAVES

You will need: *clockwork watch,*
tube 5cmx1m long.

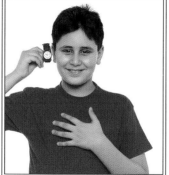

1 Place the watch close to your ear. You can hear a ticking sound coming from it. The sound becomes fainter when you move the watch away from your ear.

2 Place one end of the tube to a friend's ear and hold the watch at the other. The tube concentrates the sound and does not let it spread out. She can hear the watch clearly.

HOW TO MAKE PANPIPES

You will need: *scissors, wide drinks*
straws, modelling clay, card, sticky tape.

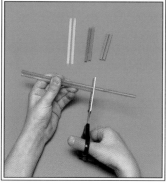

1 Cut the straws so that you have pairs that are 9cm, 8cm, 7cm, and 6cm long. Block one end of each straw with a small piece of modelling clay.

2 Carefully cut out the card to the same shape as the blue piece shown above. Tape the straws into place with the modelling clay along the most slanted edge.

3 Gently blow across the tops of the straws. You will find that the longer pipes produce lower notes than the shorter pipes. The longer pipes have a lower pitch and the shorter pipes have a higher pitch.

SEEING MORE

OVER the centuries, people have invented instruments that increase the power of the human eye. The microscope allows people to see very small things that are close to them. The telescope lets people see things that are very far away. Both microscopes and telescopes use lenses (specially shaped pieces of glass) to magnify the images that the eye sees. Spectacles help people with impaired vision to see clearly.

People knew 2,000 years ago that looking at something through a lens could magnify what they saw. At the beginning of the 1600s the Italian Galileo Galilei invented a tube with two lenses placed in it that allowed him to see details of the surface of the Moon. This was the first telescope. Later in the same century, Robert Hooke in England and Antoni van Leeuwenhoek in Holland invented the first microscopes. Since then microscopes and telescopes have become more and more powerful. By the end of the 1900s, telescopes had been built that can let us see stars trillions of kilometres away. Microscopes now exist that let us see creatures as tiny as germs.

Double vision
In the 1700s Benjamin Franklin, the American statesman, writer and scientist, invented bifocal spectacles. Bifocals are two lenses combined into one. They enable people to see clearly at both short and long distances.

Looking closely
This is one of the first microscopes ever made. It was invented in the 1600s by the English scientist, Robert Hooke. Through it he could see tiny objects such as the cork cells shown in the book on the left. Hooke shone light through the glass globe on the right to light up the objects he looked at through the microscope.

picture of cork cells

microscope

light focused through globe

Fivefold vision
Doctors soon used microscopes so that they could see the human body's parts in great detail. This microscope, invented in the 1800s, has five barrels to allow five different people to look through it at the same time. It was used in medical schools.

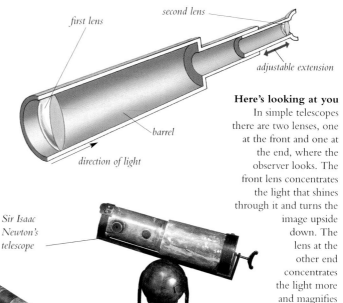

first lens

second lens

adjustable extension

barrel

direction of light

double barrelled

Binoculars such as these were invented in the early 1800s. Like telescopes, they use lenses to make distant objects seem closer but have two barrels rather than one. People using binoculars look through both barrels. Binoculars are shorter and easier to carry around than telescopes.

Here's looking at you

In simple telescopes there are two lenses, one at the front and one at the end, where the observer looks. The front lens concentrates the light that shines through it and turns the image upside down. The lens at the other end concentrates the light more and magnifies the image still further.

Sir Isaac Newton's telescope

Stargazer

When the Italian scientist Galileo Galilei learned in the early 1600s of a telescope invented in Holland he decided to make one for himself. He had soon built a telescope through which he could clearly see the craters on the surface of the Moon. Galileo's telescope allowed him to discover the four largest of the moons around the planet Jupiter, 600 million km from Earth. The telescope to the right of Galileo's was invented by Sir Isaac Newton in the late 1600s.

Galileo's telescope

FACT BOX

• The largest mirror used in a telescope is at the Mount Palomar Observatory in California, USA. The mirror is 5m wide and allows those using the telescope to see for enormous distances deep into space.

• Electron microscopes allow people to see objects as tiny as the individual cells that make up our bodies. These microscopes do not use lenses but beams of electrons (electrically charged particles).

Orbiting observatory

The Hubble space telescope was launched into space in 1990. It orbits the Earth at a distance of 600km. Instead of lenses, it uses mirrors that move to see the stars. The first telescopes like this were invented in the 1600s. The Hubble telescope is much bigger than those. The larger of its two mirrors is 2.4m wide.

BLOW UP

lens

screw

Inner world
Van Leeuwenhoek's
microscope had a spike
and a glass lens on a flat
sheet. He stuck the
object he wanted to
view on the spike and
turned the screw to bring the
object opposite the lens. Then
he turned the microscope over
and looked through the lens.

THE earliest microscope was invented by the Dutch scientist Antoni
van Leeuwenhoek around 1660. It contained a single round glass lens
about the size of a raindrop.

If you look at an ordinary magnifying glass you will see that the two
surfaces curve slightly. The curved surfaces bend light as it travels from the
object to your eye. A window pane has two flat surfaces and so does not
act as a magnifying glass. Powerful magnifying glasses have highly curved
surfaces. Van Leeuwenhoek realized that a glass sphere has the maximum
possible curvature. As a result, a spherical lens has the maximum possible
magnification of about 300 times. The invention of this microscope
opened up a whole new world. For the first time, people could see pollen
grains from flowers, bacteria and the sperm from male animals. In this
project you can make a copy of van Leeuwenhoek's microscope by using
a tiny droplet of water instead of a glass sphere.

JAM JAR MICROSCOPE

You will need: _two large jam jars,_
water, a pencil.

2 Find the
position that
gives the clearest
image with the
greatest
magnification.

1 Fill a jam jar with water and
place it at the edge of a table.
Look through the jar with one eye
and move the pencil back and forth
behind the jam jar.

4 You will find
that the image
is about four or
five times larger
than before.

3 Place a second water-filled jam
jar close behind the first one.
Hold the pencil in the water in the
second jar. Move the pencil back
and forth.

WATER DROP MAGNIFIER

You will need: *aluminium milk bottle cap, metal spoon, candle, small nail, water, flower.*

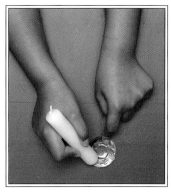

1 Place the milk bottle cap on a hard surface. Use the outer bowl of a spoon to flatten the cap. Stroke the spoon from side to side until the centre of the cap is flat and smooth.

2 Rub the milk bottle cap on both sides with the end of a candle. Make certain that both sides of the smooth centre part are coated with a thin layer of wax.

3 Push the nail through the centre of the milk bottle cap to make a small hole in it. The hole should be perfectly round and measure about 2mm across

4 Collect water on a fingertip so that a droplet hangs down. Hold the cap flat and lower the drop on to the hole. The wax holds the water in a round lens shape.

5 To use your magnifier, hold it about 1 to 2cm from the object. Now bring your eye as close to the water droplet as possible. Look at how the flower is magnified.

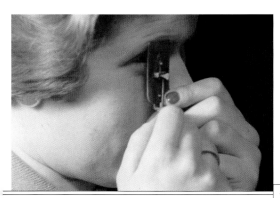

The world in a grain of sand
This woman is using van Leeuwenhoek's simple microscope by pressing it against her eye. Unlike most later microscopes, this was not a heavy instrument which could not be moved easily but a light, portable object. By using this microscope scientists were able to discover much more about the world around us, including the insides of our own bodies.

PICTURE SHOWS

Box of tricks
This early camera was so large and cumbersome that the user needed a handcart to carry it in. The extra equipment is for developing the photographs. This camera dates from the 1850s.

A SIMPLE form of photography began almost 2,000 years ago. The ancient Greeks discovered that light passing through a small hole in the wall of a dark room would make an image in the room of what was outside. In the 1500s, scientists discovered the same happened if a tiny hole was made in a completely dark room. They called the room a *camera obscura*. In the early 1800s scientists tried to find a way to permanently record the image this box made. If they were successful, it would mean that they could make pictures of the world without drawing or painting. The scientists put lenses into their cameras to sharpen the image. In 1840 William Fox Talbot invented a way of coating paper with light-sensitive chemicals that recorded the camera's image permanently.

By the late 1800s Thomas Edison had invented a camera that could record motion, and a kinetoscope, a machine that could project moving pictures. By the beginning of the 1900s, motion pictures were being made and shown commercially. Now cinema is one of the biggest forms of entertainment in the world.

Silver light
Photographs like this portrait of the English inventor Michael Faraday with his wife were made in the mid-1800s. They are known as daguerreotypes after their inventor, Louis Daguerre. They were made on small sheets of copper coated with a light-sensitive layer of silver.

Positive outlook
The images in most cameras are made on to negatives. From these, the positives (the prints) are made. Using negatives means many prints can be made from one negative. The Polaroid camera shown here was invented in the 1940s. It was called an instant camera because it produced a positive image immediately.

Polaroid camera

Freeze-frame gallops

The first accurate photographs of an animal in motion were taken by the English photographer Eadweard Muybridge. While in California in 1877, Muybridge was asked by a horse trainer to take pictures of a racehorse. The trainer wanted to prove for a bet that all four of a galloping horse's legs came off the ground at the same time for a split second during the gallop. As these photographs show, the trainer was correct.

The full works

Two French brothers, Auguste and Louis Lumière, invented this camera for moving pictures in 1895. It was both a camera and a projector and so was much better than Edison's early kinetoscope. The brothers called their invention a *cinématographe*, which has given us the modern word cinema.

cinématographe

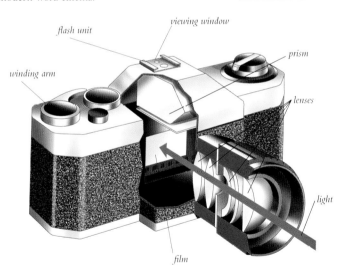

flash unit
viewing window
prism
winding arm
lenses
light
film

Reflex action

Single lens reflex (SLR) cameras became very popular after they were first developed in the 1930s. Light enters the camera through the lenses at the front and strikes the negative at the back. Users can see clearly what they are photographing by means of a prism mounted in the camera.

Picture by numbers

Digital cameras receive light through a lens in the same way as ordinary cameras. The difference in a digital camera is that the light, instead of striking a piece of plastic film, is digitally recorded by light sensors. The digital information is then stored inside the camera and can be played back on a computer screen.

WINDOW ON THE WORLD

ONCE Guglielmo Marconi had invented a way to broadcast sound and people became interested in radio, inventors soon tried to find a way to broadcast pictures. John Logie Baird, a Scottish inventor, set himself the task of achieving this. Unfortunately no one else believed it was possible to broadcast pictures and he was forced to work alone and in great poverty.

In 1926, Baird finally succeeded in sending a picture a few metres, but his way of sending pictures was not perfect. In the 1930s Vladimir Zworykin, a Russian electrical engineer, invented a better way to send pictures by using electricity to run through a cathode ray tube. Zworykin's invention was essential for modern television. The first public television programmes were broadcast by the BBC in Britain in 1936, and by the 1950s, televisions were beginning to appear in every home in the United States and Europe.

dummy *disc* *electric motor*

Spinning circle
The first picture to be captured as electrical impulses was a dummy's head. Baird placed three discs with holes in them in front of the dummy. These created flashing patterns of light that were turned into electrical impulses by a photoelectric cell (device for turning light into electricity).

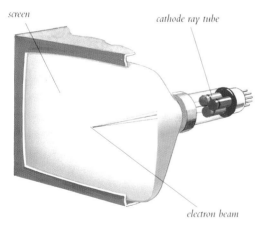

screen *cathode ray tube*

electron beam

Tube travel
The cathode ray tube is the heart of a television. Pictures are received by the aerial in the form of electrical impulses. These impulses control a stream of electrons inside the cathode ray tube. The electron beam scans across the screen and creates the picture as points of coloured light. This is the picture that the viewer sees.

1950s television

Box in the corner
The televisions that large numbers of people first began to buy in the 1950s looked very much like this one. The screens were small and the pictures could only be seen as black–and–white images. Reception was also difficult because there were very few transmitters.

Light in the gloom

When television was first widely broadcast, people saw it as something very new. Most programmes were broadcast only in the evenings and families gathered together to enjoy this new form of entertainment. Gradually more and more people bought televisions.

Moving eye

The cameras used in modern television studios are much more complicated devices than John Logie Baird's invention. This camera is on wheels and can move around the people or objects being filmed. It can move in closer and tilt up or down. Inside the camera, the image is changed into electrical impulses.

Super cool

Modern television screens are much bigger than those available in the 1950s and most are in colour. Flat-screen televisions, such as this one, first became available in the early 1990s. These televisions do not have cathode-ray tubes. Liquid crystals display the picture on the screen.

SCREEN SCENES

THE picture on a television screen is made up from thin lines of light. Follow the instructions in this project and you will also see that the picture consists of just three colours – red, green and blue. Viewed from a distance, these colours mix to produce the full range of colours that we see naturally around us. A TV picture is just rows of glowing dots of coloured light. Fax machines work in a similar way to TV, only more slowly. Feed a sheet of paper into a fax machine and a beam of light moves back and forth across it. Dark places absorb the light and pale places reflect it. The reflected light enters a detector that produces an electric current. The strength of the current depends on the intensity of the reflected light. The electric current is changed into a code made up from chirping sounds that travel down the line to the receiving fax machine. The code controls a scanner that moves across heat-sensitive paper and produces a *facsimile* (copy) of the original. The last part of this project shows how a fax machine breaks an image into tiny areas that are either black or white.

Fast messages
A fax machine sends pictures or writing down the phone line to another fax machine in seconds. The first fax machine was invented in 1904 by the German physicist Arthur Korn. They became common in the 1980s but they are slowly being replaced by electronic e-mail.

LOOKING AT A TV PICTURE

You will need: TV set, torch, powerful magnifying glass.

1 Turn off the TV. Shine the torch close to the screen and look through the magnifying glass. You will see that the screen is covered in very fine lines.

2 Turn on the TV and view the screen through the lens. The picture is made up of minute rectangles of light coloured red, green or blue.

SECONDARY COLOURS

You will need: red, green, and blue transparent plastic film, 3 powerful torches, 3 rubber bands, white card.

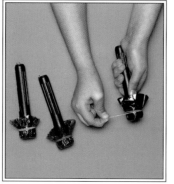

1 Attach a piece of coloured film over the end each torch. Stretch the film tightly and use a rubber band to hold it firmly in place.

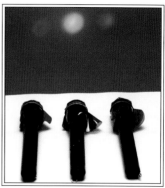

2 Shine the torches on to the white card. You can see the three different primary colours of – red, green and blue.

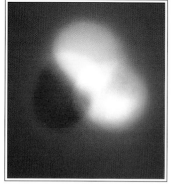

3 Position the torches so that the three circles of coloured light overlap in a cloverleaf pattern. Overlapping colours mix to give new colours.

DIGITAL IMAGES

You will need: ruler, tracing paper, photograph, black felt pen.

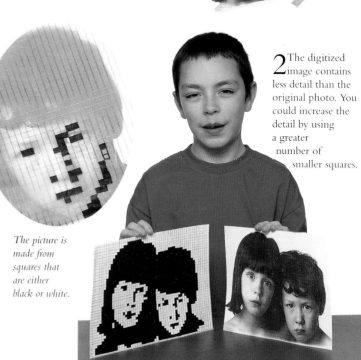

2 The digitized image contains less detail than the original photo. You could increase the detail by using a greater number of smaller squares.

The picture is made from squares that are either black or white.

1 Rule lines 5mm apart to cover the tracing paper in squares. Put the paper over the photograph. Use the pen to fill each dark square. Leave each light square.

RAW MATERIALS

Human beings have learned over thousands of years that it is possible to change raw materials so that they can be used. Between 6,000 and 3,500 years ago people discovered that they could obtain metals such as copper and iron by heating ore (rock that contains metals). The metals were then heated and shaped to make tools, weapons and ornaments. Metals are still used all over the world to make millions of useful objects.

Another breakthrough in the use of natural resources was grinding flour to bake in an oven to make bread. The Chinese discovered 2,000 years ago that tree bark, old rags and rope could be made into a pulp and then dried to make paper. In the 1800s, from rocks deep in the earth, oil was discovered as a new source of energy. Later, people learned how to use oil to make plastics and other synthetics. Today oil is the greatest single raw material used throughout the world.

The age of bronze
About 6,000 years ago, in what is now the Middle East, people first learned how to mix metals to make an alloy. They dug up ores that contained copper and tin, and smelted them together. From this new metal they created tools and weapons such as this sword. Bronze was much more useful than pure copper because it lasted longer and could be sharpened repeatedly. Gradually, other people in Europe and the Mediterranean world learned how to make bronze.

Mysterious knowledge
Lead cannot be turned into gold, but during medieval times many people such as this alchemist believed that it was possible. An alchemist drew on his knowledge of chemistry and magic to try turning lead into gold. People feared the alchemists were magicians. Although the alchemists never made gold from lead, they did pave the way for modern chemistry.

A taste of steel
The Bessemer converter marked a new way of making steel in the mid-1800s. The British inventor Sir Henry Bessemer had been making cannon out of iron for use in the Crimean War when he had the idea for the converter. Air is blown into molten iron inside the converter taking away any impurities and creating strong steel for use in many different industries.

Brand-new material

In the early 1900s, the chemist Leo Baekeland invented a way of creating a thick liquid from chemicals which, when it hardened, became a new material that no one had ever seen before. He called this material Bakelite. It was long lasting and could be shaped to make many different kinds of objects such as this radio case.

Strong and light

In the late 1800s, the electrolytic cell was invented as a way of using electricity to extract the light, strong metal called aluminium from bauxite ore. Aluminium is used when strong, light metal is needed, for example in building aircraft.

Riding on air

When motor cars were invented in the late 1800s their wheels were hard, like cartwheels. Charles Goodyear invented a process that made rubber hard and allowed people to make car tyres from it. Inside the tyres were inner tubes filled with air, which were first invented in 1845 by Robert Thomson.

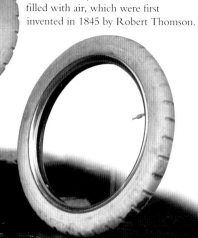

CHEMICAL CHANGE

URING the past 100 years, scientists have invented many substances that we take for granted today. Examples include plastics, medicines, detergents and fuels. These new substances are created by mixing natural substances that react to each other. These are called chemical reactions. There are just three main ways in which chemical reactions can happen: passing electricity through substances, heating them or mixing them together.

These experiments show the three ways in which chemical reactions can happen. In the first project, electricity breaks down salty water to make chlorine which is a disinfectant used to keep swimming pools clean. In the second project, you heat sugar, which is made from carbon, hydrogen and oxygen to create pure carbon. The third shows how to make the gas used in some fire extinguishers. This gas is made by mixing bicarbonate of soda and vinegar together to create carbon dioxide.

Measuring up
In a laboratory, this scientist is carefully measuring the exact amount of chemicals to add to a test tube in which the experiment will take place. In science, accuracy is very important.

ELECTROLYSIS

You will need: *screwdriver, battery (4–6 volts), bulb and holder, wire, 2 paper clips, jar, water, salt.*

WARNING!
Please take care when using electrical equipment.
Always have an adult present.

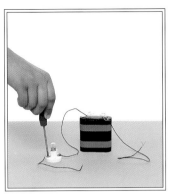

1 Connect the battery and bulb holder with wires as shown here. Remove 1cm of insulation from each end. Use the paper clips to join the wires to the battery.

2 Stir salt into a jar of water until no more dissolves. Dip the two bare wire ends into the mixture and hold them about 1cm apart. Look for bubbles forming round them.

3 The bulb should light to show that electricity is passing through. Carefully sniff the jar from 20cm away. The smell is like swimming pools.

HEAT CHANGES

You will need: old saucepan, teaspoon, sugar, cooker.

1 Make sure the saucepan is completely dry. Spread one teaspoonful of sugar across the bottom of the pan. Aim for a thin layer a few millimetres thick.

2 Place the pan on a cooker set to low heat. After a few minutes, the sugar starts to melt to give a brown treacly liquid. You may see a few wisps of steam.

3 The sugar starts to bubble as it breaks down and gives off steam. If you carry on heating, the brown sticky liquid will change to solid black carbon.

MIXING THINGS

You will need: teaspoon, bicarbonate of soda, glass bowl, spirit vinegar, matches.

1 Place three heaped spoonfuls of bicarbonate of soda in the bowl. Cooks often add this white powder to vegetables like peas and carrots. It helps to keep their natural colour.

2 Pour vinegar into the bowl. As the liquid mixes with the white powdery bicarbonate of soda, a chemical reaction happens. The mixture bubbles as a gas is given off.

3 Ask an adult to light a match and lower the flame into the bowl. The chemical reaction has made a gas called carbon dioxide. The flame goes out when it meets the gas.

WAIT A SECOND

Shadow of time
An ancient Roman sundial is cut in the shape of a shell from a block of marble. Sundials were made in many shapes and sizes. People could judge the time by watching as the shadow cast by the sun moved from one line to another.

Sometimes we say time hangs heavily on our hands. At other times we say it goes past in a flash. How do we know how much time has actually passed? The easiest way to tell the time is to watch the sun as it rises in the morning and sets in the evening. But people have always wanted to measure time more accurately. This led to the invention of the sundial. The oldest sundials known are Egyptian and more than 5,000 years old.

Today we use clocks and watches to measure time. The first clocks were invented in the 1300s. They had wheels and cogs, weights and pendulums that worked together to turn the hands of the clock. Portable, pocket-size watches were invented in the 1600s, when people discovered how to use springs rather than big weights and pendulums to turn the hands of clocks. Watches became smaller but had to be wound up regularly. In the 1920s the self-winding watch mechanism was invented. Most modern watches are now electronic, not mechanical.

The sun and stars
This clock in St Mark's square in Venice dates from the late 1300s. At this time clocks were very large and often built in or near churches because they were too big to fit in homes. Its face is decorated with astrological images of the animals and gods that were used to represent the different seasons and months of the year.

Tracking the sun
Before the 1700s, ships' captains relied on quadrants to find out where they were. They used quadrants to estimate the hour of the day, which helped them to know where on the Earth they were. This particular quadrant was designed by the English mathematician, Edmund Gunter, in the early 1600s.

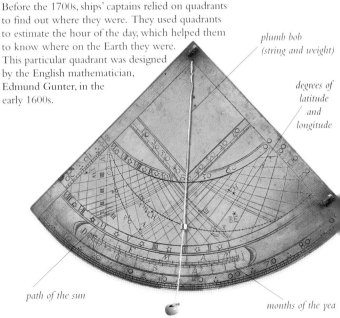

plumb bob (string and weight)

degrees of latitude and longitude

path of the sun

months of the yea

FACT BOX

• The world is divided into 24 time zones that begin and end at the Greenwich meridian in England. The meridian is the line that marks 0° of longitude and the time there is called Greenwich Mean Time.

• As trees grow they make rings in their trunks. Examining the rings on the stump of a felled tree tells us how old the tree is. Some very large trees, such as the sequoias of California, live for thousands of years.

All at sea

Sailors far from land needed to know the time to allow them to work out where they were. They needed accurate clocks to work out the time it had taken to travel a distance. In the 1700s a prize was offered by the British government to invent a marine chronometer (ship's clock) that would keep accurate time on-board ships. John Harrison worked at the problem for 34 years and invented four watches. The last of them won the prize.

hour hand cog

winding cog

minute hand cog

Precious object

A pocket watch was expensive to make and owned only by those with money to spend. A metal case protected the watch from bumps and thumps. This watch was made in 1759. Its many tiny wheels and cogs would have taken months for a skilled watchmaker to make and fit together.

All in one

Modern watches use a liquid crystal display (LCD) to show the time in digital form. In addition to giving hours and seconds, the watch also displays the day of the week, the month and the year. Other functions can be used by touching the icons at the bottom of the watch face.

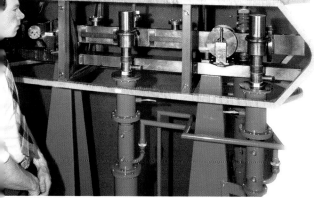

Split seconds

Willard Libby, who won the Nobel Prize for Chemistry in 1960, invented the atomic clock. An atomic clock tells the time using the extremely regular changes in the energy inside individual atoms. Clocks such as these can tell the time to within one second over thousands of years.

RIVER OF TIME

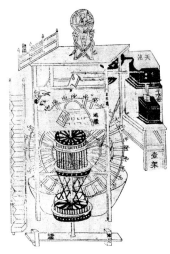

Water timer

This Chinese water clock was built in 1088. Water trickles into tiny buckets fixed to the outside of a large wheel. As each bucket fills up, the wheel clicks round to the next empty bucket. Each bucket empties as it reaches the lowest position. The position of the wheel indicates the time.

THE Ancient Egyptians invented water clocks in about 3000BC because the sundials they used could not tell the time at night. Water clocks use water that slowly drips from a bowl and the level of the surface of the remaining water indicates the time. However, a water clock cannot tell the time until you have compared it with another clock. You can make a water clock in the second part of this project.

In 1581, the Italian Galileo Galilei studied how different pendulums swinging back and forth could indicate time. He discovered that the time depends only on the length of the pendulum. It is not affected by the mass of the pendulum, or how far it swings from side to side. You can repeat Galileo's important experiment in the first part of this project. In 1641, Galileo's son Vincenzio Galilei constructed a mechanical clock that used a weighted pendulum to control the speed of hands across a clockface. All grandfather and grandmother clocks work like this. However, pendulums are not always accurate because their speed can vary depending on changes such as heat.

MAKE A PENDULUM

You will need: modelling clay, string, stopwatch.

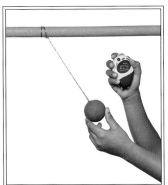

1 Roll some clay to make a ball 4cm across. Use string to hang it 30cm below a support. Pull the ball out to the position shown. Let go and time 10 complete swings.

2 Repeat the experiment. This time, use a larger heavier ball with the same bit of string. You will find that the time for ten swings is the same despite the heavier ball.

3 Increase the length of your pendulum by hanging the ball from a longer piece of string. You will find that the pendulum swings more slowly than before.

MAKE A
WATER CLOCK

You will need: *bradawl, aluminium pie dish, drinking straw, large plastic tumbler, scissors, water, jug, marker.*

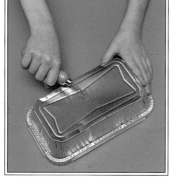

1 Use the bradawl to make a small hole in the bottom of the pie dish. The smaller the hole, the longer your water clock will run.

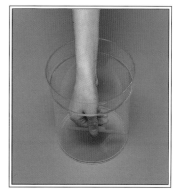

2 Place the drinking straw in the bottom of the plastic tumbler. It will act as a pointer as the water level rises. Cut the straw with a pair of scissors if it is too long.

3 Place the pie dish on top of the plastic tumbler. Make sure the hole in the pie dish is over the centre of the tumbler.

4 Pour water from a jug into the pie dish. Keep adding water until the dish is full. As soon as water starts to fall into the tumbler, note the time on your watch.

5 After 10 minutes, use the marker to mark the water level on the side of the tumbler. As the water drips into the tumbler, mark the level at 10-minute intervals.

You can use your pie-dish water clock to time your eggs for breakfast.

6 After half an hour you have three marks up the side of the tumbler. Empty out the water, refill the pie dish and you can use your water clock to measure time passing.

CROSSING THE OCEANS

O VER the centuries, people have developed ways of crossing the vast seas and oceans of the world. On board ships were pilots, navigators and captains whose job it was to navigate (find directions) across the water and arrive in one particular place. Even from the time of the earliest ship we know of, built for an Egyptian prince's funeral 6,000 years ago, seamen tried to find their way by looking at the position of the stars in the night sky and the sun during the day.

However, it is difficult to calculate exactly where you are from looking at the stars without working out complicated sums using angles and numbers. Over the years a number of instruments such as compasses and octants were invented to help seamen navigate. Maps also helped people to find their way at sea. Early maps did not have very much information. As ever more people travelled to distant places, more detailed maps were drawn of different regions and seas.

Star wheels
The astrolabe, invented by the ancient Greeks, was used for centuries to find directions at sea. The lower disc has a map of the stars and the upper disc has lines showing the heights of stars. This astrolabe dates from the AD1000s.

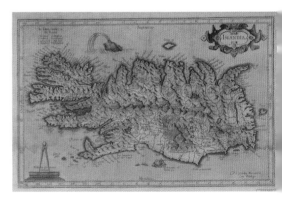

Charting the seas
Without knowing distances accurately it is very difficult to plan a journey. Making maps of large distances is difficult because the earth is round and maps are flat. It was not until the 1500s that Gerardus Mercator found a way to draw maps like this one of Iceland. It represented the distances on the surface of the earth. Using maps of this kind, travellers could find their way more easily than before.

Looking north
The compass is still one of the most widely used, simple instruments that help people find directions. Chinese and European seamen discovered 700 years ago that a tiny piece of magnetic stone floated on water will always turn towards the Pole Star in the north. Sailors began taking instruments containing pieces of magnetic stone or metal to sea with them. This one dates from the 1300s and the decoration on the top of the compass face shows the direction north.

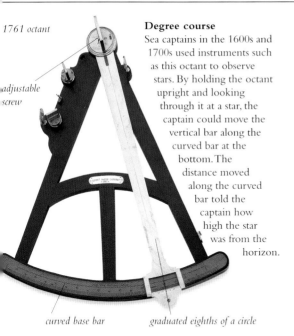

1761 octant

adjustable screw

curved base bar   *graduated eighths of a circle*

Degree course

Sea captains in the 1600s and 1700s used instruments such as this octant to observe stars. By holding the octant upright and looking through it at a star, the captain could move the vertical bar along the curved bar at the bottom. The distance moved along the curved bar told the captain how high the star was from the horizon.

Rush for a cuppa

By the 1800s, sea navigation was so highly developed that it was possible to predict how long a ship's journey would take. Very fast ships such as this tea clipper, which carried valuable tea from India, raced one another in the 1860s to see who could make the round trip from India to Britain in the shortest time.

Deep sea hunter

Modern submarines can remain submerged under water for months. Finding directions underwater is even more difficult than on the surface so submarines use a number of ways to navigate. As well as using compasses and maps, they communicate with global positioning satellites (GPS) by radio. The satellites in space send back messages to tell the submarines where they are.

Spectacular sport

Sailing is now a very popular sport and many people all over the world sail boats such as this trimaran for pleasure and in races. Every boat must carry charts, a modern compass and a direction-finding radio before it is considered safe to sail in.

DRIVING AHEAD

THE invention of the wheel was one of the most important technological advances that human beings ever made. It allowed them to travel and transport heavy weights on vehicles pulled by animals such as oxen and horses. Experts believe that knowledge of how to make wheels first developed almost 6,000 years ago in what is now the Middle East. It then spread gradually to people in neighbouring regions. In China, wheels were first made about 3,000 years ago. Some civilizations such as the Aztec and Mayan cultures in America never discovered how to make wheels. Until the invention of the steam engine in the 1800s, wheeled transport could not travel any faster than a horse could gallop. Once steam trains had been invented in the early 1800s, people began to travel faster and faster on land. Early motor cars were very slow because their engines were small and inefficient. However, as engines became bigger, cars travelled faster and faster too.

Flying squad
One immediate effect of discovering the wheel was a revolution in warfare. Racing down on their enemies in a horse-drawn chariot like this one gave the Egyptians a great advantage. War chariots were very light and fast.

FACT BOX

• The world's fastest train is the French *Train à Grande Vitesse*. It travels at speeds up to 300kph during normal journeys, but it is capable of reaching 500kph.

• The diesel engine is named after Rudolf Diesel, who invented it in 1892. Modern diesel engines power cars, trucks and trains.

Pull and push
The first wheels were solid and made out of pieces of wood cut and joined together. Gradually wheels were made lighter and stronger. The spoked wheel on this medieval wagon was the strongest kind of wheel. The spokes absorbed shocks from the wheel as it turned.

Stage by stage
In the 1800s huge numbers of people travelled to the American West when it opened up for settlement. The country was very wild and, until the railroads were built in the 1870s, stagecoaches like this were the only form of public transport. They were very uncomfortable to travel in because they pitched and swayed over rocks and holes in the badly made roads.

First of many

The invention of the steam engine changed the face of transport forever. George Stephenson's *Rocket*, shown here, was built in 1829 and was one of the first steam locomotives. He built it with his son for the Manchester–Liverpool Railway. By the late 1800s, railways stretched all over Europe, North America and much of Asia.

On the cheap

Henry Ford's Model T was the first motor car designed to be built in huge numbers very cheaply. Earlier cars had been hand-made and so were expensive, but Ford designed a system that made it possible to build cheaper cars on an assembly line in a factory. By the time the last Model T came out of the factory in 1927, 15 million had been built since 1908.

Electric engine

Steam railway engines using coal were built in their thousands throughout the 1800s. The first electric locomotives, like this one in Britain, were built in the early 1900s. They were quieter and cleaner than steam engines so they slowly replaced them.

Flash motor

Some of the earliest cars were built by Karl Benz in the late 1800s. He founded a factory that expanded to become the company that built this modern car. This Mercedes–Benz S430L can travel at a top speed of 240 kph. It is equipped with modern safety features such as airbags and uses tiny computers that control the car's stability and braking.

FLYING HIGH

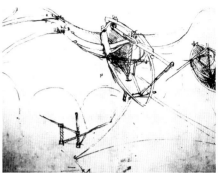

BIRDS and insects fly by using their wings to lift off the ground and support their weight on currents of air. Although humans have never had wings, they have always wanted to fly like birds. Scientists and inventors looked for ways to make artificial wings for hundreds of years.

Kites were invented in China 2,000 years ago and may have been used for military purposes. In the 1780s, the Montgolfier brothers flew in balloons over France. Balloons, however, proved too difficult to steer to be practical. Powered flight has only been possible in the past hundred years. The Wright brothers flew their first aeroplane in 1903, in the USA, and showed that it is possible to control the movement of an aircraft. Like the invention of the wheel, the discovery of flight changed warfare. Air power was used in war only 11 years after the Wright brothers' first flight. Commercial air travel became more and more popular from the 1960s onward.

Bird man
The Italian artist and inventor Leonardo da Vinci drew designs for flying machines in the early 1500s. This drawing shows wings that could be strapped to the arms to allow the wearer to fly. However, they were never built.

Keep going
This is one of the Wright brothers' first aircraft, the first successful flying machine. One engine attached to the frame turned propellers and created enough power to keep the aircraft moving forward. This provided the essential lift from air rushing past under and over the wings to keep it airborne.

Whirly bird
The man sitting at the controls of this early helicopter is the Russian-born Igor Sikorsky. After 1917, he went to live in the USA and worked as an aeroplane engineer. By 1940, he had developed the first successful vertical take-off helicopter and flew several of the early machines he built.

Blades of power
A jet turbine takes in air through the front blades. As the blades turn faster they compress the air which is ignited. The second blades are moved by the burning air which then turns the compressor. This drives the aircraft on.

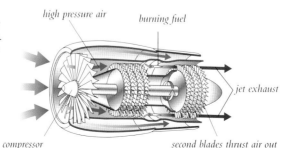

high pressure air

burning fuel

jet exhaust

compressor

second blades thrust air out

Flying boat
The largest commercial aircraft built between World War I and World War II were flying boats of the kind shown here. Because there were few long runways built on land, large planes often took off from, and landed on, water. This six-engined plane flew on routes between Italy and South America.

Two in one
The Harrier jump-jet is a unique type of aircraft. It can land and take off vertically like a helicopter, but it flies like a jet. The aircraft has movable jet thrusters that are vertical when landing and taking off but horizontal when in flight. This type of aircraft is mainly used for military purposes.

Wide blue yonder
The Space Shuttle is the ultimate aircraft. It takes off vertically attached to rocket boosters, to reach orbit around the Earth. When it returns from orbit, the Shuttle glides through the atmosphere and lands just like any jet plane.

Jetsetter
The de Havilland *Comet* shown here was the first jet aircraft to go into regular passenger service. It began flying in 1952 and halved the time for long journeys such as that between London and South Africa. By 1958, regular jet flights between Britain and the USA meant transatlantic jet travel had come to stay.

NUMBER CRUNCHERS

IT is not certain exactly when people first invented numbers. We do know, however, that numbers were in use by the time the first civilizations grew up, 6,000 years ago. In these early societies, numbers allowed people to count possessions when trading and to note the days of the week and months of the year. The Greek inventor Hero of Alexandria designed a counting machine 2,000 years ago and, in the early 1500s, Leonardo da Vinci also designed one. In 1835 Charles Babbage invented a mechanical calculator called the difference engine. A mechanical calculator was later used to break codes (secret communications) during World War II. These machines were the first computers. Afterwards, ever larger electronic computers were built, and in the 1980s small personal computers (PCs) appeared in offices and at home.

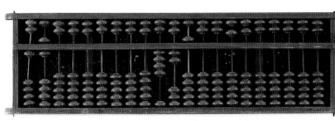

Counter culture
People have been using this kind of counting device for thousands of years. It is known in China as a *suan pan* and as an abacus in English. Beads are arranged on vertical, parallel strings. Each string represents different kinds of number. For example, on the extreme left are 1s, next left 10s. By sliding the beads up and down, a person can quickly perform complicated arithmetic.

Brass and steel
The difference engine is a complicated arrangement of metal cogs and ratchets designed to count numbers mechanically. It was invented by Charles Babbage in 1835 but he never succeeded in finishing it. Building such a machine out of solid metal parts without any electrical circuits is extremely difficult.

Code breaker
Colossus was the name given to this computer built at Bletchley in Britain during World War II. It was used to break codes used by German commanders who sent orders by radio. The orders were sent as constantly changing groups of letters that only made sense to those who knew the key. *Colossus* performed the millions of calculations necessary to read the code even though the British did not have the key.

FACT BOX

• The most complex computer is the human brain. Modern PCs can perform an average of 100 million calculations every second and the fastest computers now available achieve 1.6 trillion calculations per second. This is 10,000 times slower than the brain, which makes an average of 10 quadrillion calculations per second.

• Many different ways of writing numbers have been invented. The number system used in this book was first invented by Arab mathematicians about 1,200 years ago, so these numbers are called Arabic numbers. The ancient Romans used a different system in which, for example, the year 1950 would be written as MCML.

Micro-maze
Silicon chips allow modern computers to perform millions of calculations in a second. Before chips were invented, enormous boxes were needed to hold all the wires required to calculate electronically. Then miniaturization was invented. This made it possible to put many tiny circuits on to one piece of silicon.

Carry on computing
A small computer can be carried and used anywhere. Batteries inside supply power for the hardware. Portable computers are often called laptops because they are small and light enough to place on a sitting person's lap.

A boring box
This very uninteresting looking box is in fact one of the world's fastest computers. There is little to look at on the outside because everything interesting is inside, where thousands of chips can calculate trillions of numbers every second.

Out into space
To operate in space without human help, spacecraft such as the *Voyager* probe are equipped with computers that control them. Without small computers, spacecraft would never be able to leave earth. They would need to carry machines to control them so large that the spacecraft would weigh far too much to leave the earth's surface.

THROUGH THE LOGIC GATE

INFORMATION flowing inside a computer is called data. It is in the form of electrical pulses. Data changes as it passes through part of the computer called the central processing unit (CPU). The CPU has thousands of separate high-speed switches called logic gates. These logic gates are microscopic transistors cut into a silicon chip. They can flick on and off up to 300 million times a second. Data flows into the input side of each gate. It only flows out again if the gate is switched on. The computer program sets up how the gates switch on and off and so controls the data flow through the computer.

There are three main types of gates, called AND, NOT, and OR gates. Working together, they act as counters or memory circuits to store data. Logic gates are also used to control things like washing machines. In this project, you can make a model AND gate to show how the output depends on the settings of the two input connections.

AND gate

Input A	Input B	Output C
OFF	OFF	OFF
OFF	ON	OFF
OFF	ON	OFF
ON	ON	ON

OR gate

Input A	Input B	Output C
OFF	OFF	OFF
OFF	ON	ON
ON	OFF	ON
ON	ON	ON

On or off?

AND and OR gates both have two inputs (A and B) and one output connection (C). The tables show how the ON/OFF states of the inputs affect the ON/OFF state of the output. These tables are called "truth tables".

MAKE A LOGIC GATE

You will need: *felt-tipped pen, ruler, stiff card in 3 colours, scissors, stapler, pencil, red and green sticky circles.*

1 Mark and cut out three pieces of card. Referring to the colours shown here, the sizes are: dark blue 15 x 10cm, light blue 10 x 7cm and yellow 4 x 20cm.

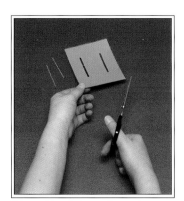

2 On the 10 x 7cm card, draw two slots that are slightly more than 4cm wide and 4cm apart. Cut each slot so that it is about 2 – 3mm wide.

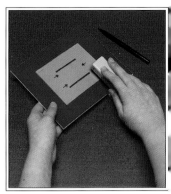

3 Place the card with slots in the centre of the dark blue card. Staple them together with one staple at each corner of the top card. Draw the three arrows as shown.

4 At 2cm intervals, stick coloured circles in the order shown on to the left side of the long card strip. This is the input side.

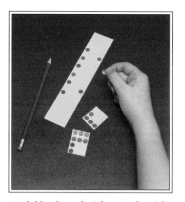

5 Add coloured stickers to the right (output side) at 4cm intervals in this order: green, red, red, red. Notice that each sticker is midway between the two on the left.

6 Push the strip between the two stapled cards and feed it through the lower slot. Keep pushing the strip and feed it through the top slot and out between the stapled cards.

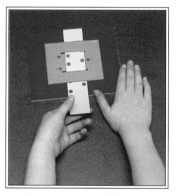

7 Move the strip until there is a green dot at the top of the input side. There should be a green dot on the output side, showing that both inputs must be ON for the output to be ON.

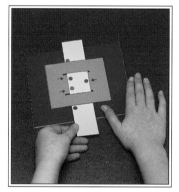

8 When the input shows red at the top with a green dot below, then a green dot appears on the output side. Your model is showing that the output is OFF when only one input is ON.

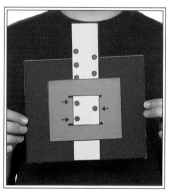

9 Here is your completed model AND gate. Now make a similar model with the stickers in the right places to show how an OR gate works. You will find that AND gates and OR gates are very different.

A completed AND model

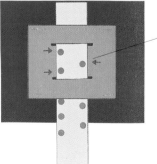

Red dots indicate both inputs on model AND are OFF.

10 When both inputs on your model AND gate show red, then a red dot appears opposite the output. As you might expect, the output of an AND gate is OFF when both inputs are OFF.

THINGS TO COME

THE pace of invention has increased dramatically since the 1800s and there is no sign of it slowing down. Almost every week new inventions are announced. A recent invention for replanting trees by dropping saplings from the air could make forests grow again in many parts of the earth. Computerized map systems have been developed that make it impossible to get lost when travelling.

Many new inventions are things we hardly notice, such as the material Velcro which holds surfaces together and is used in place of buttons and zips on clothes. Some inventions are useful only in special situations. Kevlar is a recently invented, bullet-proof material that is very valuable for soldiers and policemen but little used in everyday life. Understanding of the genetic structures of living bodies is increasing all the time. In the future people may be able to choose what colour their baby's hair will be! One thing is certain. Whatever happens, people will not stop inventing.

Electronic circuits
Semiconductors are essential for making many of the electronic devices that we use every day, from pocket calculators to personal computers. Semiconductors are used to make electricity flow through tiny circuits in complex patterns that control how machines work.

Solar energy
People are trying increasingly to find new sources of energy because the old ones, such as coal and gas, will be used up in the future. Solar energy (the heat and light of the Sun) is one new energy source. This Russian space module, part of the international space station (ISS), is powered by the solar energy panels that fan out on either side of it. The panels convert heat and light into energy.

Russian space module

Village in orbit
The international space station is due to be completed in 2004. It is being built with the co-operation of 16 different countries throughout the world. They hope that having this permanent space station in orbit will allow scientists to make discoveries in space that will advance medicine, science and engineering.

Touchy-feely

Virtual reality is an invention that allows users wearing a headset and gloves to see and feel scenes which exist only on computer. Looking and touching in this way can be a very helpful way of training people to use machines. For example, pilots can be trained to fly a new aircraft without actually going into the air.

Talk to me

A scientist is looking at a graph that shows the word "baby" on a computer screen. It is part of research into how computers can reply to human voices. If people could talk to computers, using them would be easier.

Safe energy

The biggest problem with energy produced using nuclear fuel is the danger of radiation that can kill people. Some scientists recently believed that they had found a way to generate energy using the cold-fusion process shown here. The process creates energy by nuclear fusion without making radioactivity. It is uncertain whether this process can be used on a large scale or even repeated easily.

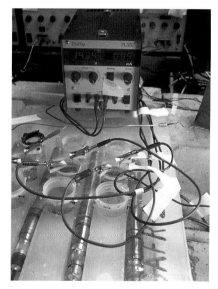

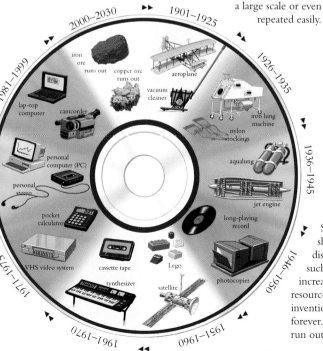

2000–2030
1901–1925
1981–1999
1926–1935
iron ore runs out
copper ore runs out
aeroplane
vacuum cleaner
lap-top computer
camcorder
iron lung machine
nylon stockings
personal computer (PC)
aqualung
1936–1945
personal stereo
pocket calculator
jet engine
long-playing record
VHS video system
cassette tape
Lego
photocopier
1946–1950
synthesizer
satellite
1971–1975
1961–1970
1951–1960

Still turning

Some of the many inventions since 1900 are shown inside the circle of this CD (compact disc). In the last 40 years electronic inventions, such as video and CD technology, have been used increasingly in homes everywhere. However, the resources on which people rely to make new inventions, such as copper and iron, will not last forever. In particular, copper ore will start to run out in 25 years' time.

PART TWO

MACHINES

However complex modern machines are, many of them use very simple devices that have been employed for thousands of years. The wheel, the pulley and the lever all helped to build the ancient pyramids of Egypt. Added to other simple devices such as the screw and the gear wheel, they allowed people to make spectacular advances in what they could accomplish. The engines and motors developed in the 1800s allowed another great leap forward, and the computers of today are creating a revolution that may be even more wide-reaching.

AUTHOR
Chris Oxlade
CONSULTANT
Graham Peacock

WHAT IS A MACHINE?

Thousands of different devices can be called machines, from calculators and televisions to trucks and aircraft. Scissors and staplers are very simple machines, while computers and cars are complicated. All machines have one thing in common – they help us do jobs and so make our lives easier.

Think about what you did yesterday. Make a list of every machine you can remember that you used or saw, from when you woke up to when you went back to bed. Many things that we take for granted, such as opening a tin can, cutting paper or tightening a screw, can only be done with a machine. Other jobs, such as washing clothes, used to be done by hand but nowadays are usually done by machine. Machines are being improved – and new ones invented – all the time. We may find that tasks that take a long time today become much easier and faster to do in the future.

screwdriver

pliers

scissors

hammer

Allen keys

Simple machines
Tools such as these are simple machines that are useful to have at home. They each do a task that would be much more difficult without them. Can you think of a job for each tool?

Useful screws
The parts of this model helicopter are fixed together with screws. The screws are machines because they do the job of holding the helicopter parts in place.

Domestic machines
A microwave oven is one of the many machines that people use at home to make preparing and cooking food quicker and simpler. Other domestic machines include vacuum cleaners and washing machines.

Using tools
This girl uses a spanner to tighten the nuts on her model helicopter. A spanner is a simple tool that is used to tighten up, or undo, nuts. Using the spanner is more efficient than if the girl used her fingers alone, because the spanner can make joints much tighter and more secure.

FACT BOX

• Leonardo da Vinci (1452–1519) was an Italian artist and inventor. He drew plans for machines, such as tanks and aircraft, that were hundreds of years ahead of their time.

• Greek scientist Hero of Alexandria lived in the 1st century AD. He invented a steam engine, a slot machine and a screw press.

Old farm machines

People use many different machines to help them farm the land in this picture, which was painted in about 1400. Some of the first machines ever invented were used by farmers. At the bottom of the picture is a plough, and halfway up on the right-hand side is a water-wheel. At the top, by a church, is a machine called a shaduf, which was used to raise water from a deep well. Next to the shaduf is a machine that was used for sowing seed.

Construction machines

Diggers and cranes are used on a construction (building) site. These huge machines are clearing the site of rubble before the buildings are restored. Construction machines have powerful engines for moving and lifting heavy loads, such as soil, rocks, steel and concrete.

Calculating machine

Unlike most of the other machines shown here, a computer does not help lift, move or cut things. Instead it makes life easier by remembering information and doing calculations. Computers help us to work faster and more accurately. They can do amazing work – such as controlling the flight path of a spacecraft.

Travel by machine

To travel from place to place you need a machine to get you there. The space shuttle is a machine that transports people into space. Its powerful rocket engines launch it through Earth's atmosphere. Other transport machines, such as cars and trains, also have engines. Their engines are much less powerful than those on a spacecraft.

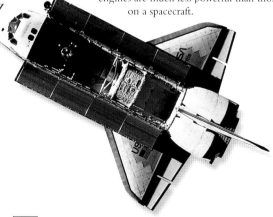

Chopping machine

A hand axe is used to chop large logs into smaller pieces. When the woman brings the axe down, the sharp blade slices into the wood, forcing it to split apart. The axe is a simple machine, but it is very effective. It does a job that is impossible to do by hand.

POWERFUL LEVERS

Six simple machines that were invented thousands of years ago are still the basic elements of all machinery. These machines are the lever, the wheel and axle, the inclined plane or ramp, the wedge, the screw and the pulley. The simplest, and probably the oldest, is the lever. A lever is a bar or rod that tilts on an object called a pivot. You only need a small push down on one end to raise a large weight on the end nearer to the pivot. Any rod or stick can act as a lever, helping to move heavy objects or prise things apart. The lever makes the power of the push into a much larger push. This is known as mechanical advantage.

Did you know that some parts of your body are levers? Every time you brush your hair or get up from a chair, the bones in your arms and legs act as levers, helping you to lift your limbs.

Shut the door
Closing a door near the hinge is hard work. It is easier to press on the handle because the door is a lever. Its pivot is made by the hinges. The door turns your small push on the handle into a bigger push.

How a lever works
A lever tilts on a pivot, which is nearer to the end of the lever with the load on it. The effort, or force, is the push you make on the long end of the lever to lift the weight of the load.

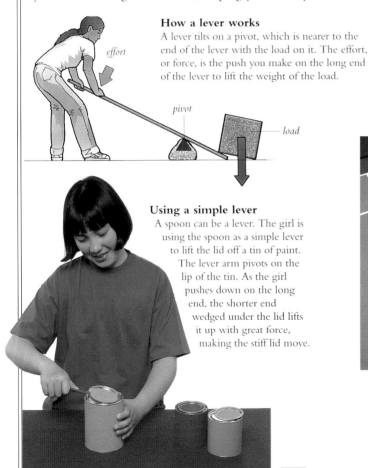

effort

pivot

load

Using a simple lever
A spoon can be a lever. The girl is using the spoon as a simple lever to lift the lid off a tin of paint. The lever arm pivots on the lip of the tin. As the girl pushes down on the long end, the shorter end wedged under the lid lifts it up with great force, making the stiff lid move.

Levers in the body
A tennis player uses muscle-powered levers in her shoulders and elbows to serve the ball at high speed. Small movements of the muscles cause large movements of the racket, which gives the racket the speed for a fast serve.

LEVERS AND LIFTING

1 A ruler can be used as a lever to lift a book. With the pivot (the box) near the book, only a small effort is needed to lift the book up. The lever makes the push larger.

2 When the pivot is moved to the middle of the lever, the effort needed to lift the book up is equal to the book's weight. The effort and the load are the same.

3 When the pivot is near where the boy is pressing, more effort is needed to lift the book. The force of the push needed to lift the book is now larger than the book's weight.

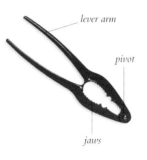

lever arm

pivot

jaws

The strong crushing action of the nutcracker's jaws is produced by pressing the two lever arms together.

Raising water

In Middle Eastern countries, farmers use a machine called a shaduf to lift water to irrigate their crops. The arm of a shaduf is a lever with a bucket on one end and a weight on the other, pivoted on the top of a wooden frame. The shaduf operator pulls the empty bucket down into the water using a rope. The weight at the other end acts as the effort, lifting the bucket of water (the load). The shaduf is an ancient machine, used by farmers for thousands of years.

Cracking a nut

A pair of nutcrackers, like a pair of scissors or a pair of pliers, has two lever arms joined at a pivot. Pressing the ends of the nutcracker arms together squashes the nut in its jaws. The levers make the effort you use about four times bigger, allowing you to break the nut quite easily. Putting the pivot at the end of the levers rather than towards the centre (as in a pair of scissors) means that the arms of the cracker can be shorter but still create a force just as big.

BALANCING LEVERS

Levers are used for lifting, cutting and squashing. A lever on a central pivot can also be used as a balance. The lever balances if the effect of the force (push) on one side of the pivot is the same as the effect of the force on the other. A see-saw is one sort of balancing lever. It is a plank balanced on a central post or pivot. Someone small and light can balance a much bigger person if they sit in the right position on a see-saw.

Outside the playground, balancing levers have other important uses. By using a lever to balance one force with another, the size of one force can be compared to the size of another. This is how a weighing machine called a balance scale works. It measures the mass (weight) of an object by comparing it with standard weights such as grams and kilograms.

weights *pivot* *pan* *lever arm*

Weighing up
Balance scales like this one were once used for weighing things in shops or in the kitchen. To make the lever arm balance, the weights on the left must equal the weight in the pan.

Using a balance scale
An object, such as a pile of strawberries, is put in a pan resting on one end of the lever arm. Weights are added to the other end of the arm until the arm balances. Then the individual weights are added up to find the weight of the object. We call the result 'weight' because we measure the force needed to balance the weight of the object. In fact, a balance scale measures kilograms.

Balanced crossing gates
A level-crossing gate is actually a balanced lever. The pivot is at the side of the road, with the gate to one side and a heavy counterweight on the other side to balance it. This means that only a small effort is needed from electric motors to move the lever up or down. The gates are operated automatically by electronics linked to the railway's signalling system.

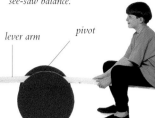

Two children of equal weight, the same distance from the pivot, make the see-saw balance.

lever arm   pivot

Balancing a see-saw

A see-saw shows the effect of moving a weight nearer or farther from the pivot of a lever arm. Two children of equal weight, the same distance from the pivot, make a see-saw balance. If another child is added to one end, the arm overbalances to that side. By moving the single child farther from the pivot, or the pair closer to it, the arm balances again.

By adding another child to one side, that side overbalances. The pair's greater weight easily lifts the lighter boy.

FACT BOX

• Stone Age people were probably the first to use levers. They may have used branches as levers to move heavy rocks.

• Balance scales were invented by the ancient Egyptians so that they could weigh gold. Gold was precious, so it needed to be weighed accurately.

• A trebuchet was a medieval war machine like a giant catapult. It was based on the lever arm. It was used to hurl boulders at the enemy up to 0.5km away.

By moving the pair nearer the pivot, their weight can be balanced by the lighter boy moving farther away.

Investigating balance

Make a ruler balance on a tube. Now put different-sized piles of coins at different positions on each end so that they balance. For example, you can make one coin balance two coins if the single coin is twice as far from the pivot as the other coins.

ALL KINDS OF LEVERS

Levers are very common machines. Look around you and see how many levers you can spot – don't forget the levers in your own body! Each of the machines shown here has a diagram to show you where the pivot, effort and load are, to help you to see how the lever is working.

Levers are divided into three different basic kinds, or classes. The most common type is a first-class lever, where the pivot is always between the load and the effort, as with a see-saw, a pair of pliers or a spade. In second-class levers, the load is between the pivot and the effort. Nutcrackers and wheelbarrows are examples of these. In a third-class lever, the effort is between the pivot and the load, as with hammers, tweezers and fishing rods.

Spade work
A spade is a first-class lever for lifting and turning soil. A sharp blade makes it easy to push the spade into the soil. Pressing down on the handle is the effort, the pivot is your foot on the blade and the load is the soil. Pushing the handle down levers the soil up.

In a pair of pliers, the effort is pressing down on handles. The load is the resistance that an object has to being crushed in the jaws of the pliers.

Lifting the handles of a wheelbarrow lifts a heavy load nearer the pivot, or wheel.

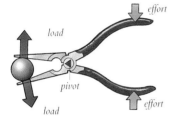

First-class levers
A pair of pliers has two lever arms linked at the pivot by a hinge. They are first-class levers because the pivot is between the load and the effort. The handles are on one side of the pivot and the jaws are on the other.

Second-class levers
A wheelbarrow does not look like a lever, but it is one. The lever arm goes from the end of the handle to the centre of the wheel, which is the pivot. A small effort pulling up on the handles lifts the load in the barrow.

A hammer acts as a lever when you use your wrist as a pivot. Your fingers make the effort to lift the hammer's head.

Third-class levers

A hammer may not look like a lever, but it is. The handle joins with your hand to make the lever arm, with your wrist as the pivot. Your fingers supply the effort to make the hammer head move down. The load is the weight of the hammer head. The small movement of your arm makes a large movement in the hammer head to drive the nail into the wood.

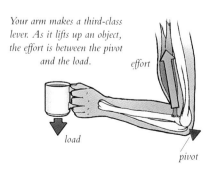

Gone fishing

A fishing rod is a third-class lever, similar to the hammer above. The pivot is at the fisherman's wrist. The effort is made by his hand, and the load is the weight of the rod and the fish on the line. An effort much greater than the load is needed to lift the rod. The advantage of the rod is that a small movement of the fisherman's arm makes a large movement at the end of the rod. So a flick of the wrist casts the line which floats far across the water.

Your arm makes a third-class lever. As it lifts up an object, the effort is between the pivot and the load.

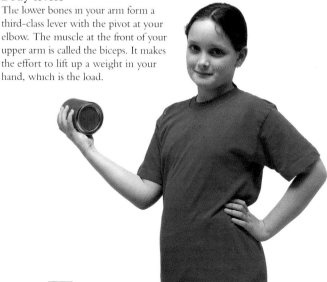

FACT BOX

• The longer a lever arm, the greater the force. Using a lever (it would have to be a strong lever) 10m long, with a pivot 10cm from the end, you could lift an elephant with one finger!

• A piano is full of levers. Each key is a lever with other levers attached to it. When you press a key, the levers make hammers fly at the strings.

Body levers

The lower bones in your arm form a third-class lever with the pivot at your elbow. The muscle at the front of your upper arm is called the biceps. It makes the effort to lift up a weight in your hand, which is the load.

MAKING LEVERS WORK

MAKE A GRIPPER

You will need: *short pencil, two pieces of wood each about 15cm long, thick elastic bands, objects to pick up or squash such as sweets or grapes.*

You can find out how to make two different lever machines in the projects here. The first is a simple gripper for picking up or squashing objects. It can act both as a pair of nutcrackers (a second-class lever) or a pair of tweezers (a third-class lever). In a pair of nutcrackers, the load (in this case a sweet) is between the pivot (the pencil) and the effort (where you push). In a pair of tweezers, the effort is between the pivot and the load. Draw a lever diagram that shows both ways of using lever machines to help you understand how each one works.

The second machine is a balance scale. It is like the ones used by the Romans about 2,000 years ago. It works by balancing the weight of an object against a known weight, in this case a bag of coins. The coins are moved along the lever arm until they balance the object being weighed. The further away from the pivot the weighted bag is, the greater turning effect it has on the lever arm. The heavier the weight being measured, the further the bag must be moved to balance the arm. The weight is read off against the scale along the arm.

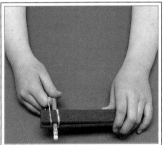

1 Put the pencil between the two pieces of wood, near one end. Wrap the elastic bands tightly around the pieces of wood to make a pivot. You have now made the gripper.

2 Hold the gripper near the pivot to make it act like a pair of tweezers. See if you can pick up a delicate object, such as a sweet or a grape, without crushing the object.

3 Holding the gripper at the other end makes a pair of nutcrackers. It increases the force you make. Try using the nutcrackers to crack a small nut or to crush a small sweet.

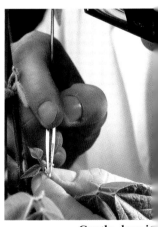

Gently does it
A pair of tweezers is used to pick up minute grains of pollen. Tweezers make it easier to pick up tiny or delicate objects. The tweezers act as a third-class lever, so the force that squeezes the object is smaller than the effort you use

MAKE A BALANCE SCALE

You will need: *thick card about 50cm x 8cm, thin card, scissors, string, ruler, hole punch, 12-cm circle of card, sticky tape, 100g of coins, felt-tipped pen, objects to weigh.*

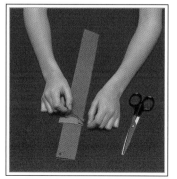

1 Make the arm by folding the thick card in two. Make a loop of thin card and attach it to the arm so that its centre is 11cm from one end. Tie a piece of string to this support.

2 Make a hole 1cm from the arm's end. Make the card circle into a cone-shaped pan and tie it to the hole. Make an envelope and tie it to a loop so that it hangs over the arm.

3 Put the 100g of coins in the envelope and seal it up. Starting from the centre of the support, make a mark every 5cm along the arm. This scale will enable you to work out the weight of any object you put in the pan because each mark equals 50g.

4 To weigh an object, put it in the pan and slide the envelope of coins backwards and forwards along the arm until the arm balances. In this picture, the arm balances when the envelope of coins reaches the third mark. The object being weighed is about 75g because each mark equals 50g.

WHEELS AND AXLES

The wheel is one of the most important inventions ever made. About 6,000 years ago, people discovered that using logs as rollers was a more efficient way to move heavy loads than to drag them. A slice from a log was the first wheel. Then people found that they could attach a wheel to the end of a pole. The pole became an axle.

A wheel on the end of an axle makes a simple machine. Turning the wheel makes the axle turn, too. It is a machine because turning the axle is easier using the wheel than turning the axle on its own. Wheels and axles increase mechanical advantage – turning the wheel makes the axle turn with greater force. The bigger the wheel compared to the size of the axle, the greater the force, making turning even easier. Wheels are used in millions of machines. One of the most obvious is in wheeled vehicles, which were in use more than 4,000 years ago and are still the most common form of transport today. Sometimes wheel and axle machines can be difficult to recognize. Can you find a wheel and axle in a spanner or a door key?

Pedal pusher
Pushing on the pedals of this child's tricycle turns the axle and drives the tricycle's front wheel.

handle

spindle

Winding up
The key of a wind-up toy has a handle that acts as a wheel and a spindle that is an axle. The large handle makes it easier to turn the spindle.

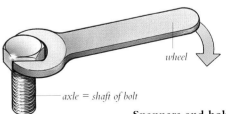

wheel

axle = shaft of bolt

Spanners and bolts
A spanner and a bolt make up a wheel and axle system. The threaded shaft of the bolt is the axle and the handle of the spanner is the wheel. By turning the spanner, it is much easier to tighten or loosen the bolt.

Lock and key
A key doesn't look like a wheel and axle machine, but it is. A key has a small handle on the end which makes it easier to turn in the lock. The handle acts as a wheel. The key's shaft is the axle.

Putting the spoke in

A cart full of grapes is pulled by oxen in this Roman mosaic, which was made about 1,700 years ago. Using wheeled carts meant oxen could pull a much heavier load than they could carry. The first cart wheels were made from slices of tree trunk. About 4,000 years ago, the Romans hollowed the wheels out and added spokes to make them lighter. Vehicles could now go faster.

Potters' wheels

A potter in India uses a wheel to cast his pots. Casting pots was one of the first uses of the wheel. Simple potter's wheels are still used around the world. The massive wooden wheel can be turned either by foot or by hand.

Keep on spinning

The rim of this grinding wheel moves at very high speed as it sharpens tools. The wheel is very heavy, which means that it tends to keep spinning even when the tool is pressed against it.

Racing wheels

A racing car is moved along by its rear wheels (which are called the driving wheels). Each driving wheel is turned by an axle called a driveshaft. In most cars the driving wheels are the front wheels.

Driving in a screw

A screwdriver is a machine. Its shaft is an axle and its handle is a wheel. The handle increases the force on the shaft when it is turned to drive in a screw.

Steering wheels

A car's steering wheel is attached to the end of an axle, called the steering column. The wheel increases the force from the driver's hands, so giving the driver enough force to control the car.

WHEELS AT WORK

MAKE A CAPSTAN WHEEL

You will need: pencil, small cardboard box such as a shoe box, ruler, card tube, scissors, dowelling, sticky tape, string, a weight, thin card, glue, thick card.

There are hundreds of different examples of wheels and axles. Some are very old designs, such as the capstan wheel. A capstan is a wheel on an axle with handles that stretch out from the edge of the wheel. The handles are used to turn the wheel, which turns the axle. Large capstan wheels can be turned by animals as they walk round and round, or by several people who each push on a handle. In the past, they were a familiar sight on ships and in dockyards where they were used to raise heavy loads such as a ship's anchor. This project shows you how to make a simple capstan wheel for lifting a weight. At the end of the project a ratchet is attached to the axle. A ratchet is a very useful device that acts like a catch. It prevents the capstan wheel turning back on itself once you have stopped winding it.

1 Draw a line around the box about one-third from the top. Place the tube on the line, draw around it and cut out a circle. Repeat on the opposite side of the box, so the circles match.

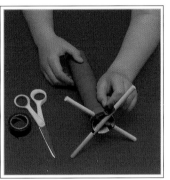

2 Cut four slots in one end of the tube. Lay two pieces of dowelling into the slots so that they cross over. Tape the dowelling in place. You have now made the capstan wheel.

3 Push the tube into the holes in the box. Tape the end of a piece of string to the middle of the tube inside the box. Tie a heavy object to the other end of the string.

Round in circles

Sailors on board a sailing ship turn a capstan wheel. The wheel turns a drum that pulls the ship's heavy anchor up from the sea bed. The longer the handles on the capstan wheel, the easier it is to turn the drum, but the farther the sailors have to walk. Pulling up the anchor by hauling in the cable would be far more difficult.

4 Stand the box on a table edge so the weight hangs down. Turn the capstan wheel to lift the object. Try turning the handles at their ends and then near the wheel's centre.

5 To make a ratchet, cut four small rectangles of card and carefully glue them to the tube at the opposite end to the capstan wheel. These will form the ratchet teeth.

6 From a piece of thick card, cut an L-shaped piece. Bend one of the legs of the L at a right angle to the other leg. This will form the part that locks into the ratchet teeth.

7 Glue the L card to the top of your box so that the end hanging over the edge just catches in the ratchet teeth. Leave the glue to dry before trying your ratchet.

8 Wind up the capstan wheel to lift the weight up again. You should now be able to let go of the capstan without the weight dropping back to the ground. The teeth will catch on the L shape, stopping the axle from turning backwards.

Crushing the grapes

A wine press crushes grapes from a vineyard to release the grape juice that is used for wine-making. The press is operated by turning a nut at the top that forces a screw thread downwards into the tub. The horizontal bar on the nut works like a capstan. Pushing in opposite directions on its ends turns the nut. The longer the bar, the greater the turning force on the nut, and the greater the squashing force on the grapes.

SLOPING RAMPS

How can an inclined plane, or ramp, be a machine? It is a type of machine because it makes going uphill, or moving an object uphill against the force of gravity, much easier. Think about a removal van and people trying to lift a heavy box inside it. It might take two people working together to lift the box up high enough to reach into the van. One person could push the box up a gently sloping ramp on his or her own.

Ramps are useful in many different situations. You often see ramps on building sites, and stairs are ramps, too. The shallower (less steep) the slope, the easier it is to move an object up it, but the further the object must move to gain the same amount of height. For example, when you are walking uphill on a zig-zag path you are using ramps. Walking along the gently sloping sections of the path is easier than walking straight up the steep hillside, but you have to walk much further to reach the top. Railways have to use winding routes to go up hills because trains cannot get up very steep hills without sliding backwards.

Mud-brick ramp
These are the remains of a ramp made of mud bricks. The ramp was built by the Ancient Egyptians about 3,000 years ago. Egyptian pyramid and temple builders had no cranes. They used ramps to move building materials up to where they were needed.

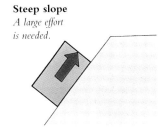

Steep slope
A large effort is needed.

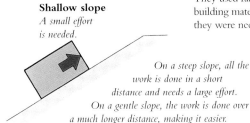

Shallow slope
A small effort is needed.

On a steep slope, all the work is done in a short distance and needs a large effort. On a gentle slope, the work is done over a much longer distance, making it easier.

Ramps for building
A ramp is being used to construct a building in this picture, which was copied from an ancient Egyptian tomb painting. Without construction machines such as cranes, the Egyptians had to build huge sloping ramps to pull stone blocks to the upper levels of the building.

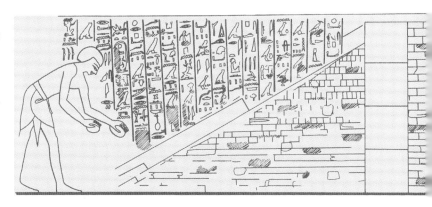

Ramps for loading

A car is driven up a ramp on to the back of a delivery truck. Long, gently sloping ramps are easier to drive up than short, steep ones. Loading and unloading cars from a transporter truck is easy using ramps because the cars can be driven on and off the truck. No winches or cranes are needed.

Access ramps

A disabled man is using a ramp to get down to the beach. Ramps make it much easier for vehicles with wheels to travel from one level to another. Many public buildings, such as libraries, sports centres and hospitals, often have ramps leading up to their doors as well as steps. Without ramps, people with wheelchairs or push-chairs often find it difficult to get in and out of buildings.

Fast track

When engineers plan roads such as motorways, they try to avoid steep carriageways. Cuttings and embankments are built into hillsides to provide gentle slopes. Vehicles are able to climb the slopes without having to slow down too much.

Zigzag roads

Mountain roads, such as this one in South Africa, zigzag upwards in a series of gentle slopes. A road straight up the side of the valley would be far too steep for most vehicles to drive up

FACT BOX

• Most canals have flights of locks to move boats up and down hill, but a few use inclined planes, or ramps. In a 1.6km-long inclined plane in Belgium, the boats float inside huge 5,000-tonne tanks of water. The tanks are hauled up the inclined plane on rails.

• The railway line from Lima to Galera, in Peru, climbs 4,780m. In some places the track zigzags backwards and forwards across the very steep hillsides.

WEDGES AND SCREWS

A pair of scissors and your front teeth have something in common. They are simple machines called wedges that use inclined planes (ramps) to work. A wedge is a type of ramp, or two ramps back-to-back. Pushing the thin end of a wedge into a narrow gap with a small effort makes the wedge press hard on the edges of the gap, forcing the gap apart. Chisels, axes and ploughs all work with wedges. If you look closely at their blades you will see that they widen from the cutting edge.

Screw threads are also a type of inclined plane. Imagine a long, narrow ramp wrapped around a pole. This is what a screw thread is. Screw threads make screws, nuts and bolts and car jacks work. It only takes a small effort to turn a screw thread to make it move in or out with great force. Screw threads provide a very secure way of fixing something together, or of raising a heavy load.

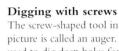

Wedging a door

A door wedge stops a door from opening or closing. Pulling on the door pulls the bottom of the door further up the wedge's ramp. This makes the wedge press even harder against the bottom of the door and the floor.

Wedges as cutters

An axe is used to cut down a tree. The axe head is wedge-shaped. When it hits the wood, its sharp edge sinks in, forcing the wood apart and splitting it. The handle allows the person operating the axe to swing it with great speed and lever out pieces of wood.

Wedges for woodworking

Wedges are useful for shaping materials. The axe in the foreground uses a wedge to split wood. The woodworker in the background is using a small wedge-shaped tool to remove small amounts of material from the wood, which is spun at high speed by a foot pedal.

Digging with screws

The screw-shaped tool in this picture is called an auger. It is used to dig deep holes for fence posts, or for filling with concrete, to make secure foundations for buildings. The auger is operated by a mechanical digger. The auger both loosens soil from the bottom of the hole and transports the soil to the surface.

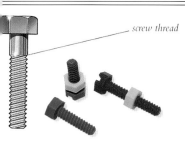

screw thread

Screws

A screw uses a screw thread to attach itself firmly into wood or metal. A screw thread is a ramp wrapped around a pole. Turning the thread is like moving up or down the slope.

bolt   nut

Nuts and bolts

A nut and bolt are used to join objects together. The screw threads on the nut and bolt interlock so that turning the nut makes it move down the bolt.

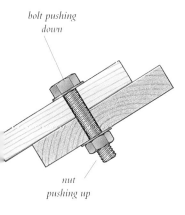

bolt pushing down

nut pushing up

When the nut is screwed on to the bolt the combined force of the nut and bolt squeezes the two pieces of wood tightly together.

Spiralling slope

A corkscrew has a screw thread that makes it wind into a cork as the handle is turned. The screw only moves a small way into the cork for each turn of the handle. This makes winding the corkscrew quite easy.

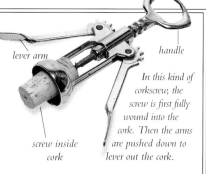

lever arm   handle

In this kind of corkscrew, the screw is first fully wound into the cork. Then the arms are pushed down to lever out the cork.

screw inside cork

Uncorking a bottle

A corkscrew such as this one combines three simple machines: the wheel and axle, the wedge and the lever. The handle of the corkscrew acts as a capstan to make turning in the screw easier. One end then folds down to rest on top the bottle's neck, and the other end forms a lever for pulling out the cork.

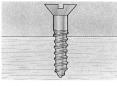

The point of a wood screw helps it to sink into the wood. The thread makes the point go in deeper as the screw is turned.

Driving force

Using a screwdriver increases the force with which you can turn a screw. As it turns, the screw thread bites into the wood. The screw is also wedge-shaped to help it force its way into the wood. Using screws is a strong and secure way of fixing all sorts of materials together.

PLANES AT WORK

Although screw threads are most commonly used for joining things together, they can also be used to lift a weight upwards. In a screw jack, the force made by turning the screw thread is used to lift a weight upwards. With a screw jack, a huge weight, such as a car, can be lifted easily, but slowly. One turn on the handle of the jack using a small effort raises the heavy load a few millimetres.

The first project on these pages shows you how to make a simple type of screw jack. The second project shows you how to make a device to measure force, or the effort needed to raise an object. Use it to compare how a gentler slope makes lifting an object easier.

MAKE A SCREW JACK

You will need: long bolt with two nuts, a washer, strong glue, piece of wooden board or thick card, lolly stick or short piece of wood, cardboard tube, card, a weight to lift.

Squashing with screws
The apple press uses a screw to squash the juice from apples. Turning the screw is quite easy, but it makes a huge force for squashing the apples.

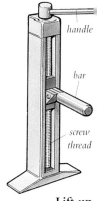

Lift up
If a car gets a puncture, the driver can lift the car with a screw jack before changing the wheel. The driver places the jack on the ground with the bar underneath the car. As the driver turns the handle, the bar moves up the screw thread and lifts the car.

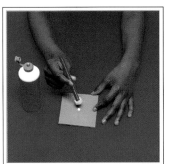

1 Fix a nut on one end of the bolt. Glue the bolt to the middle of a square piece of wooden board or thick card so that the thread is pointing upwards. Leave to dry.

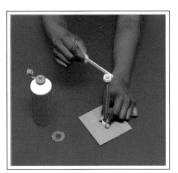

2 Glue the end of the lolly stick to the side of a nut (the nut must fit the bolt) to make a handle. When the glue is dry, wind the nut on to the bolt and put the washer on top.

3 Stick the tube to a rectangle of card. Place tube over the bolt so it rests on top of the washer. Move a weight up and down by turning the handle on the nut.

MAKE A FORCE MEASURER

You will need: *piece of wood or thick card, elastic band, paper fastener, string, pencil or felt-tipped pen, ruler, model vehicle, materials to make a slope (such as a plank and books).*

1 Measure and cut a piece of wood or card about 15cm x 5cm. Attach the elastic band near one end with a paper fastener. Tie a piece of string to the other end of the band.

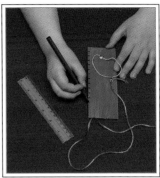

2 Mark centimetres along one edge of the wood, for recording how far the elastic band stretches when it is pulled by the weight. You have now made your force measurer.

On a level

The Ancient Egyptians used ramps to lift huge stone blocks to build their pyramids. As the building progressed, more ramps were added so that they were always level with the top the building.

3 Use your force measurer to find the weight of the model vehicle. Hang the model from your measurer and note where the band stretches to. Write down the measurement.

4 Make a slope – try using a plank propped up on books. How much force is needed to pull the vehicle up the slope? Is it less or greater than the model's weight? Try again with a shallower slope. Does the force needed change? You should see that it needs less force to pull the model vehicle up the shallower slope.

LIFTING WITH PULLEYS

Using a pulley is often the easiest way to lift a heavy load high up. The pulley is a simple machine. The most basic pulley system is a wheel with a groove in its rim in which a rope is fitted. The wheel rotates around an axle. The rope hangs down either side of the wheel, with one end attached to a load. Pulling down on the rope lifts the load hanging on the other end. It does not reduce the amount of force needed to lift an object, so there is no mechanical advantage. It does, however, make lifting the load easier, because it is easier to pull down than it is to pull up. A pulley's special advantage is that it changes the direction of the force.

Using several pulleys together makes lifting even easier and many pulley systems have more than one wheel that operate together. A pulley system such as this is called a block and tackle. Pulleys are useful for lifting loads on building sites and dockyards, and for moving heavy parts and machinery in factories.

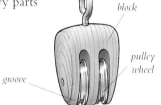

block

pulley wheel

groove

A block and tackle has two blocks like the one shown above, arranged one above the other. The pulley wheels are designed to turn easily as the rope runs around them, through the groove.

Pulling down
The simplest pulley system is a single pulley wheel with a rope running over it. It changes the direction of the pull (the effort) needed to lift an object (the load) off the ground. Instead of pulling up on the object, the boy is pulling down on the rope. He can use his weight to help.

Winching with pulleys
An air-sea rescue helicopter uses an electric winch to lift sailors from the sea on the end of a wire. The wire runs from the winch over a pulley wheel on the side of the helicopter.

Pulleys for building
Workmen use a pulley to lift building materials to construct the walls of a great city in the 1500s. The workman at the bottom turns a handle to haul up the bucket. The pulley was probably devised by Ancient Greeks about 2,500 years ago and has been in use ever since.

Half the effort

This pulley system has two pulley wheels. Pulling the rope raises the lower wheel and the load. With two wheels, the effort needed to lift the load is halved. This makes it easier, but the rope has to be pulled twice as far.

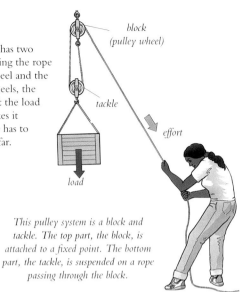

block (pulley wheel)

tackle

effort

load

This pulley system is a block and tackle. The top part, the block, is attached to a fixed point. The bottom part, the tackle, is suspended on a rope passing through the block.

Up and away

A light pull on the loop of chain lifts a very heavy boat engine. This pulley system has a very high mechanical advantage – it takes little effort to pull a massive weight.

Boats away!

A ship's lifeboats hang on pulley systems ready to be lowered quickly into the sea if the ship has to be abandoned. The pulley systems allow the heavy boats to be lowered by one person standing inside the boat itself.

Dockyard block and tackle

The lower end of the block and tackle on a dockyard crane can be seen in this picture. The crane is lifting heavy pallets of cargo from the deep hold of a ship.

Higher and higher

A dockyard crane uses pulley systems to lift very heavy loads. The cable from the pulley is winched in and out by an engine to make the lifting hook rise and fall. Other engines move the crane's arm up and down.

PULLEYS AT WORK

The two projects on these pages illustrate how pulley systems work. In the first project, a simple double pulley system is constructed. It does not have pulley wheels. Instead, the string passes over smooth metal hoops. This would be no good for a real system because friction (a force that slows things down) between the rope and metal would be too great, but it does show how a pulley system is connected together.

The second project investigates how adding more turns on a block and tackle reduces the effort needed to move a load. You may notice, however, that the more turns you make, the greater the friction becomes. Using wheels in a block and tackle cuts down this friction.

Lifting materials
Construction cranes make use of pulleys to lift heavy materials to the upper floors of a building. Pulleys make the hook move up and down and backwards and forwards along the cranes boom.

MAKE A SIMPLE PULLEY

You will need:
lengths of string,
two large paper clips,
a weight.

Linking up
Heavy-duty block and tackle systems, like this one in a dockyard, are used for lifting the heavy cargo. They have metal chain links, which are much stronger than a rope would be. The chain links interlock with the shaped pulley wheels.

1 Take a short length of string. Use the string to tie a large paper clip to a door handle, or coat hook fixed to a wall. Make sure the paper clip is tied securely to its support.

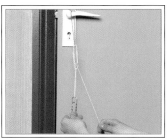

2 Cut a long piece of string and feed it through the paper clip's inner hoop. Now feed it through the top of a second paper clip and tie it to the outer hoop of the top clip.

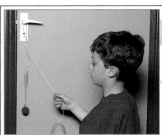

3 Fix a weight, using another piece of string, to the bottom paper clip. Pull the end of the long string to lift the bottom paper clip, which will lift the weight.

MAKE A BLOCK AND TACKLE

You will need:
two broom handles or lengths of thick dowelling, strong string or thin rope, two friends.

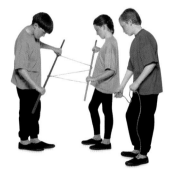

1 Ask each of your friends to hold a broom handle, or length of dowelling, between outstretched hands. Tie the end of a long piece of string, or rope, to one handle.

2 Wrap the string around each handle once, keeping the loops fairly close together on the handles. Now pull on the string. How easy was it to pull your friends together?

FACT BOX

• Using a block-and-tackle system with a mechanical advantage of 20 (with ten wheels at each end), you could lift an elephant easily by hand!

• One of the first people to make use of block and tackle systems was the famous Greek scientist Archimedes. He is said to have pulled ships ashore with them, in the third century BC.

---

3 Now wrap the string twice around each handle, making sure you keep the turns close together. Now pull on the end of the string again. What differences do you notice this time? Is it any easier?

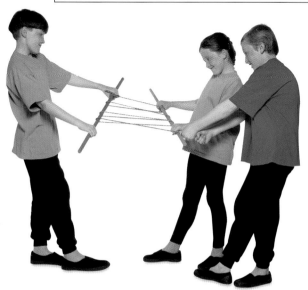

4 Make more turns around the handles and try pulling again. Do more turns make the effort you need to make smaller? Do you have to pull the rope farther than before?

GEAR WHEELS

A gear is a wheel with teeth around its edge. When two gear wheels are put next to each other their teeth can be made to interlock. Then when one wheel turns, the other one turns, too. Gears are used to transmit movement from one wheel to another. If both wheels are the same size, the wheels turn at the same speed. If one wheel is bigger than the other, the gears can be used to speed up or slow down movement, or to increase or decrease a force. Many machines, from kitchen whisks to trucks, have gears that help them to work.

Belt drives and chain drives are similar to gears. In these, two wheels are linked together by a belt or a chain instead of teeth. This is another way of transferring power and movement from one wheel to another. Speed can also be varied by changing the size of the wheels.

Tooth to tooth
This is a simple gear system. One gear wheel turns the other because the teeth interlock with each other. The larger wheel will make the smaller wheel turn faster because it is bigger, so the smaller wheel takes less time to turn a full circle. The larger wheel is twice the size of the smaller one.

Mining with gears
Huge gear wheels are part of an old lift mechanism from a mine. The teeth on the interlocking gear wheels press very hard against each other. They need to be very wide and thick so that they don't snap off.

Transmitting a force
In the centre of this kitchen whisk is a set of gears. They are used to transmit the turning movement of the handle to the blades of the whisk. The gears speed up the movement, making the blades spin faster than the turning handle. The gears turn the movement through a right angle, too. These sort of gears are called bevelled gears.

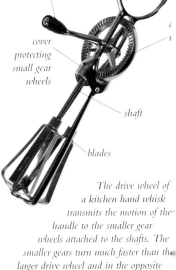

turning handle

cover protecting small gear wheels

shaft

blades

The drive wheel of a kitchen hand whisk transmits the motion of the handle to the smaller gear wheels attached to the shafts. The smaller gears turn much faster than the larger drive wheel and in the opposite direction to each other.

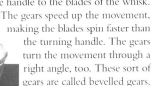

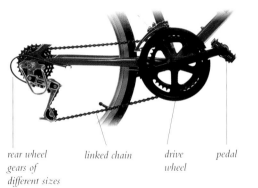

All geared up

Bicycle gears use wheels and a chain to transmit the drive from the pedals to the bicycle's rear wheel. As a rider turns the pedals, the drive wheel is moved around. This moves a linked chain, which turns a set of gear wheels of different sizes attached to the rear wheel. With the chain on the largest of these gears (in low gear), pedalling is easy but the bicycle travels slowly. With the chain on the smallest gear (in high gear), pedalling is harder but the bicycle moves faster.

rear wheel gears of different sizes

linked chain

drive wheel

pedal

interlocking gears

winder to wind up spring

Wind-up watch gears

The back has been removed from this wind-up watch so you can see the tiny gear wheels inside. Different-sized gear wheels are arranged so that they move the hands of the watch at different speeds. The clock is powered by a spring, wound up by hand. The spring makes a gear wheel turn, which moves the minute hand. Another gear slows down this movement to turn the hour hand.

gears transmit energy from spring

Swinging time keeper

This pendulum clock uses gear wheels to control its speed. A spring drives one gear round, which drives other gears that show time. The speed that gears turn at is controlled by a swinging pendulum that interlocks with the teeth on a gear wheel called the escape wheel. The escape wheel gives the pendulum a small push on each swing to keep the pendulum moving.

Belt drives

Wide belts, called belt drives, stretch between wheels in the roof and the machines of a factory. The photograph was taken in about 1905. The wheels in the roof are turned by an engine, and the belts transmit this movement to drive the machines.

MAKING GEARS WORK

Before engineers used metals, they made gear wheels from wood. One way of making gear-wheel teeth was to fix short poles on to the edge of a thick disc. The poles on different gear wheels interlocked to transmit movement. Gears like this were being used 2,000 years ago. If you visit an old mill, you might still see similar wooden gears today. The first project shows you how to make a simple gear wheel system. What do you notice about how the wheels turn? They turn in different directions and the smaller wheel (with fewer teeth) turns one and a half times for every one rotation of the larger wheel. The second project shows you how to make a simple belt drive and how it can turn an axle at different speeds.

Slow pedal power
Old sewing machines, such as this one, were powered by a foot pedal that turned a large pulley wheel. This wheel was linked by a drive belt to a small pulley wheel on the machine. So pedalling slowly made the small wheel turn quickly.

MAKE A SET OF GEAR WHEELS

You will need: pair of compasses and pencil, protractor, thick card, scissors, used matchsticks or thin dowelling, glue, paper fasteners, small cardboard box.

Spiral gears
A computer graphic image shows part of a car gear box. These gears are helical (spiral) gears, which are more efficient than gears with straight teeth.

3 Use paper fasteners to attach one wheel to the top of the box and the other to the side so that the teeth interlock. Turn one disc to turn the other.

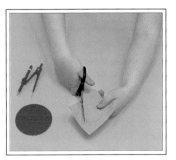

1 Using a pencil and compasses, mark out two discs on card and cut them out. Make the diameter of one disc twice the diameter of the other, for example 8cm and 4cm.

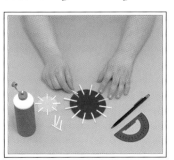

2 Glue eight matches around the edge of the small disc. First glue four matches in a cross shape, then add four more half-way. In a similar way, glue 12 matches to the large disc.

MAKE A BELT DRIVE

You will need: cardboard box, dowelling, scissors, strips of thin card, glue, thick elastic band, felt-tipped pen.

1 Cut two pieces of dowelling each about 5cm longer than the width of the box. Cut two holes in both sides of the box. Slide the dowelling through to make two axles.

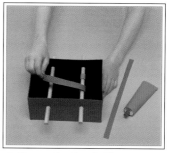

2 Cut a strip of card. Glue it to one of the axles. Wrap it round and glue the end down to make a wheel. Make a bigger wheel with a strip of card three times longer than the first.

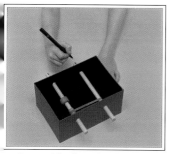

3 Put a wide elastic band around both axles. The band should be slightly stretched when it is in place. Make a mark at the end of each axle so you can see how fast they turn.

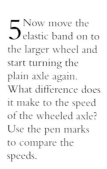

Printing gear
Computer printers use gears driven by electric motors to move sheets of paper past the print head (where the ink is fired onto the paper) bit by bit at the correct speed. More gears move the print head from side to side, making up lines of the image.

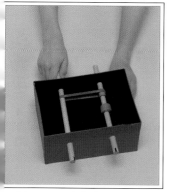

4 To test your belt drive, put the elastic band on to the smaller wheel and start turning the plain axle. Does the wheeled axle turn more or fewer times than the plain?

5 Now move the elastic band on to the larger wheel and start turning the plain axle again. What difference does it make to the speed of the wheeled axle? Use the pen marks to compare the speeds.

POWER FOR MACHINES

Early machines, such as axes and ramps, relied on human muscle power to make them work. Then people started using animals to work many simple machines. Animals, such as oxen, can carry, pull and lift much heavier loads than people can. Eventually people realized they could capture the energy of the wind or flowing water by using windmills and water-wheels. These became the first machines to create power that in turn was used to make other machines work. This energy was used to do such things as grinding grain to make flour or pumping up water from underground.

Today, wind and water energy are still captured to generate electricity, which we use to light and power our homes, schools, offices and factories.

Wind for milling

A windmill uses the power of the wind to turn heavy mill stones that grind grain to make flour. The whole building can be turned around so that the sails are facing into the wind. The speed of the mill is controlled by opening and closing slots in the sails.

Power walking

A man is operating a treadmill in Australia in the 1840s. He is walking up the rungs so that his weight turns the wheel. The movement of the wheel is used to operate machinery. Human treadmills are no longer used.

Overshot water-wheel

There are two different types of water-wheel. This one is called an overshot wheel because the water flows over the top of the wheel and falls into buckets on the wheel. The water's weight pulls the wheel around.

Undershot water-wheel

The second type of water-wheel is called an undershot wheel because rushing water in a stream or river flows under the wheel and catches in the buckets at the bottom of the wheel. The force of the water spins the wheel.

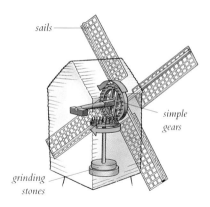

sails

simple gears

grinding stones

Grinding stones

Many windmills and watermills generate power to turn millstones. The grinding stones in this picture are used to squeeze oil from olives. Only the top millstone turns while the bottom stone stays still.

Inside a windmill is an arrangement of wooden gear wheels, which transfers power from the sails to the grinding stones. Mills like this have been in use for centuries.

Modern mills

Wind turbines, like these shown on a wind farm, are a modern type of windmill. The wind spins the huge propellers, which turn an electricity generator inside the top of each turbine.

Power from water

A hydroelectric station generates electricity from the water of a fast-flowing river. The water is stored behind a huge dam. As it flows out, it spins a turbine, which is like a very efficient water-wheel. The turbine turns a generator, which makes electricity.

Underground power

In the underground turbine hall of a hydroelectric power station, each of the generators can produce about a gigawatt of electricity – enough electricity to work about 10 million light bulbs.

WIND AND WATER POWER

Modern windmills are called wind turbines and are used to generate electricity. The most efficient wind turbines only have two or three blades, as in the propeller of an aircraft. Hundreds of wind turbines can be grouped together to make a wind farm. Sometimes one or two large turbines generate enough electricity to power a small community. There are several shapes of wind turbine. One of the most efficient is the vertical-axis type. This has an axle standing vertical to the ground. It is very efficient because it works no matter which way the wind is blowing.

The first project shows you how to make a vertical-axis turbine. The second project shows you how to make an overshot water-wheel. This captures the energy of falling water to lift a small weight. Try pouring the water on to the wheel from different heights to see if it makes a difference to the wheel's speed.

MAKE A WINDMILL

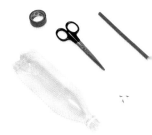

You will need:
plastic bottle, scissors, sticky tape, thin dowelling, drawing pins.

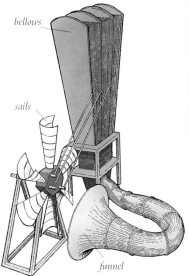

bellows

sails

funnel

Round and round again
This machine was devised in the 1500s by an Italian inventor. He believed that as the sails turned, they would operate a set of bellows. The bellows in turn would provide enough wind to drive the sails to set up a continuous cycle of movement. It cannot work because the sails do not provide enough energy to squeeze the bellows.

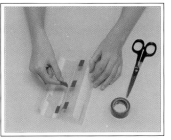

1 Cut the top and bottom off the bottle to leave a tube. Cut the tube in half lengthwise, then stick the two halves together in an S shape, so the edges overlap by 2cm.

2 The piece of dowelling should be about 4cm longer than the vanes. Slide it into the slot between the vanes. Press a drawing pin gently into each end of the dowelling.

3 To make the windmill spin, hold it vertically with your fingers on the drawing pins at each end of the dowelling. Blow on the vanes. The windmill will spin easily.

MAKE A WATER-WHEEL

You will need: *large plastic bottle, scissors, wire (ask an adult to cut the bottom out of a coat hanger), cork, craft knife, sticky tape, string, weight, jug of water, large plate.*

1 Cut the top third off the plastic bottle. Cut a small hole in the bottom piece near the base (this is to let the water out). Cut a V-shape on each side of the rim.

2 Ask an adult to push the wire through the centre of the cork to make an axle. From the top third of the plastic bottle, cut six small curved vanes as shown.

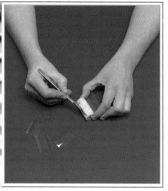

3 Ask an adult to cut six slots in the cork with a craft knife. (This might be easier without the wire.) Push the plastic vanes into the slots to make the water-wheel.

4 Rest the wheel's axle in the V-shaped slots. Tape a length of string towards one end of the axle and tie a small weight to the end of the string. Fill a jug with water.

FACT BOX

• In a strong breeze, the world's largest wind turbine, in Hawaii, USA, would be capable of operating more than 4,000 microwave ovens.

• China's Three Gorges Dam will generate 18 gigawatts of electricity – enough to work 24 million microwave ovens!

5 Put the water-wheel on a large plate or in the sink. Pour water on to the wheel so that it hits the upward-curving vanes. The weight should be lifted up.

Animal power

A water-raising wheel such as this one would be operated by an animal or a person walking in a circle, pulling the horizontal pole on the right. Buckets attached to a chain driven by the wheel go down into the well, scoop up water, lift it, and empty it into a chute.

ENGINES AND MOTORS

Many modern machines are powered by engines and motors, which are complicated machines themselves. An engine is a machine that makes movement energy from heat. The heat is made by burning a fuel, such as petrol. The first engines were driven by steam.

Most engines today, such as the ones used in cars, are internal combustion engines. This means that the fuel is burned inside the engine. In a car engine, as the petrol explodes, it produces hot gases that push pistons inside cylinders up and down. The pistons turn a crankshaft, which carries the movement energy from the engine to the wheels of the car. An electric motor is a machine that makes movement energy from electricity rather than from burning fuel. Most of the electricity we use is made in power stations or from the chemicals inside batteries.

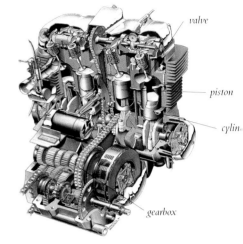

valve

piston

cylin

gearbox

Burning inside
This diagram shows the pistons inside the internal combustion engine of a car. At the top are valves that let fuel and air into the pistons and let exhaust gases out. At the bottom is the gearbox that sends the power from the engine to the wheels.

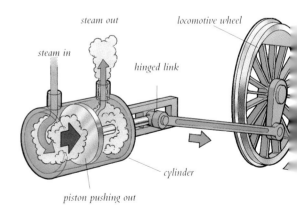

steam out

locomotive wheel

steam in

hinged link

piston pushing out

cylinder

Piston powe
In a steam engine, steam made by heating water in a boiler is forced along a pip into a cylinder. The pressure of the stear pushes a piston in the cylinder outwards. The moving piston then turns a whee that is used to drive a locomotive o power a machine

Early steam power
An atmospheric engine was one of the first types of steam engines. Steam was fed to a cylinder, where it was cooled and turned back to water, forming a vacuum. The atmospheric pressure outside the cylinder pushed the piston in.

Engines for cars

A car's internal combustion engine is usually fitted under the bonnet. The engine's cylinders are inside the large black engine block. You can see the exhaust pipes that carry away waste gases from the cylinders.

Under the bonnet

The top of an internal combustion engine in a small truck. On the left are the starter motor (an electric motor that makes the engine turn to start it up) and the alternator, that makes electricity for the electrical parts, such as the lights, of the truck.

Electric motors

Electricity is turned into movement by an electric motor. When the motor is connected to a battery, its shaft spins around. Electric motors are small and clean, which makes them useful for household gadgets.

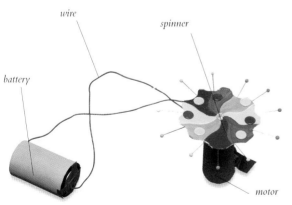

wire

spinner

battery

motor

An electric motor with a colourful spinner on top is connected to a battery by two wires. This makes an electric circuit.

HYDRAULICS AND PNEUMATICS

Did you know that a machine can be powered by a liquid or a gas? Machines that have parts moved by a liquid are called hydraulic machines. Those that have parts moved by a gas are called pneumatic machines. A simple hydraulic system has a pipe filled with oil and a piston (a cylinder that moves to and fro) fitted at each end. Pushing one piston into the pipe forces the piston at the other end outwards, transmitting power from one end of the pipe to the other. In a simple pneumatic system, compressed air is used to force a piston to move.

Hydraulic and pneumatic machines can be very powerful. They are also quite simple and very robust. Machines that work in dirty and rough conditions, such as diggers, drills and tipper trucks, often have hydraulic or pneumatic systems instead of motors. Most dental drills are also worked by a pneumatic system. Air, pumped to the drill, makes a tiny turbine inside the drill spin very fast.

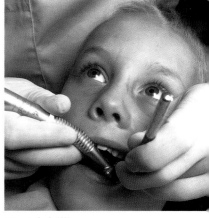

Dental drilling
The high-pitched whine of a dental drill is made by the air that powers it. Inside is an air turbine that spins an amazing 10,000 times a second as air is pumped through it.

Pump it up
Using an air pump is a simple way to blow up a balloon. A valve in the pump's outlet allows air to be pumped into the balloon as the piston is pushed in. It prevents the air being sucked out again when the piston is pulled out.

Lift it up
Pneumatic power can lift up a book. The girl blows air into the inflated balloon and pushes the book upwards. Less effort is needed to lift the book like this than is needed to lift it by hand.

air outlet

cylinder

piston

Sucking in air
All pneumatic machines need a device to suck in air from the outside and push it into the machine. This is called an air pump, or a compressor. The simple air pump above sucks in air as the piston is pulled back, and forces air out as the piston is pushed in.

Hydraulic lift

Lifting and moving a heavy load is made easy with a hydraulically-powered machine such as a fork-lift truck. The forks are lifted by hydraulic rams. Each ram consists of a fixed cylinder and a piston that moves inside it. Pumping special oil, called hydraulic fluid, into the cylinder makes the piston move in or out, depending on which end of the cylinder the oil is pumped into.

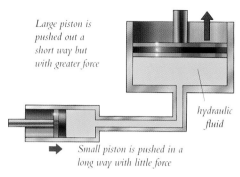

Large piston is pushed out a short way but with greater force

hydraulic fluid

Small piston is pushed in a long way with little force

Pushing in, pushing out

A simple hydraulic system has two pistons connected by a cylinder filled with hydraulic fluid. Using different-sized pistons creates a mechanical advantage. Pushing the small piston creates a greater force at the large one.

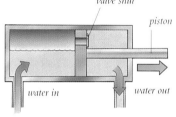

valve shut

piston

water in

water out

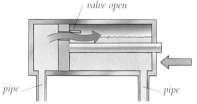

valve open

pipe

pipe

Pumping water

Moving a water pump's piston in and out moves water from the pipe on the left to the pipe on the right. The valve opens to let water through as the piston moves in. The valve shuts automatically as the piston moves out because the water presses the valve closed.

Hydraulic digging

The sections of the arm of a digger are moved by powerful hydraulic rams, each with a cylinder and piston. Hydraulic fluid is pumped to the cylinders by a pump powered by the digger's diesel engine. The fluid flows along very strong pipes called hydraulic lines, which you can see on the upper part of the arm.

Breaking through

A pneumatic drill is an air-powered drill used to break up road surfaces and concrete. The air forces the drill's heavy blade to jump up and down very quickly. The drill needs a supply of compressed air to make it work, which comes along a strong, rubber pipe from a machine called a compressor.

LIQUID AND AIR AT WORK

MAKE AN HYDRAULIC LIFTER

You will need: large plastic bottle, scissors, airtight plastic bag, plastic tubing, sticky tape, plastic funnel, spray can lid, heavy weight, jug of water.

Hydraulic machinery uses a liquid to transmit power, while pneumatic machinery uses compressed air. The first project shows you how to make a simple hydraulic machine that uses water pressure to lift an object upwards. A central reservoir (a jug of water) is poured into a pipe. The water fills up a plastic bag, which is forced to expand in a narrow cylinder. This forces up a platform, which in turn raises a heavy object. Many cranes, excavators and trucks use this principle to lift heavy loads, using hydraulic rams.

The second project shows you how to make a simple air pump. An air pump works by sucking air in one hole and pushing it out of another. A valve stops the air being sucked in and pushed out of the wrong holes. When the air tries to flow through one way, the valve opens, but when the air tries to flow through the other way the valve stays shut.

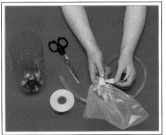

1 Cut the top off the large plastic bottle. Make sure the plastic bag is airtight and wrap its neck over the end of a length of plastic tubing. Seal the bag to the tube with tape.

Firing water
Fire-fighters spray water on to fires through hoses so that they can stand back from the flames. The water is pumped along the hoses by a powerful pump on the fire engine.

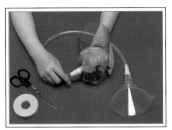

2 Fix a funnel to the other end of the tube. Make a hole at the base of the bottle and feed the bag and tubing through. The bag should sit in the bottom of the bottle.

3 Put the spray can lid on top of the bag and rest a book, or another heavy object, on top of the bottle. Lift the funnel end of the tubing up, and slowly pour in water. What happens to the can lid and the book?

PROJECT

MAKE AN AIR PUMP

***You will need**: large plastic bottle, scissors, hammer, small nails, wooden stick or dowelling, card, sticky tape, table tennis ball.*

1 Cut around the large plastic bottle, about one third up from the bottom. Cut a slit down the side of the bottom part of the bottle so that it will slide inside the top part.

2 Ask an adult to help you nail the bottom of the bottle to the end of a wooden stick or piece of dowelling. You have now made a piston for your air pump.

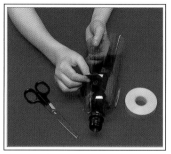

3 Cut a hole about 1 cm across near the neck of the bottle. Cut a piece of card about 2cm x 2cm. Tape one edge of the card to the bottle to form a flap over the hole.

4 Drop a table tennis ball into the top part of the bottle so that it rests in the neck. Push the bottom part of the bottle (the piston) into the top part (the cylinder).

FACT BOX

• A fire-engine pump can pump 1,000 litres of water a minute – enough to fill eight large fizzy drink bottles a second.

• Fire-fighters free people trapped in crashed cars with hydraulically powered cutting and spreading machines.

Skip-lifting truck
A skip truck has hydraulic rams to lift a full skip. The rams are controlled by levers near the cab, and powered by a pump operated by the engine.

5 Move the piston in and out to suck air into the bottle and out of the hole. Can you see how both the valves work? The flap should automatically close when you pull the piston out.

MACHINES AT HOME

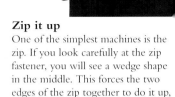

zip
fastener

Your home is full of machines. Look in the kitchen, the bathroom, the living room and bedroom. In your kitchen you should find several simple gadgets, such as can-openers, taps, scissors and bottle openers. There might also be more complicated machines, such as a washing machine or a dishwasher. Other machines you might find include a vacuum cleaner and a refrigerator. In other rooms there may be a hairdryer, a shower and a television. Even the zips on your clothes are machines. Think about how each one might save you time and effort. What would life be like without them?

Most machines not only save you work, but also improve the results – a modern washing machine cleans clothes better than an old-fashioned tub and a vacuum cleaner is more efficient than a broom. Many machines save time, too. For example, it is far quicker to heat food in a microwave oven than over an open fire. Many of these machines need electricity to work and are powered from the mains supply.

Zip it up

One of the simplest machines is the zip. If you look carefully at the zip fastener, you will see a wedge shape in the middle. This forces the two edges of the zip together to do it up, and apart again to undo it. Before there were zips, people had to do their clothes up with buttons or hooks and eyes, which took longer.

wheel and axle

lever arm

wedge

Can-opener

Can you see four different types of machine in a can opener? You should be able to find levers, a wedge, a wheel and axle and a gear wheel. Together, they make it simple to open a can.

FACT BOX

• The zip was invented in 1893. The first zips were unreliable until tiny bumps and hollows were added to the end of each tooth, to help the teeth interlock.

• Electrically powered domestic machines were only possible once mains electricity was developed in the 1880s.

• One of the earliest vacuum cleaners was built in England, in 1901. It was so large that it had to be pulled by a horse and powered by a petrol engine!

• The the spin dryer was thought of by a French engineer in 1865, but it was not developed until the 1920s.

How a fridge works

Inside a refrigerator is a pump that squeezes a special liquid called a refrigerant. As the refrigerant expands again, it uses up heat, making the compartment cold.

What, no bag?

This clever bagless cleaner spins the dusty air at high speed, which throws the dust to the sides of the dust-collecting container. Most vacuum cleaners have a bag that lets air through but traps dust, and the bag has to be replaced regularly. The bagless cleaner's container lasts for much longer.

Washing by machine

A modern washing machine is a combination of several machines. It has electric motors (to turn the drum), pumps (to pump water in and out) and valves (that let water in or out). All these machines are controlled by an automatic programme timer.

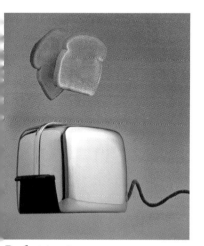

Perfect toast

A toaster is a machine that heats bread using electric heating elements until it detects that the surface of the bread is hot enough. Then it ejects the toast and turns off the elements.

Hairdryer

Small, mains-powered electric motors make it possible to make compact machines such as hairdryers. The motor in a hairdryer works a fan. This blows air across a coil of wire that is heated instantly by electricity, making the air warm.

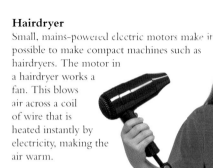

DOMESTIC HELP

MAKE A CAN CRUSHER

You will need:
*two short planks of wood about
50cm x 10cm and 1–2cm thick,
hinge, screws, screwdriver, two
coffee-jar lids, glue.*

Household machines are designed to make life easier. Here you can make a really useful can crusher and a hand-operated vacuum cleaner. Use the can crusher to flatten empty drinks cans before you take them for recycling or to the tip. Crushed cans take up far less space than empty, full-sized ones. This makes them easier to store and to carry.

The crusher is a simple machine that uses a lever action to press on the ends of the can. It is much easier to crush a can with the machine than it is with your hands. The vacuum cleaner is based on the air pump that you have already made. It uses the same principles to pick up bits of paper as a more sophisticated vacuum cleaner does to pick up household dust. Tissue paper is used for the collection bag because it allows air to pass through it and filters out the bits of paper. Securing the table tennis ball to the neck of the pump makes the cleaner more efficient, as it prevents the ball from falling too far out of place.

Shredded in seconds
A blender has high-speed chopping blades at the bottom that will cut vegetables and other foods to shreds in seconds. The blades are based on a simple machine: the wedge. Many kitchens are full of gadgets to help make food preparation faster.

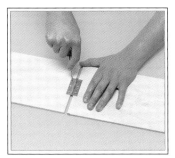

1 Lay the two planks of wood end to end. Ask an adult to help you screw them together with a hinge, using screws and a screwdriver. Make sure the hinge is secure.

2 Glue a jar lid to each plank of wood with the top of the lid face down. The lids should be about half-way along each plank and the same distance from the hinge.

3 To crush a can, put the can in between the lids so that it is held in place. Press down hard on the top piece of wood

MAKE A VACUUM CLEANER

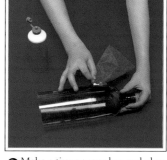

1 Make the air pump from the last project without the valve. Tape string to the ball, feed it through the bottle's neck and tape it down so that the ball falls out a few millimetres.

2 Make a tissue paper bag and glue it over the hole in the bottle. Air from the pump will go through the bag and anything the vacuum picks up should be trapped.

You will need: *large plastic bottle, scissors, hammer, small nails, wooden stick or dowelling, table tennis ball, string, sticky tape, tissue paper, glue.*

FACT BOX

• One of the first vacuum cleaners used small pumps like bellows that were attached to the bottom of shoes. The user had to run on the spot to suck up dust!

3 Try picking up tiny bits of paper with the vacuum. Pull the piston out sharply to suck the bits of paper into the bottle. Push the piston back in gently to pump the paper into the tissue bag. How much can you pick up with your home-made cleaner? Can you pick anything else up, such as grains of salt?

Up the tube
Modern vacuum cleaners have an air pump operated by an electric motor. The pump creates a vacuum inside the cleaner, and dusty air rushes in from the outside to fill the vacuum. A bag at the end of the pipe lets air through but traps dust.

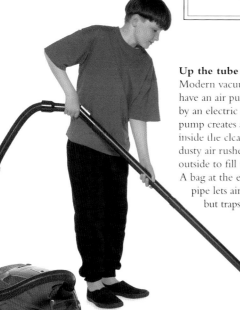

TRANSPORT MACHINES

Bicycles, cars, buses, trucks, trains, ships and aircraft are all machines used for transport. They all make it easier and quicker to travel from one place to another by making wide use of different types of engines, motors, gears and wheels. The bicycle is one of the most complicated machines that relies on human muscle power to work. A bicycle includes several types of simple machine, such as wheels, axles and levers, and is designed to reduce effort to a minimum.

Larger transport machines have engines and motors to power them. Many also make use of hydraulic, pneumatic and electronic systems. The different systems combine to make the machine efficient, so that it uses the minimum amount of fuel or electricity, and safe, so that there is a low risk of accidents, and passengers are well protected.

Hopalong hobbyhorse
The first bicycles had no gears and no pedals. They were called hobbyhorses and the riders had to push them along the ground with their feet. They were still quicker than walking.

The gear system allows a cyclist to travel quickly or slowly and still pedal at a comfortable rate.

On your bicycle
A cyclist uses her energy to push down on the pedals. The gear system uses this push to turn the back wheel and drive the bike forwards. The tyres rub against the road, causing friction, a force that slows things down. Air hitting her body, and her weight, cause her to slow down, too.

The brake lever on the handlebar pulls a cable that makes a brake block press on the wheel rim.

A smooth ride
A pump is used to pump air into the tyres. A valve in the tyre lets air in, but stops it escaping. Tyres are pumped full of air to give a smoother, easier ride.

FACT BOX

• The first locomotives were built in the early 1800s. They were powered by steam, but they were not used for pulling passenger carriages. Instead they were used for hauling coal trucks at mines and ironworks.

• In 1845, two British naval ships fought a tug-of-war. One had paddles and the other was fitted with a propeller. The Navy wanted to test whether paddles or propellers were best. The propeller won the contest easily.

Electric trains

Overhead cables suspended above the track provide the power for the electric motors that move fast express trains, such as this Swedish X2000. Electric motors work well at low speed and high speed, so no complicated gears are needed for the train to speed up or slow down. Inside the locomotive cars at each end of the train are electric circuits that control the flow of electricity to the motors. The driver controls the speed of the train from the cab at the front. The train is also streamlined (shaped to move smoothly) so that it cuts easily through the air.

Car parts

All modern cars, from sports cars to small family cars, have similar parts. They are moved by an internal combustion engine (at the front) which burns petrol or diesel fuel stored in a tank (at the rear). All the parts are attached to a steel body shell.

Aircraft parts

The flaps that extend from an aircraft's wings to provide extra lift during take-off and landing are controlled by hydraulic systems. Airliners, such as this Airbus A340, are the most complex transport machines of all, with thousands of parts. They are moved through the air by powerful jet engines, which are complex machines themselves. Safety is very important, so most of the aircraft's systems have back-up systems in case they go wrong.

BUILDING MACHINES

Constructing houses, office blocks, bridges, roads and railways involves digging into the ground, moving rock and earth, and transporting and lifting steel, concrete and other heavy building materials. There are specialized construction machines, such as diggers, bulldozers, concrete mixers and cranes, to carry out all these jobs. Many of them use the principles of simple machines to work. For example, cranes use pulleys and balanced levers to help them lift. Most construction machines have large diesel engines to provide the power they need, and some have hydraulic or pneumatic systems to move their parts.

Machinery of old
The Flemish artist Pieter Brueghe painted the mythical Tower of Babe in 1563. It shows the sort of construction machines that were in use in the 1500s, such as chisels, levers pulleys and simple cranes, operated by large treadmills. The huge cathedral found in many European cities wer built with simple machines like these

---

FACT BOX

• The height of a tower crane's tower can be increased. A new section of tower is hauled up and positioned on top of the existing tower.

• Tunnels that go through soft rock, such as chalk, are dug with tunnel boring machines. The machine bores its way through the rock with a rotating cutting head.

• Around 2,000 years ago the Romans used cranes for building. The cranes were powered by slaves walking round in a giant treadmill.

Earth mover
A bulldozer is used to push rock, soil and rubble away to clear a building site ready for work to start. Its wide tracks, called caterpillar tracks, stop it sinking into muddy ground.

Digging out
A mechanical excavator is used to dig up rock and soil. It makes trenches for pipes, and holes for foundations. Its powerful digging arm is operated by hydraulic rams.

Loading machine

A machine called a loader has a wide bucket that skims along the ground scooping up waste soil. When the bucket is full, hydraulic rams lift it into the air so that the loader can carry it to a waiting tipper truck.

Mixing it up

A concrete mixer carries concrete to the building site from the factory. Inside the drum a blade, like a screw thread, mixes the concrete. The blade stays still while the drum rotates.

Hammering in

A pile driver hammers piles, or metal posts, into the ground. It repeatedly lifts a large weight with its crane and drops it on to the top of the pile. The piles form the foundation of a new building.

Towering crane

These tower cranes look flimsy, but they do not topple over even when they are lifting heavy weights. This is because of a concrete counterweight behind the cab.

Tipping out

Dumper trucks are used to deliver hardcore (crushed up stones used for foundations) and to take away unwanted soil. To empty the load on to the ground, the back of the dumper is tipped up by hydraulic rams. The load slides to the ground.

ON THE FARM

Some of the oldest types of machines in the world are used for agriculture. Farmers use machines to prepare the soil, to sow and harvest their crops, and to feed and milk their animals. One of the first, and still one of the most important farm machines, was the plough. Archaeologists have found evidence of ploughs from about 9,000 years ago. They began as a simple, sharpened stick that was used to turn up the soil. Today, a seven-furrow plough hauled behind a modern tractor can cover 40 hectares of land – as much as 80 football pitches – in a day.

Modern farming uses many specialized machines to make cultivated land more productive. In some parts of the world, powered machinery, usually operated by a tractor, does all the work. But in many countries, ploughs are pulled by animals, and crops are harvested using simple hand tools.

Tractor and plough
Modern, tractor-pulled ploughs have several individual ploughs in a row to break up the soil into furrows. This makes it much quicker to plough a field than with a single plough. At the rear end of the tractor is a rotating shaft called a take-off shaft. It provides the power for the plough.

FACT BOX

• On many farms in arid areas, the pumps used to raise water from wells or streams for irrigation, and for animals to drink, are powered by small windmills.

• One of the most important agricultural inventions was the seed drill, which planted seeds in neat rows and at the correct depth. It was invented more than five thousand years ago.

Steam power
Steam-driven traction engines were the first type of tractor. This one was built in 1880. It replaced the farm's horses and powered other machines, such as the thresher shown here.

Animal power
A water buffalo pulls a plough through the soil. Animals, especially oxen, are still widely used by farmers who cannot afford machinery or who live in hilly or mountainous areas.

Pneumatic milking

In a milking parlour, milk is sucked from cows' udders by pneumatic milking machines. A large parlour can milk dozens of cows at the same time. The milk pours into tanks, where it is measured and then pumped to a refrigerated tank to wait for collection by a milk tanker.

Hay wrapper

A baling machine automatically makes hay into bales and wraps them in plastic to keep them dry. Here, the machine is spinning the bale one way as it wraps plastic sheeting around it the other way.

Combine harvester

A combine harvester cuts and collects crops. A reel sweeps the crop into a cutter bar that slices the stalks off at ground level. The stalks are pushed into the machine and grain is stripped from them. Special screws, called impeller screws or augers, are often used to move the grain around inside the harvester.

A close shave

A sheep farmer uses electrically operated shears to cut the fleece from a sheep. The shears work like a pair of scissors. The electric motor moves the blades together and apart at high speed.

MAKING FARM MACHINES

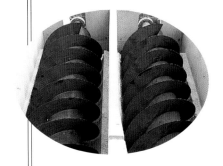

Screwed-up water
Inside an Archimedean screw is
a wide screw thread. Water is
trapped in the thread and is
forced to move upwards as the
screw is turned. A screw thread
like this is also called an auger.

The two projects on these pages will show you how to
make two simple machines like those used on farms.
The first is an Archimedean screw. In parts of the world where
water pumps are expensive to buy and run, Archimedean
screws are used to move water uphill in order to irrigate crops.
The machine is made up of a large screw inside a pipe. One
end of the machine is placed in the water and, as a handle is
turned, the screw inside revolves, carrying water upwards. This
water-lifting device has been in use for centuries and it is
named after the ancient Greek scientist, Archimedes.

The second project is to make a simple plough. By pushing
the plough through a tray of damp sand you will be able to see
how the special, curved, wedge shape of a real plough lifts and
turns the soil to make a furrow. A furrow is a trench in which
the farmer plants the seeds.

MAKE AN ARCHIMEDEAN SCREW

You will need:
*small plastic bottle, scissors,
plastic tubing, waterproof
sticky tape, two bowls.*

1 Cut the top and bottom off the
bottle. Wrap a length of plastic
tubing around the bottle to make a
screw thread shape. Tape the tubing
in place with waterproof sticky tape.

2 Put one end of the bottle in a
bowl of water and rest it on the
bowl's edge. Place the other bowl at
the end of the tubing. Slowly turn the
bottle. After a few turns, the water
will pour out of the top of the tubing

FACT BOX

• Every year Australian farmers have to shear tens of millions of
sheep. As an experiment in 1986, Australian engineers built a
robot that could shear a sheep in about 90 seconds.

• The first ploughs were made from wood or from stag antlers.
They were invented in Egypt and India about 5,500 years ago.

MAKE A SIMPLE PLOUGH

You will need:
small plastic bottle,
scissors, strip of wood or
dowelling, drawing pin,
tray of damp sand.

1 Start by cutting a triangle of plastic from one side of the small plastic drinks bottle. This triangle will form the blade of your plough.

2 Cut a slot in the triangle, as shown above. Fold the triangle in half along the line of the slot against the curve of the plastic.

3 Holding the two sides of the blade together, fix it to the length of wood or dowelling with a drawing pin. Make sure the blade is securely attached to the handle.

Soil-turning wedges

Each metal blade on this plough works as a wedge. The front point slices easily through the soil, splitting it up. As the soil slides along the blade's side, the curved shape lifts and turns it over. The plough buries weeds and brings fresh soil to the surface for new crops to grow in. This is called tilling.

Guided plough

The wheels on a plough from the 1400s stop it from sinking too far into the ground. The farmer guides the plough to make a neat furrow, while a helper urges on oxen and horses.

4 Fill up the tray with damp sand and push the plough through the sand in lines. Does your plough lift and turn the soil to make a furrow?

ELECTRONIC MACHINES

Most of the machines we use have moving parts that are operated by hand or by an engine or motor. These devices are called mechanical machines. Many modern machines, however, such as computers, have no moving parts. They are called electronic machines. Inside an electronic machine lots of components are connected together to form a continuous wire, called a circuit, around which an electric current flows. The components control the way electricity flows around the circuits and so control what the machine does. Complicated electronic circuits, containing hundreds of thousands of components, can be contained on a single microchip a few millimetres across.

Some electronic machines, such as weighing scales and digital watches, do the same job as mechanical machines. Many modern machines, such as robots, are combinations of mechanical and electronic parts.

Weighing scale
When an orange is put on a scale, it presses on an electronic device called a strain gauge. The gauge controls the strength of a tiny electric current. Electronics inside the machine detect the size of the current, work out the orange's weight, and show it on a display panel to be read.

Internet on the phone
A mobile phone is an extremely complex machine in a tiny case. It is a combination of a telephone and radio receiver and transmitter. As well as being a phone, this machine can send and receive e-mails, and download web pages from the Internet and display them on its screen.

Palm-top computer
The personal digital assistant (PDA) is a small but powerful type of electronic machine. It is a palm-sized computer that stores personal data.

Microscopic microchips
A photomicrograph (a photograph taken through a microscope) shows the tiny components on a microchip, each too small to see with the naked eye. The chip starts as a thin layer of silicon, and the components are built up using complex chemical and photographic processes.

The first computers

One of the first electronic computers was called ENIAC (Electronic Numerical Integrator And Calculator). It was built in the 1940s. It took up a huge amount of space because its electronic parts were thousands of times bigger than today's microchips. ENIAC needed several rooms to fit in all its valves, wires and dials, but it was less powerful than a modern pocket calculator.

display shows words and pictures

Inside a computer system

A computer is an extremely complicated machine, but the way it works is quite easy to understand if you think of it in several parts. Each part does its own job, such as storing or sending information.

memory stores data and programs

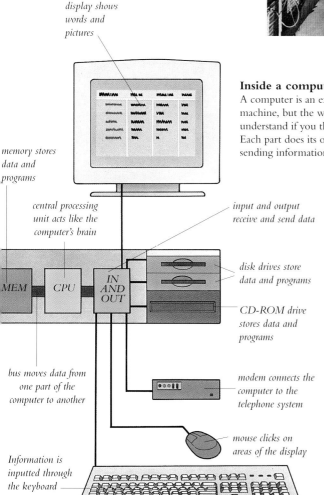

central processing unit acts like the computer's brain

input and output receive and send data

disk drives store data and programs

CD-ROM drive stores data and programs

bus moves data from one part of the computer to another

modem connects the computer to the telephone system

mouse clicks on areas of the display

Information is inputted through the keyboard

FACT BOX

• In the 1830s, British scientist Charles Babbage designed a mechanical calculator called an Analytical Engine. Unfortunately, although it would have worked, it was never made because its parts were too complex.

• The first PC (personal computer) went on sale in 1975. It had 256 bytes of memory. PCs today have around 128 megabytes of memory – or more than 128 million bytes.

• The fastest supercomputers can add together more than a quarter of a million million numbers in a second.

MACHINES IN INDUSTRY

In a spin
A steam-powered circular saw is used to cut large logs into shape. The saw has a razor-sharp blade with teeth that cut into the material as it spins. The object that is being cut is moved backwards or forwards across the blade.

Machine tools are machines used in factories to manufacture objects. The operations they are used for are cutting, drilling, grinding, turning and milling. Each of these operations is done by a special machine. For example, the operation of turning (forming a curve in the material) is done on a lathe, and cutting is done with a saw. All machine tools have a cutting blade or edge, which is normally made of metal, but may include diamond or other tough materials. The blade moves against the object being cut, called the workpiece, shaving off unwanted material.

Machine tools are used to make engine parts and other complex machines in which the parts have to fit together perfectly. Industrial robots are versatile machines that can be programmed to do many jobs, such as moving workpieces or drilling very accurately.

A perfect fit
Under computer control, this miniature milling machine is shaping a piece of ceramic material so that it will fit perfectly into a cavity in a dental patient's tooth. A milling machine cuts away areas of a piece of material. The cutting tool has rotating teeth, similar to a gear wheel.

Pedal power
A pole lathe is powered by a foot-operated pedal. The lathe spins the workpiece around very fast. The operator presses cutting tools against the spinning wood, shaving away a layer each time. How accurately the workpiece is finished depends on the skill of the lathe operator.

Pressed panels
A machine called a die press flattens sheets of steel into shaped panels, such as those used for car bonnets. The top part of the machine moves down to press the panel into shape. Each sheet of steel is pressed to exactly the same shape every time.

Digital control

An engineer makes a heating element from a graphite rod using a computer-controlled milling machine. Data describing the shape and size of the heating element is fed into the machine's computer, normally from another computer on which it has been designed. The computer then works out the cutting movements required to make the heating element from the rod, and operates the milling machine very precisely.

Keeping cool

The milky liquid pouring on to this drill is, in fact, coloured water. As the drill bit cuts into the metal workpiece, it gets very hot. The water keeps the drill cool, stopping the tool melting and washing waste metal away.

Industrial robots

Robots are used for welding car components together. The robot is shown how to do the job once and can then do it over and over again much faster than a human worker.

FACT BOX

• In some industries, high-energy lasers are used for cutting and shaping materials instead of traditional machine tools. The most powerful lasers can cut through 6cm of steel.

• In some car-making factories, parts for the cars are delivered by robot vehicles that are programmed to drive themselves around the floor of the factory.

MACHINES OF THE FUTURE

Machines that do complicated jobs need controls. Some of these machines need a human operator who controls the machine manually. For example, a car needs a driver to control its speed and direction. Other machines control themselves – once they are turned on, they do their job automatically. For example, an automatic washing machine washes and spins your clothes at the press of a button. One of the first machines to use a form of automatic control was the Jacquard loom, which wove material. Punched paper cards were fed into the loom and told it which threads were to be used. Today, many machines are controlled by computer to perform a set task whenever it is required. The most advanced machines are even able to check their own work and change it if necessary.

Flying by wires
Airliners and fighter aircraft may have a "fly-by-wire" control system, where a computer, rather than the pilot, actually flies the plane. The pilot monitors how the plane is working by watching a computer screen instead of dials.

Journey through space
Shuttle-like space planes, such as the experimental X-33, will eventually be used to transport passengers via Space. Space planes could reduce the usual flight time from New York to Tokyo from nearly 14 hours to just a couple of hours.

Robotic rover
A toy robot dog has built-in artificial intelligence. It knows nothing at first, but it gradually works out the layout of its new home and learns to respond to its new owner's commands.

Tiny machine
The rotor in this photograph is actually only about 0.5mm across. It is part of a meter that measures liquid flow. It is made of silicon and was manufactured using similar methods to those used to make microchips. Tiny machines such as this are called micromachines.

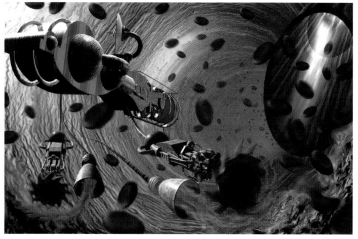

Robotic surgeon

In the future, it is possible that microscopic machines will be used in surgery. In this futuristic painting a microscopic robot is repairing a human body. The robot, just 0.1mm long, has been injected into a blood vessel through the needle on the right. Around the robot are red blood cells. With its rotating blades, the robot is cutting away a blockage made of debris (shown in grey). The robot sucks up the debris for removal.

Invisible gears

These gear wheels look quite ordinary, but they were made using microscopic experimental technology called nanotechnology. The width of the wheels is less than the width of a human hair. A hundred of these gear wheels piled up would be only as tall as the thickness of a sheet of paper!

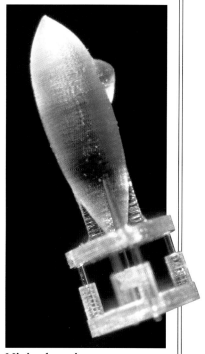

Handy android

An android (a human-like robot) uses electronic eyes and ears to work out where objects are, and its hand to pick them up. With its artificial intelligence, it can decide what sort of object it is holding. Androids help scientists to research how robots can be made to act like humans.

Car control

Many of this car's systems are controlled by a microchip called a microprocessor. It continually checks signals from sensors and sends a control signal back again. It calculates the speed, distance and fuel consumption of the car and displays them on the dashboard.

Mini submarine

A miniature submarine that measures just 4mm from top to bottom was made using an experimental technique for creating microscopic machine parts. The technique uses tiny laser beams to solidify selected parts of a pool of liquid plastic to form the submarine's shape.

AUTOMATIC CONTROL

CONTROLLING A ROBOT

You will need:
blindfold, egg and egg-cup.

1 Ask a friend to put on the blindfold. Use the list of commands opposite to direct your friend to where the egg is located.

2 Your friend should not know where the egg is or what to do with it. Instruct your friend to carefully pick the egg up. Only use commands in the list.

Machines that perform very difficult, complicated tasks need to be controlled with precision. Robots are machines that are programmed with instructions for different situations. They can respond to each situation in an 'intelligent' way, rather like human beings. However, although robots seem to be very clever, they can only do what they are told to do. The project below will show you how tricky it is to programme a robot to do even the simplest job. Using only the words that are from the list of commands, see if a friend can carry out the task successfully.

The second project shows you how to make a simple control disc. This is the sort of device used to control some washing machines. The metal track on the disc is part of an electric circuit. As the disc turns, the track completes or breaks the circuit, turning parts of the machine, such as lights and motors, on and off.

Robot commands
FORWARD
STOP
TURN LEFT
TURN RIGHT
ARM UP
ARM DOWN
CLOSE FINGERS
OPEN FINGERS

3 Now ask your friend to accurately place the egg on another surface. See if your friend can put it in the egg-cup. How quickly was your friend able to complete the task? The faster your friend completes the task, the better you are at programming.

MAKE A CONTROL DISC

You will need: *pair of compasses and pencil, ruler, card, scissors, aluminium foil dish, glue, sticky tape, paper fastener, wire, three plastic-coated wires, battery, torch bulb and holder.*

1 Use a compass to mark out a 10cm disc on the card and cut it out. Also cut a 6cm ring from the foil dish and glue it on to the card.

2 Put pieces of sticky tape across the foil track. The bare foil will complete the circuit. The pieces of sticky tape will break the circuit.

Loom control

The Jacquard loom, invented in 1801, was one of the first machines with automatic control. Cards with patterns of holes in them, called punched cards, controlled how threads were woven together to create patterns in the fabric that the loom made. The pattern created could be changed simply by changing to another set of cards with a different pattern of holes.

3 Push a paper fastener through the middle of the disc and mount it on to a piece of card. Using the wire, make two contacts with a bend in the middle, as shown.

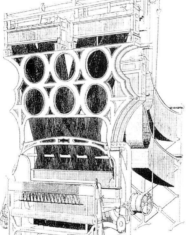

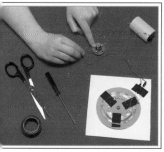

4 Stick the contacts to the card so they press on the foil. Connect a battery to a bulb with plastic-coated wire. Attach a second piece of plastic-coated wire to the bulb, and a third to the battery.

5 Attach the two loose wires to the two contacts on the card. You have now made a circuit. Turn the disc slowly. The light bulb goes on and off as the disc turns. As the contacts go over a piece of sticky tape, the circuit is broken and the light goes out. When they touch the foil again, the circuit is completed and the light comes back on.

PART THREE

CAMERAS

When you understand how different cameras work, it will make a huge difference to how well or badly your photographs turn out. Learning about lenses, apertures, shutter speeds and film speeds gives you the knowledge and confidence to take photographs in different lighting and weather situations. It is even possible to pick up some tips used by professional photographers and to print your own photographs. It is important to keep up with new developments too, for digital and video photography offer exciting new opportunities for those interested in taking and using pictures.

AUTHORS
Chris Oxlade • Al Morrison
CONSULTANT
John Freeman

YOU AND YOUR CAMERA

What is the one vital piece of equipment you must not forget if you are off on holiday or having a birthday party? Your camera! To most people, a camera is simply a device for taking snapshots of their favourite places or people. Cameras are really sophisticated machines that make use of the latest breakthroughs in science and technology. A camera is designed to do a specific job. It makes a copy of a scene on film by collecting light from that scene and turning it into a picture. It works in a very similar way to your eyes, but it makes a permanent record of the scene instead of simply looking at it.

As simple as blinking
Using a camera is like looking through a special window. Blink your eyes. This is how a camera records light from a scene. A shutter opens to let light pass through a glass lens and fall on to the film.

With your camera, you can record all kinds of events, such as parties and holidays. A simple point-and-shoot compact camera is all you need.

Early cameras
The first practical cameras with film were developed in the 1830s. Today, cameras do the same job, but are much easier to use. In the early days, it could take half an hour to take a photo. Modern cameras have a far shorter exposure time. Scenes can be recorded in a fraction of a second.

Producing prints

A camera is no use without a film inside to record the images the lens makes. If you want prints, then the film is developed, or processed to produce negatives. Prints are then made from the negatives and can be enlarged to a variety of different sizes. Frame numbers and details of the type of film used appear on the edge of the strip. The notches are for the use of the processing mini-lab. You can see which of the negatives on this strip produced the print next to it.

negative

print

The winning picture

If professional photographers are shooting a sports or news event, they must get a clear image. Their pictures appear in magazines and newspapers and help us to understand the story.

Professionals at work

These professional photographers are using telephoto lenses to get a closer picture of the event they are recording. Professionals need to use sophisticated equipment and usually carry two or three cameras, a selection of lenses, a tripod, a flash and rolls of film of different speeds.

WHAT IS A CAMERA?

All cameras, from disposable to professional models, have the same basic parts. The camera body is really just a light-proof box. This keeps the light-sensitive film in complete darkness. A section of film is held flat in the back of the body. At the front of the body is the lens, which collects light from the scene and shines it on to the film. Between the lens and the film is a shutter. When you take a photograph, the shutter opens to let light come through the lens on to the film. Many cameras have additional features that help you to take better photographs. In some cameras, the shutter timing and lens position are automatically adjusted to suit different conditions.

Disposable cameras come with the film already inside. You take the whole camera to the film processor when the film is finished.

Compact camera
A compact camera is a small camera that will fit in your pocket. With many models, all you have to do is aim at the scene and press the shutter release button. Simple compacts are also called point-and-shoot cameras.

shutter release button

viewfinder

flash unit, to light up dark scene.

lens protected by plastic flap when camera is not in use

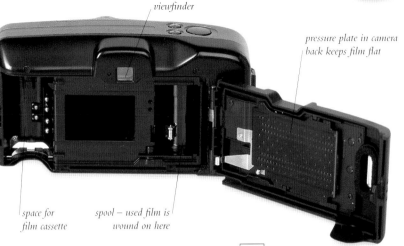

viewfinder

pressure plate in camera back keeps film flat

space for film cassette

spool – used film is wound on here

Inside the camera
You open the back of the camera to load and unload the film. There is space for the film cassette and a spool where the used film is stored. The film is advanced, or wound on, either by an electric motor or by hand.

Close-up care

The view that you see in the viewfinder of a compact camera is not quite the same as the view that the lens sees. This is because the viewfinder is higher up than the lens. Remember to leave some space around close-up objects in the viewfinder.

lens view

viewfinder view

You look through a viewfinder to see what will be in your photo. The guidelines you see in many viewfinders (seen in red here) show you what area of the scene will be included in your picture. If the photographer takes this picture, the boy's hat will be cut off.

Instant photos
The Polaroid camera uses special film which produces prints almost instantly.

SLR camera

Focusing on an image

Most modern 35mm cameras (those needing 35mm format film) use a single lens reflex (SLR) design. When you look into the viewfinder, you see exactly what the lens sees. You can change the lens of an SLR camera to achieve different effects.

HOW A LENS WORKS

Making your own simple viewer will show you just how a camera lens collects light from a scene and makes a small copy of it on the film. The copy is called an image. Just like a real camera, the viewer has a light-proof box. At the front of the box is a pin-hole, which works like a tiny lens. The screen at the back of the box is where the film would be in a real camera. This sort of viewer is sometimes called a camera obscura (which just means a dark box used to capture images of outside objects). In the past, artists used these to make images of scenes that they could paint.

MATERIALS

You will need: ruler, scissors, small cardboard box, card, sharp pencil, sticky tape, tracing paper.

Light rays
Light travels in straight rays. You can see this when you shine a torch. When you look at a scene, your eyes collect rays that are coming from every part of it. This is just what a camera does.

MAKE YOUR OWN VIEWER

1 Using scissors, cut a small hole, about 1.5cm by 1.5cm, in one end of the cardboard box.

2 Now cut a much larger square hole in the other end of your cardboard box.

3 Cut a square of card 4cm by 4cm. Pierce a tiny hole in the centre with a sharp pencil.

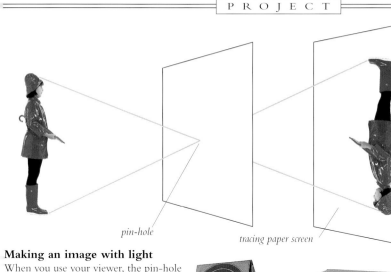

If you look at a person through your viewer, light rays from their head hit the bottom of the viewer's screen. Rays from their feet hit the top of the screen. So the screen image is upside down. Left and right are swapped, too.

pin-hole

tracing paper screen

Making an image with light

When you use your viewer, the pin-hole lets in just a few light rays from each part of the scene. The rays keep going in straight lines and hit the tracing paper screen, making an image of the scene.

A Camera Obscura

Some camera obscuras are more like rooms than boxes, but they work in the same way. Light from a small hole or simple lens creates a reversed and upside down image on a flat surface. This can be seen in the darkened interior of the room.

6 Now look out of a window, through the screen of tracing paper. Try tracing the image you see on to the paper.

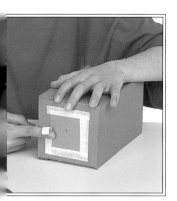

4 Place the card over the box's smaller hole. Make sure that the pin-hole is centred over the hole. Now tape it into place.

5 Cut a square of tracing paper slightly bigger than the larger hole. Stick it securely over that hole. Your viewer is ready to use.

PROJECT

EXPERIMENT WITH LIGHT

MATERIALS

MATERIALS

You will need: ruler, two pieces of card, scissors, torch, glass of water, magnifying glass, mirror.

Light is refracted and reflected inside cameras by lenses and mirrors. The best way to see how this happens is to send some light beams through lenses and then bounce them off mirrors yourself. You can make narrow light beams by shining a torch through slots in a sheet of card. Try these experiments and then see if you have any ideas of your own. Vary the size of the slots to see how the light beams change. Carry out the experiments in a room with the lights off and the blinds or curtains closed.

Converging light rays

The lens of a magnifying glass makes light rays from objects converge, or bend inwards, towards each other. So, when the rays enter the eye, they seem to have come from a bigger object.

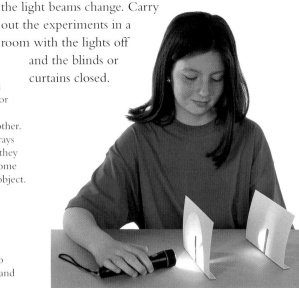

HAVING FUN WITH BEAMS

1 Cut a slot about 2mm wide and 5cm long in two pieces of card. Bend the bottom edges so they stand up. Shine the light beam of a torch through both.

2 To see how the beam can be refracted put a glass of water in its path. Move the glass from side to side to see how the beam widens and narrows.

3 Replace the second piece of card with one with three slots in it. Put a magnifying glass in the path of the three beams to make them converge, or bend inwards.

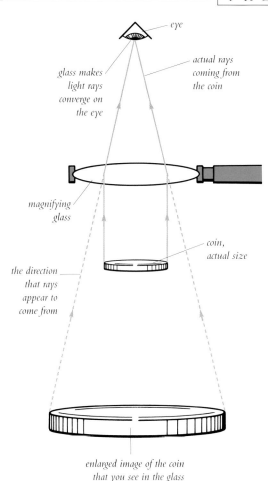

eye

glass makes light rays converge on the eye

actual rays coming from the coin

magnifying glass

coin, actual size

the direction that rays appear to come from

enlarged image of the coin that you see in the glass

Water mirror

Unlike other cameras, single-lens reflex cameras (SLRs) give crisp, clean images. To see why, try this simple experiment. Hold a glass of water up so that you can see the underneath surface of the water clearly. Now poke your finger into the water from above. You should see a clear, single reflection of your finger in the surface. This is because the surface acts just like a mirror *(now see box below).*

4 Now try each of the experiments, but put a mirror in the way of the different beams. Can you see how the pattern of rays stays the same?

MIRRORS AND PRISMS

Stopping reflections
If you look carefully at a reflection in a normal mirror, you will see a "ghostly" second image. The water mirror above does not make a "ghost" image. To stop you from getting "ghost" images on your pictures, the SLR has a glass block called a pentaprism (a five-angled prism), which treats reflections in the same way as the water mirror.

The same view
The pentaprism in an SLR camera also makes sure that the image you see in the viewfinder is exactly the same as the image on your developed photo.

COMING INTO FOCUS

Before taking a photograph, you need to make sure that your subject is in focus. When it is, all the rays of light that leave a point on the subject are bent by the lens so that they hit the same place on the film. This makes a clear, sharp image on the film. Parts of the scene in front or behind the subject will not be in focus. On some cameras you have to choose the part of the scene that you want to be in focus yourself. Autofocus cameras focus the lens by automatically choosing the object at the centre of the focal plane.

In this photograph (above), the subject is in sharp focus. You can see all the fine detail. When the same shot is out of focus (below), it makes the subject look blurred.

focal plane

The focal plane
When the image of a subject is in focus, the light rays meet on the film focal plane. The camera's film is held flat by th focal plane by a plane by a pressure plate, visible if you open the back of your (empty) camera.

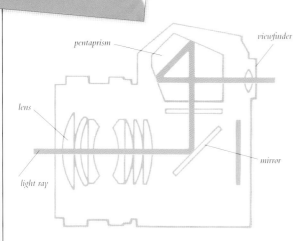

pentaprism

viewfinder

lens

mirror

light ray

Focusing SLRs
With an SLR camera, you see exactly what the image looks like through the viewfinder. On a manual-focus SLR, you turn a ring around the lens to get your subject in focus.

Getting closer
Use a magnifying glass and lamp to make an image of an object on a sheet of paper. Move the magnifying glass closer to and farther from the paper to bring different parts of the scene into focus.

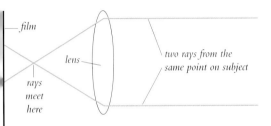

The lens, here, is too far away from the film. Rays from the subject meet in front of the film, so it is out of focus.

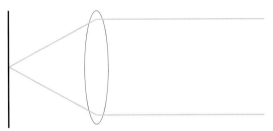

To focus, the lens is moved backwards, towards the film. The rays now meet on the film.

In and out of focus

A camera focuses on a subject by moving the lens backwards and forwards so it gets closer to, or farther from the film. This brings parts of the scene that are at different distances from the camera into focus. When the lens is set closest to the film, objects from the distance are in sharper focus.

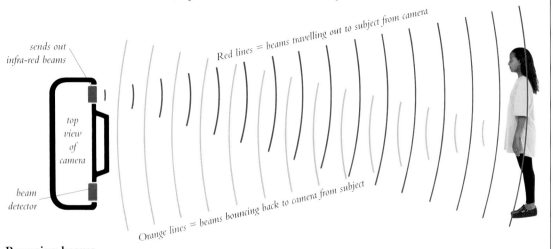

Red lines = beams travelling out to subject from camera

Orange lines = beams bouncing back to camera from subject

Bouncing beams

With the type of autofocus system shown here, the camera emits a wide beam of invisible infra-red light. It works out how long the infra-red light takes to bounce back, and so knows how far away the subject is. A small electric motor then moves the lens.

Autofocus errors

Most autofocus cameras focus on objects that are in the centre of the scene in the viewfinder. If your subject is off to one side, the camera focuses on the background, and your subject will be blurred *(left)*. If you have a focus lock, you can beat this by aiming at the subject first, and then using your focus lock before recomposing the shot and shooting *(right)*.

MAKE YOUR OWN CAMERA

M A T E R I A L S

You will need: pin-hole box viewer, kitchen foil, scissors, sticky tape, pencil, 1m black paper, thin card, thick cloth or plastic, photographic paper, elastic band.

MAKING A PIN-HOLE CAMERA

You can make your very own simple camera with just a few basic pieces of equipment. This project combines all the main principles that lie behind photography. For simplicity, this camera uses photographic paper (paper with a light-sensitive coating on one side) instead of film, and a pin-hole instead of a lens. When the "film" (paper) is processed, you will have a negative. Then turn to the 'Printing and Projecting' project to find out how you can make a print from the negative. Find out about the equipment you need in the 'Recording an Image' project.

1 Make the pin-hole viewer from the 'How a Lens works' project, but remove the tracing-paper screen. Replace the 4cm card square with kitchen foil. Pierce a hole, about 2mm across, in the centre of the foil using a sharp pencil.

2 Open the back of the box and line the inside with black paper. Alternatively, colour the inside with a black felt pen.

3 Cut a square of card large enough to cover the kitchen foil. Tape just the top edge to the box, so that it will act as a shutter.

4 Cut a square of card to fit right across the other end of the box. Tape it to one edge so that it closes over the hole like a door or flap.

5 Find some heavy, black, light-proof cloth or a plastic sheet. Cut a piece large enough to fold around the end of the box.

6 In a completely dark room, feeling with your fingers, put a piece of photographic paper under the flap at the end of the box.

7 Close the flap, then wrap the cloth or plastic sheet tightly over it. Next, put an elastic band tightly around the box to secure it.

8 Now you can turn the light on. Point the camera at a well-lit object and open the shutter. Leave the camera still for about five minutes and then close the shutter.

Throwaway camera
Single use cameras have the film already loaded and ready to use. You send off the whole camera when you want the film to be developed.

Opening the shutter allows light to strike the piece of light-sensitive paper. The paper is coated to turn dark where light strikes it. This gives you a negative, on paper instead of on film. Next, you need to develop the image on the paper with developing fluid (see the 'Printing and Projecing' project). This will give you the negative image on the sheet of paper as it appears here.

USING FILM

The camera's job is to create a focused image of a scene, but this would be no use without a way of recording the image. This is the job of the film. Film is coated with a type of silver that is affected by light. So when an image strikes the film, the silver records the patterns of light, dark and colour. You cannot look at film straight away. It must be developed first with chemicals that turn the silver black or gray where light has struck it. Until then, it must be kept in complete darkness. If undeveloped film is exposed to direct light, it turns completely black.

Always load and unload a film in dim light or in shadow, to prevent light from leaking into the film canister.

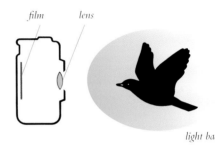

film   lens

The film is exposed by th camera whe you photograp something, such as this bird against a light background (left)

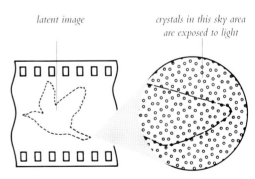

latent image

crystals in this sky area are exposed to light

Crystals in the light area of the image change. Crystals in the dark area do not. The image has been recorded chemically. Nothing shows up on the film, and the image is called the latent (hidden) image.

Types of film

There are several different types of film. The one most people use is film for colour prints. This is called colour negative film. Other common types are black-and-white negative film for making black-and-white positive prints and colour reversal film for making slides.

Exposing a film

Black-and-white film contains millions of microscopic light sensitive crystals that contain silver. When a photograph is taken, some of the crystals that are exposed to light begin to break down, leaving silver metal. In the areas where more light falls, more crystals begin to change.

Processing film

Amateur photographers develop black and white films at home, in a small developing tank. In the dark, the film is wound carefully onto a plastic spiral. The spiral is then placed in the tank and a lid is put on. A chemical called developer is poured into the tank and left for a few minutes before being poured away. Then chemical fixer is poured in. Finally, the film is washed.

Film drying

After washing, films are carefully dried. They are usually hung up to dry in a dust-free area, sometimes in a special drying cabinet. Once the films are dry, the photographer can cut them into manageable strips and choose which ones to print.

black background with white bird

changed crystals

unchanged crystals

During developing (above), all the crystals that had begun to break down change completely to silver. They look black. The unchanged crystals stay as they are.

black background with clear bird

Changed crystals

no crystals

Fixing gets rid of all the unchanged crystals, leaving clear film. The result is a negative, where dark areas on the original subject are light, and light areas are dark.

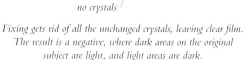

Developed colour negative film looks strange because the colours are in negative. The true colours are revealed when the positive prints are made up.

When colour reversal, or slide film, is developed, the actual colours of the scene are reproduced as a positive image.

THE RIGHT FILM

There are three basic types of film. They are colour negative film, colour-reversal film and black-and-white film. Films come in different sizes (called formats). Most cameras take 35mm film which comes in a preloaded container called a cassette. Films also come in different lengths. The lengths are measured by the number of exposures, or photographs, that will fit on the film. The usual lengths are 24 and 36 exposures. You also have to decide which speed of film to use. Fast films react to light more quickly than slow films. Film speed is referred to by its ISO (International Standards Organisation) rating. The most common speeds are ISO 100 and ISO 200, which are medium-speed films.

Automatic coding

On one side of a film cassette is a pattern of black and silver squares. This is called a DX code and it indicates the film's ISO rating and length. Modern cameras have sensors that can read the code and display it in the viewfinder. On older cameras, you have to set the ISO rating manually on a dial.

All the details of a film (format, speed and length) are printed on the film carton and the film cassette. The carton also has the expiry date to indicate its freshness.

Which film speed?

The difference between films of different speeds is the size of their crystals (or grains). Fast films (ISO 400 and above) are perfect for shooting in dim light and for action shots (or when the subject won't sit still). They have larger grains than slow films. This is because larger grains can react to much less light than small ones. These large grains often show up in the final picture *(above right)*. Slow films (ISO 50 and below) are perfect for fine, crisp detail *(above left)*.

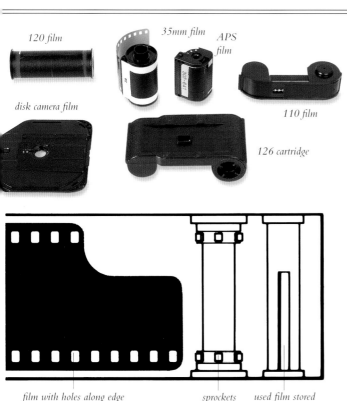

120 film

35mm film

APS film

disk camera film

110 film

126 cartridge

Film and photo formats

Format is the size of the film and the size and shape of each image recorded on the film. Large-format films give much more detail. Smaller formats are more convenient. Some cameras can take photographs of different formats on the same film using adaptors or masks.

film with holes along edge   *sprockets*   *used film stored on spool*

Winding on

35mm and APS (Advanced Photographic System) films have small holes along each side. The holes fit over sprockets in the camera that turn to wind on the film. This brings a fresh part of unexposed film behind the lens. Roll films have a backing paper that shields the film from stray light. This film is wound from one spool to another as it is exposed.

Indoor films

Most colour films are designed for use in daylight. If you use them indoors, with light from light bulbs, the photos come out yellowy. You can buy indoor film called tungsten film, which gives the right colours, or use a conversion filter that compensates for indoor light.

Polaroid film

The film used in Polaroid cameras is very different from other films. As well as the chemicals to record the image, it has developing chemicals inside. After a photograph is taken, the film is squeezed through a roller, which releases the developer. This turns the film into a finished photograph.

FACT BOX

• Infra-red film is coated with chemicals that react to heat, rather than to the visible light rays, coming from a scene.

• The largest negative that has ever been used measured 7m by 25cm. This massive negative was made for a huge panoramic picture of 3,500 people, photographed in the USA in 1992.

• 35mm format film was originally developed for movie cameras. It is still the most common format for cine camera film.

PROJECT

RECORDING AN IMAGE

MATERIALS

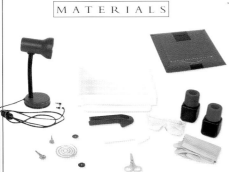

You will need: lamp, photographic paper, different-shaped objects such as keys, discs and scissors, rubber gloves, protective goggles, plastic tongs, plastic dishes, chemicals (see right).

You do not need a camera to see how film works. In fact you do not need a film either! You can use black and white photographic paper instead. Photographic paper is the paper that prints are made on. It works in the same way as film. Here, you can see how to make a picture called a photogram. It is made by covering some parts of a sheet of photographic paper with objects and then shining light on the sheet. When the paper is developed the areas that were hit by the light turn black, leaving you an image of the objects.

Photographic chemicals

You will need two photographic chemicals: developer for paper (not film) and fixer. Buy them from a photographic supplier. Ask an adult to help you follow the instructions on the bottles to dilute (mix with water) the chemicals and make sure you protect your eyes and hands when handling them. Store the diluted chemicals in plastic bottles. Seal the bottles and label them clearly.

MAKE YOUR OWN PHOTOGRAM

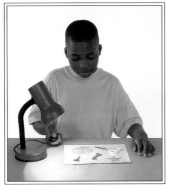

1 Turn off the light. Lay a sheet of photographic paper down, shiny side up. Put objects on it. Turn the light on again for a few seconds.

2 Pick up the paper with the tongs and put it into the dish of developer. Push it down so that the paper is all under the liquid.

3 After a minute, use the tongs to move the paper into the fixer. Leave it right under the liquid for a minute, until the image is fixed.

P R O J E C T

This symbol, on photographic chemical bottles, means that they can be dangerous if not used with care. Always wear gloves and goggles.

Photographic paper

For black and white prints, you need a paper called monochrome paper. Buy the smallest size you can, and choose grade 2 if possible, with a gloss finish. The paper comes in a light-proof envelope or box. Only open the envelope in complete darkness. The paper is in a second, black polythene envelope.

The finished photogram should show the objects in white on a black background. Try experimenting with other ideas. How about cutting out letters and making your name, or crunching up transparent materials to create more exciting effects?

4 Now you can turn the light back on. Using the tongs, lift the paper out of the fixer and wash it with running water for a few minutes. Then lay the paper on a flat surface to dry. This technique is an excellent way of producing unique invitations or greetings cards quickly and effectively.

THE CAMERA SHUTTER

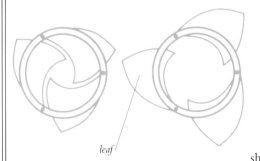

leaf

A leaf shutter has thin metal plates called leaves. These overlap each other to close the shutter (left) *and swivel back to open it* (right).

All cameras have a shutter between the lens at the front and the film at the back. The shutter is rather like a door. It is closed most of the time, so that no light gets to the film. When you press the button to take a photo, the shutter opens briefly and then closes again, to let light from your subject reach the film. The time for which the shutter is open is called the shutter speed. Compact cameras have a leaf shutter close to the lens. SLR cameras, which have interchangeable lenses, have a focal-plane shutter which is located just in front of the film. You should take care not to touch the shutter when loading film in this type of camera.

first curtain

Focal-plane shutter
This has two curtains. When the camera takes a photograph, the first curtain opens to let light hit the film. The second curtain follows closely behind, covering up the film again. The smaller the gap between the curtains, the faster the shutter speed.

second curtain

Shutter speeds
Most photographs are taken with a shutter speed of between 1/60 and 1/250 of a second. On some SLR cameras, you have to set the shutter speed by turning a dial *(below)*. Each setting gives a shutter speed about twice as fast as the one before.

Camera shake
When the shutter is open, even tiny camera movements make the image move across the film, causing a slightly blurred picture. This is called camera shake. It can happen if the shutter speed is below about 1/60 of a second

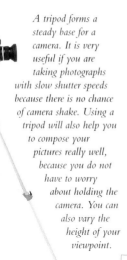

A tripod forms a steady base for a camera. It is very useful if you are taking photographs with slow shutter speeds because there is no chance of camera shake. Using a tripod will also help you to compose your pictures really well, because you do not have to worry about holding the camera. You can also vary the height of your viewpoint.

The above picture shows the famous sprinter and long jumper Carl Lewis in action. The photographer has panned the camera (moved it to follow the athlete), which has blurred the background, enhancing the impression of speed. Only Lewis' arms and feet are blurred, which adds to the feeling of action.

Panning, or moving your camera to follow a moving subject, helps to stop the area that is travelling across the frame from being blurred. The stationary elements (background) of the photo will still appear fuzzy.

When you photograph action, such as people running, a fast shutter speed will freeze the action, and avoid a blurred shot. Panning will also help, especially if your subject is moving across the scene. To pan, aim at your subject and swing the camera to follow it, squeezing the shutter release button when the subject is where you want it.

There are several ways of keeping your camera steady as you take a photograph, even if you do not have a tripod. For example, stand with your legs slightly apart, or crouch down with one knee on the ground. Squeeze the shutter release button slowly. For extra steadiness, lean yourself against a tree, or try resting your camera on a wall. A friend's shoulder or bean bag are also good ideas.

WHAT AN APERTURE DOES

The aperture ring on an SLR lens. Aperture size is measured in f-numbers (such as f/8).

The aperture is basically a hole, situated behind the camera lens, that can be made larger or smaller. When the aperture is small, some of the light rays that pass through the lens are cut off so that they do not reach the film. This does not cut off any of the image on the film, but it does reduce the amount of light that hits the film, making the image darker. Changing the size of the aperture also affects how much of the scene is in focus. Some cameras, such as the disposable variety, have a pre-set aperture.

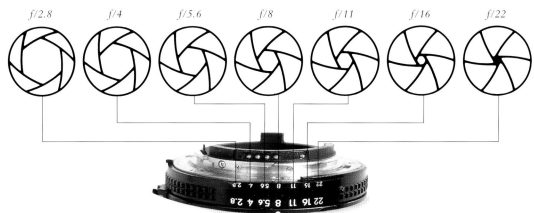

Aperture sizes

The mechanism that changes aperture size has interlocking metal leaves. These fold in to make the aperture smaller. The f-number is a fraction – f/4 means a quarter of the focal length of the lens. (Focal length is the distance from the lens to the focal point, where light rays from an object come together.) So an aperture of f/8 is half the width of one of f/4, and lets in one-quarter of the amount of light.

Changing depth of field

Depth of field is the distance between the nearest part of the scene that is in focus and the farthest part of the scene that is in focus. As f-numbers get bigger, the aperture gets smaller and the depth of field increases. Shooting on a sunny day will let you use a small aperture. This makes it easier to get a large depth of field. The depth of field can be set on some cameras.

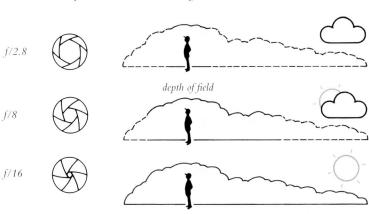

This photograph was taken with a much smaller aperture than the photograph on the far left, making the depth of field far deeper. Almost everything in the scene is in focus. Greater depth of field is useful for photographs of scenery or architecture where you want to show clear detail. It is also useful if you have people in the foreground and want both the people and the background to be in focus.

In this photograph, the subject (the two boys) is in focus, and the background is totally out of focus. This is called a shallow depth of field because only the objects that are a certain distance from the camera are in focus. Using shallow depth of field is ideal if you want to make parts of the scene that might confuse your picture disappear into a blur.

FACT BOX

• A lens always has its maximum aperture written on it. For example, a lens described as 300 f/4 has a focal length of 300mm and a maximum aperture of f/4.

• Large maximum apertures tend to be very expensive, because the lenses have to be much bigger. For example, an f/1.4 lens can cost several times as much as an f/4 lens.

• A pin-hole camera the size of a shoe-box has an aperture of about f/500 (1/500th of the focal length).

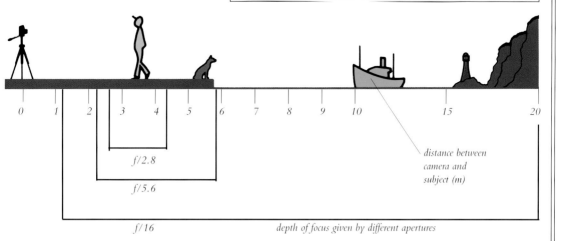

distance between camera and subject (m)

f/2.8

f/5.6

f/16

depth of focus given by different apertures

Try focusing your camera at a certain object and then changing the aperture. You will see how different areas of the picture come into focus.

Lens focused at 3m
Aperture at f/2.8
Depth of field=1.5m

Lens focused at 3m
Aperture at f/5.6
Depth of field=3.5m

Lens focused at 3m
Aperture at f/16
Depth of field=20m

THE RIGHT EXPOSURE

Exposure is the word for the amount of light that reaches the film in your camera when you take a photograph. Exposure depends on the shutter speed (slower shutter speeds give more time and allow more light through) and the aperture (larger apertures also allow more light through). You might see exposure stated on your camera as a combination of shutter speed and aperture, for example, f/16 at 1/60 sec. All but the simplest cameras measure the amount of light coming from the scene and work out what exposure is needed for the speed of the film in the camera. They do this with an electronic light sensor called a metering system.

In this picture, too little light has reached the film, and the chemicals have not reacted enough. This is called under-exposure. The finished photo looks too dark and usually has a grainy quality. Nothing can really be done to improve it in processing.

Here, too much light has got to the film, and the chemicals in the film have reacted too much. This is called over-exposure. The final photo is washed out. It can be corrected in printing, unlike under-exposure.

When this photograph was taken, the exposure was correct and exactly the right amount of light reached the film. The finished picture is well-balanced – neither too light, nor too dark.

Shutter speed and aperture

Try using different combinations of shutter speed and aperture, each of which lets in the same amount of light *(see right)* and see what difference it makes. For example, f/8 at 1/125 sec gives the same amount of light as f4 at 1/500 sec. But a narrower aperture (f8) gives a greater depth of field. You might use the wider aperture (f4) for a fast, action shot and the narrower aperture (f8) for a landscape shot where you want greater depth of field.

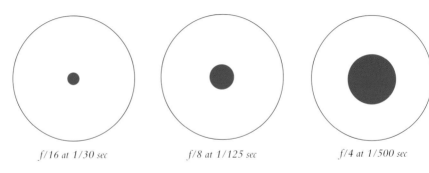

f/16 at 1/30 sec   *f/8 at 1/125 sec*   *f/4 at 1/500 sec*

FACT BOX

• Some cameras can measure the changes in brightness across a scene automatically and then take an average reading for the whole scene.

• There are certain advanced APS (Advanced Photographic System) cameras that can remember the exposure settings for each picture on a film.

• It is more important to get the exposure right if you are using slide (colour reversal) film, rather than print film (colour negative). This is partly because it is possible to correct mistakes when making prints, but not when making slides.

In the picture on the left, the light shining through the window is brighter than the main subject – the girl. This means that the camera measures more of the light coming from the brighter area. As a result, the background is correctly exposed, but the girl is under-exposed and so she looks too dark.

In this picture, the background was still by far the brightest part of the picture. The problem was solved, however, by using a much larger exposure and the balance is just right. Bright lighting coming from the background is called back lighting.

LETTING IN THE LIGHT

Changing a camera's aperture affects both the brightness of an image and the depth of field. You can see how it works with a few simple experiments. First, look at your own eyes. Like an aperture, your pupils automatically narrow in bright light to protect your retinas, and open wide to let you see in dim light. To see a shutter at work, open the back of your camera (when there is no film in it). Now look for a leaf shutter near the lens or a focal-plane shutter just behind where the film would be.

MATERIALS

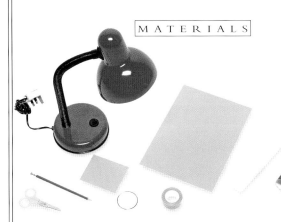

You will need: magnifying glass, cardboard tube, sticky tape, scissors, thin card, tracing paper, table lamp, pencil.

Use your eyes
Look closely at one of your eyes in a mirror. Close it and, after a few seconds, open it again quickly. You should see your pupil go from wide to narrow as your eye adjusts to the bright light.

INVESTIGATING APERTURES

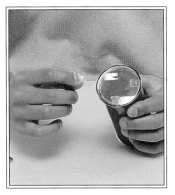

1 Carefully attach the magnifying glass to one end of your cardboard tube using small pieces of sticky tape.

2 Roll a piece of thin card around the other end of the tube. Tape the top edge down to make another tube that slides in and out.

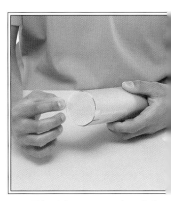

3 With sticky tape, attach a circle of tracing paper across the end o the sliding card tube. This will form your viewing screen.

See a shutter at work

To see just how a shutter works, open the back of your camera (when there is no film inside) and carefully place a small strip of tracing paper where your film usually goes. Now aim the camera at a subject, preferably one that is brightly lit, and press the shutter release button. You should see a brief flash of the image on your tracing paper – although there will be no lasting picture! Take great care not to put your fingers on the shutter blades in the focal-plane cameras.

4 With the screen nearest to you, aim your tube at a table lamp that is turned on. Can you see an image of the bulb on the screen?

5 Slide the tubes together until the image of the bulb is clear. Now adjust them again so that the image is slightly out of focus.

6 Mark then cut a small hole (about 5mm wide) in a piece of card, to make a small aperture. Look at the light bulb again and put the card in front of the lens. The smaller aperture will bring the light bulb into focus. Is it clearer? Can you read the writing on the bulb?

PRINTING

When a film is developed, the images on the film are usually too small to look at. You can view slide films with a projector, which makes a large copy of the image on a screen. But before you can look at photographs taken with negative film, you have to make prints. The paper used for prints is light-sensitive, just like film. To make a print, the negative image is projected on to the paper. When the paper is developed, you get a positive image, so that the scene appears as you saw it originally.

If you are using black-and-white film, bear in mind that bright areas of the image change the chemicals in the film more than dark areas.

Negatives

When black-and-white film is processed, light areas of the scene appear dark and dark areas appear light. This is a negative.

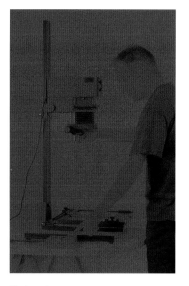

Developing and fixing

The paper is processed in the dark, using chemicals. The three trays hold the developer, water or stop bath (to stop the developer) and fixer. Areas where light has hit the paper come out dark. So light areas of the negative come out dark, as in the original scene.

Enlarging

This is the first stage in making a print. An enlarger projects the negative on to paper placed below it. This must be done in the dark, so that no stray light spoils the paper. Lighter areas of the negative allow more light to reach the paper than darker areas.

The final print

After processing, the final print must be dried carefully, to prevent it from getting scratched or curling at the edges. Once developed, take care of your prints by mounting them on card using a glue such as photo spray mount. You can then frame your favourite pictures, or keep them in a photograph album.

Printing in colour

Colour prints are produced in the same way as black and white prints. The negative *(above)* is projected on to colour photographic paper. When the paper is developed, the colours are reversed once again, so that they come out looking natural.

Colour photos

When you take a photo with colour negative film, the film records the patterns of colour in a scene. When the film is developed, the colours on the film look very strange, but the prints come out correctly. Colour film has three layers, one on top of the other. These react to three primary colours, yellow, magenta (blue-red) and cyan (blue-green), which together can produce all of the different colours in the light spectrum.

FACT BOX

• The negative/positive method of photography was invented in 1839, by an Englishman called William Fox Talbot.

• High-contrast printing paper makes blacks look blacker and whites look whiter. Low-contrast paper creates less of a difference between the blacks and the whites.

• Professionals can make parts of a print look lighter or darker by using special techniques on the enlarger. For example, they can "burn" certain areas, which means making more light get to them.

Processing and printing

Most people have their films sent away to be processed and printed *(above)* by a special photographic laboratory. Some shops, however, have their own automatic processing and printing machines, often called mini-labs. These can produce prints on the spot in a very short space of time.

PRINTING AND PROJECTING

If you have just taken a photograph with your own pin-hole camera, you can find out how to turn it into a print below. There is also a simple projector for you to make. A projector lets you look at slide film. On this type of film the colours of the image on the developed film are the same as the colours in the original scene. Projecting a slide is rather like the reverse of taking a photograph. First, light is shone through the slide. The light then passes through the lens of the projector and is focused on a flat surface such as a wall, where an enlarged version of the slide appears.

You will need: photographic paper and chemicals, negative from pin-hole camera, torch or table lamp, safety goggles, rubber gloves, plastic dishes, plastic tongs or tweezers.

A slide viewer is a special magnifying glass with an opalescent (milky-colour) screen used for looking at slides. It is an alternative to a projector. You can also use a light box (a glass box with a light inside) to look at your slides before viewing in a projector.

QUICK AND EASY PRINTS

1 In a totally dark room, lay a fresh sheet of photographic paper on a flat surface, shiny side up. Lay the negative from your pin-hole camera face-down on top.

2 Shine a torch or a table lamp on to the top of the two papers for a few seconds. Turn the torch off and remove your paper negative. Put on the goggles and gloves.

3 Put the fresh paper into a tray of developing fluid, then fix and wash the fresh paper (see the pages on 'Printing'). You should end up with a print of the original image.

P R O J E C T

DO-IT-YOURSELF PROJECTOR

M A T E R I A L S

You will need: cardboard tube, scissors, developed colour negative film, thin card, sticky tape, magnifying glass, tracing paper, torch.

Old projector

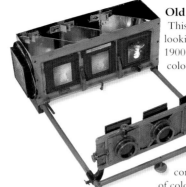

This device *(left)* provided a way of looking at colour slides around 1900. Instead of three layers of colour on the film, three separate negatives were taken. Blue, green and red light were projected simultaneously at the same place as the black-and-white slides. The three colours combined to produce the range of colours in the slide scene.

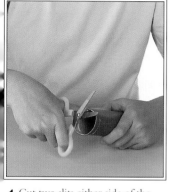

1 Cut two slits either side of the cardboard tube at one end. They must be wide enough for a strip of negatives to slide through. Only use old negatives that you do not want.

2 Wrap a piece of card around the other end of the tube. Tape down the edge to make another tube that slides over the first tube.

3 Tape the magnifying glass to the end of the adjustable tube. Now tape a disc of tracing paper over the slotted end of the main tube.

4 Hold the projector about 2m away from a light-coloured wall. Slot the negative into the tube and shine a torch through it. Adjust the tubes until an image of the negative appears on the wall. You can also try this with slide film, but only use old, unwanted slides.

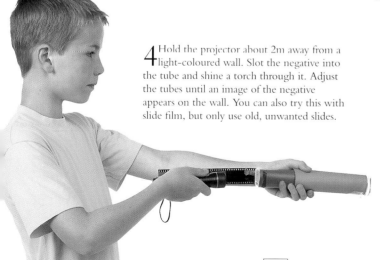

the image as projected on the wall or screen

WIDE AND NARROW

All camera lenses have their own focal length, which is written somewhere on the lens. The focal length is the distance between the centre of the lens and the focal plane inside the camera where the light coming through the lens creates an image of the object being photographed. Lenses of different focal lengths produce images on the film that contain more or less of a scene. If you use a 50mm lens, you see the same scene as you do with your eyes. Lenses with shorter focal lengths take in more of the scene, and longer lenses take in less than you would normally see.

What the lens sees

Put your hands either side of your face. Your view is similar to what a 50mm lens can see. Keeping your hands the same distance apart, move your hands steadily away from your face. The view between your hands will show you what a telephoto lens sees.

a wide angle lens has a wider angle of view (about 50% more) than the human eye

only light rays that pass through the very centre remain straight

Ultra-wide angle

The widest type of lens collects light from a complete half-circle (180 degrees). It makes straight lines appear curved, and the centre of the scene seems to bulge outwards. It is called a fish-eye lens because fish have eyes that gather light from a huge angle.

Long-lens wobble

With telephoto lenses, which have very long focal lengths (300mm or more), the tiniest bit of camera shake blurs the image. Professionals always use a tripod or monopod with these lenses, to keep the camera steady. This is also important because the amount of light that reaches the lens is quite small, and so slow shutter speeds are often needed.

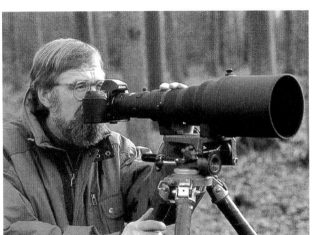

View from a compact camera

The simplest compact cameras usually have a 35mm lens. This gives a slightly wider view *(left)* than you see with your own eyes. Many compacts now come with a built-in zoom lens enabling you to get a closer shot of your subject while you are still far away from it. These are especially useful for taking portraits (see 'Close-up Shots' to find out more).

Compact camera with variable lens.

The view through a telephoto lens.

Telephoto lens view

Any lens that gives you a magnified view of a scene is called a telephoto lens. A telephoto lens is a bit like a telescope, because it homes in on just one part of the scene. Telephoto lenses are often used to photograph portraits and distant wildlife, and for coming in close on the small details in a scene.

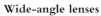

A wide-angle lens view.

Wide-angle lenses

Any camera lens that gives a wider view than we usually see with our eyes is called a wide-angle lens. Extremely wide-angle lenses (of 28mm and less) allow you to get a huge amount of a scene into your photograph. A really wide-angle lens is perfect to use for panoramic photographs of scenery – such as cityscapes.

CLOSE-UP SHOTS

To save carrying several lenses with different focal lengths, many photographers use one lens, called a zoom lens. These can change their focal length. A zoom lens usually consists of three separate lenses, with adjustable distances between them. They allow you to change how much of a scene will be in a shot without having to move your body.

The built-in lens on many compact cameras, and the lens that comes with most SLRs, is a zoom. A common zoom is 35–70, which means the lens can have focal lengths between 35mm and 70mm. It goes from wide angle to short telephoto (which brings objects closer). Macro, or close-up, lenses can focus on things that are very close to the lens. They are ideal for shots of flowers and insects.

A compact camera with a built-in zoom lens. Pressing a button on the camera makes the zoom get longer or shorter.

Super-zooms

A super-zoom lens has a very large range of focal lengths. For example, a 28–200 zoom goes from very wide angle to long telephoto.

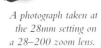

A photograph taken at the 28mm setting on a 28–200 zoom lens.

SLR zooms

With an SLR and two interchangeable zoom lenses, such as 28–70 and 75–300, you can have a huge range of focal lengths. The focal length is changed by turning or sliding a wide ring on the lens. Because zoom lenses are so complicated, they can make straight lines in a scene look slightly bent, especially at the picture's edges. A special streaked effect can be produced if you zoom in on a subject during a long exposure.

Zooming in for detail with a 200mm setting.

Close-up equipment

Special high-powered microscope cameras, such as the one on the right, are used for some very close-up shots, such as the close-up of an insect on the left. SLR camera lenses can be removed and replaced with a microscope adaptor.

Extension tubes

Extension tubes fit between the camera body and the lens. They move the lens farther from the film. This means that the lens can bend light rays into focus from objects that would usually be too close. A set of extension tubes has three tubes of different lengths for different magnifications.

FACT BOX
• A telephoto doubler fits between an SLR and its lens. It doubles the focal length of the lens.
• A 500mm telephoto lens with a maximum aperture of f/8 weighs several kilograms.
• The longest lenses you can buy have a focal length of 1000 to 1200mm.
• A standard 50mm lens might be made up of five glass lenses. Most zoom lenses contain at least twelve lenses.

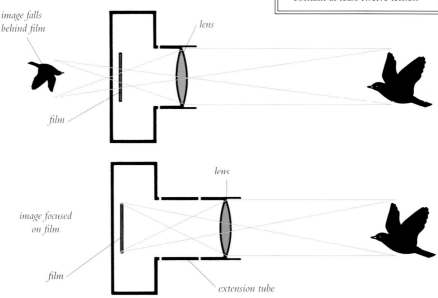

Usually, the light rays from a close-up object are not bent enough to form a focused image.

image falls behind film

lens

film

With an extension tube, the lens moves forwards, giving room for the rays to become focused.

image focused on film

lens

film

extension tube

FOCAL LENGTHS

If you have either an SLR camera or a compact camera with a zoom lens, then you will probably have taken photographs at different focal lengths. The simple experiments shown on these two pages will help to explain how different focal lengths make more or less of a scene appear on the film. These will help you to give more impact to your pictures. In the mini experiment on the left, try to find as many convex lenses as you can to experiment with. You will find that weaker lenses, which have longer focal lengths, make larger images. This is the opposite to what happens if you use them as a magnifying glass.

Working with lenses
Standing by a window, use a magnifying glass to form an image of the window on a piece of paper. See what happens when you use different convex lenses.

M A T E R I A L S

You will need: cardboard tube, thin card, sticky tape, scissors, sharp pencil, tracing paper.

Camera lenses
Some camera lenses consist of several lenses, or elements. As rays of light pass through a lens, they are refracted (bent) at different angles. These rays can distort, resulting in multi-coloured edges on your print. Multiple-element lenses, like the ones seen here, help to prevent the light rays distorting.

ZOOMING IN AND OUT

1 Cover one end of a cardboard tube with thin card and tape it down. Pierce a small hole in the centre with a sharp pencil.

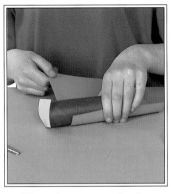

2 Wrap a large square of card around the other end of the tube. Tape the edge down to form another tube that slides over the first.

3 Cut a circle of tracing paper big enough to stick over the end of your sliding tube. Tape it firmly in place. This is your focal plane.

P R O J E C T

*Record what you see
through your zoom lens.
Slide the tubes in and out
to make the image bigger
(left) or smaller (below)*

4 Aim the tube at a window or
bright light (with the tracing
paper end at your eye). Hold it
right up to your eye to get it
level with your line of sight,
and then hold it at least
10-15cm away from your eye.
You should now see an image
on the tracing paper screen.

Flat and curved mirrors

Some cameras have
one or more
mirrors instead of
a lens. All the rays
that hit a mirror
are reflected. A
flat mirror *(right)*
reflects all rays in
the same way, so
your image looks
unchanged (although left
and right seem reversed).

A convex
mirror reflects
and bends
light *(left)*. It
works like a
mirror and a
lens together
to distort
the image.

Simple close-ups

Put a small object, such as a coin, on a flat surface. Hold a
magnifying glass (the larger, the better) in front of the
viewfinder and move the camera until the coin fills about a
quarter of the frame. Put the magnifying glass in front of the
camera lens and take the photograph. Take a few more shots
with the camera a bit nearer and then try moving the camera a
bit farther away. A macro lens can be fitted to a camera to take
close-ups, and some have a mini-macro lens fitted permanently.

LIGHTING AND FLASH

Lighting is one of the most important parts of photography. The kind of light you take your picture in, how that light hits the subject, and where you take the picture from, all affect the result. Outdoors, most photos are taken with natural light. Artificial light is needed indoors, or outdoors when there is not enough natural light. Photographs can be taken in dim natural light without additional artificial light, but only with very long exposures. Lighting can also create dramatic effects. Flash lighting makes a very bright light for a fraction of a second. Most small cameras have a small, built-in flash unit.

Lights and reflectors

Photographic studios have lots of strong lights. They allow the photographer to create many different lighting effects, without worrying about natural light. Some lights make light over a wide area, others make narrow beams. Using umbrellas and sheets of reflecting material can direct the light, too. These can be used to help reduce the contrast on bright sunny days.

With front lighting, light is coming to the subject from the same direction as the camera position or slightly above. It lights the subject evenly, but gives a flat look because there are no strong shadows or highlights.

Back lighting means that the subject is between the light and the camera. It can make your subject look darker. The light does not have to be directly behind. Here, two lights have been set at a 45° angle behind the subject, one on either side.

If a picture is side-lit from the back, the the light is coming across your subject. Side lighting will often give the most interesting or dramatic photographs, because it creates shadows that give more shape and depth to the subject.

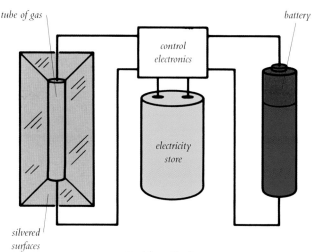

tube of gas

battery

control electronics

electricity store

silvered surfaces

Light in a flash

Light from a flash unit only lasts for a fraction of a second. It is carefully timed to flash when the camera's shutter is open. Many cameras have a built-in flash unit. A more powerful flash gun can be added to an SLR camera *(above)*. Most cameras have a signal that tells you when you need to use the flash.

Inside a flash

Flash *(above)* is made by sending a very large electric current through a narrow tube of gas. This makes a lightning-like flash. The flash's batteries gradually build up a store of electric charge, which is released very quickly. It is like filling a jug from a dripping tap and then pouring all the water out at once, or blowing up a balloon and then bursting it.

Bouncing and diffusing

Direct flash from the camera to the subject can cause harsh shadows and red-eye (where the flash creates red reflections in a person's eyes). Bounce flash means aiming the flash at the ceiling, so that the light spreads out. Some photographers diffuse flash with a sheet of material attached to the top of the flash, as on the right.

These people are sitting at different distances from the flash. This means that some of them are overexposed (have too much light), while others are underexposed.

Arrange people so that they are all about the same distance from the camera. This should ensure that everyone is properly exposed.

WORKING WITH LIGHT

Y ou can improve many of your photographs by giving
thought to the lighting before you shoot. For pictures
of people, try some of the simple suggestions here. If you're
taking pictures outside, move around your
subject to study the effects of light as it
falls at different angles. You can also ask
people you are photographing to tilt
their head at different angles, so that
the sunlight lights up their faces. If
there isn't enough light, some cameras
have a back light button that lengthens
the exposure time for dark subjects.
You could also use flash to light up
the darker areas. This is known as
using fill-in flash.

*Red-eye is caused by light from a flash
unit near the camera lens bouncing off
the retina (at the back of the eye) and
back into the lens. With SLR
cameras, the flash can be moved
to one side to avoid red-eye.*

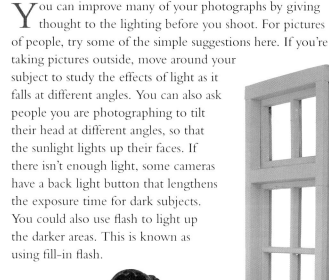

CREATING LIGHTING EFFECTS

M A T E R I A L S

*You will need: a camera, large sheets of
white and coloured paper or card,
kitchen foil, desk lamp, torch,
coloured tissue paper.*

1 Sit your
subject near
a window and
ask them to turn
their head
into different
positions. Move
around the room
to see the effects
of front, side and
back lighting.

2 Hold a sheet of white paper or card near your subject to reflect some light from the window back on to their face. The reflected light fills in the shadows caused by the side lighting. Do the same with coloured paper. This will add colour to your subject's face.

3 Try the same with kitchen foil or a piece of shiny card. See how this gives a much brighter reflected light. Crushing the foil and then smoothing it out again will diffuse the light in interesting and creative ways.

4 For pictures with some really spooky lighting effects, light your subject from below with an ordinary lamp or a torch. Do it in a darkened room with your camera's flash turned off. To try out this kind of effect, you will need to get a friend to help.

5 To take this approach even further, experiment with putting your hand in front of the light. As with the previous step, turn off your camera's flash if you can, and hold the camera very still. If you have a tripod, use that to free your hands.

6 For less harsh lighting, put a sheet of tissue paper in front of the lamp or torch. Try this with coloured tissue paper to see what effects you can achieve. You can also take flash photos with a small piece of tissue paper over the flash unit.

USING FILTERS

A photographic filter changes the light as it enters the camera's lens. There are hundreds of different filters, and each one creates its own effect. The most common filter is called a skylight filter. It lets all visible light through the lens but stops invisible ultra-violet light from getting in, as ultra-violet light can make photographs look unnaturally blue. Filters called graduate filters make some parts of the scene darker. They are often used to darken very bright skies. Coloured filters, such as red or yellow, can make black-and-white photograps look very dramatic. There are other special-effect filters that you can buy for adding different effects to your photographs. Smearing petroleum jelly on the edges of a clear filter can give a photograph a soft effect.

Normally filters are only used on SLR cameras. Some filters are circular, and screw on to the end of the camera's lens. Others are designed to slot into a filter holder at the front of the lens.

Bright lights
You will not always want strong reflections and bright light in a picture *(right)*.

Polarizing filter
Here *(left)*, putting a polarizing filter in front of the lens has made the reflections and strong light disappear. These filters cut out certain light rays from a scene, but let others through. They can also have a dramatic effect on skies, making them a much darker blue. If you want to take pictures through a window, a polarizing filter will reduce reflections in the glass.

Creating a sunset

With a sunset filter, you can turn a daytime sky *(left)* into a beautiful sunset *(below)*. Half the filter is clear and the other half has a slight orange tint. Position the tint at the top of your shot and the sky appears reddish.

Making your own

You can make filters from transparent, coloured sweet wrappers. Put clean wrappers in front of the viewfinder to see what effect they have. Then attach them to the front of the lens with small pieces of tape.

Interesting shapes

A frame filter is a black mask with a shape cut in it. This makes the scene you are shooting come out in that shape. The other parts of the scene will be black. Frame filters come in simple shapes, such as squares and ovals, and more complex shapes, such as keyholes. Shooting through holes in walls or old trees can give you the same creative effects.

USEFUL TIPS

Here are a few simple tips that should help you to improve your photographic technique and avoid some common mistakes. Good technique is made up of technical skill and an eye for an interesting subject. Remember that a complicated SLR camera does not necessarily take the best photographs, and that great shots are perfectly possible with a simple point-and-shoot camera. The first thing to decide is the type of film you want to use (colour print, colour slide or black-and-white). Always load and unload your film in dim lighting. Once it has all been exposed, place it in its container and get it processed as soon as possible.

Hold a camera steady with both hands. Be careful not to put your fingers over the lens, flash or autofocus sensor. Keep your elbows close to your body and squeeze the shutter release button slowly. Do not stab at it.

Check the background
When you are taking portraits, or photographs of groups of people, always look at the background as well as at your subject. If necessary, recompose your picture to avoid the sort of accident that has happened in this shot. Many cameras have a portrait setting that gives a shallow depth of field. This automatically makes the background go out of focus.

Fill the frame
Do not be afraid to get close to your subject. For example, if you are taking a portrait, make sure the person's head and shoulders fill the frame *(right)*. But be careful not to get too close, because the camera may not be able to focus *(far right)*. If you get too close with an autofocus camera, it will not let you take a picture.

Natural frames

Try adding some interest to photos by shooting through archways or doors to frame the subject. With photos of groups or scenery, you can include overhanging branches in the foreground.

The rule of thirds

Try using the rule of thirds: place the subject a third of the way across or up or down the frame. This makes the shot more interesting. With autofocus cameras, you often have to use your focus lock to point at the subject first and then recompose the picture before shooting. Try this with landscapes, for example, having a mountain range in the top third of the frame.

A different viewpoint

Photographs taken from a standing position have the same viewpoint as your eyes usually do. Changing the camera's viewpoint can give more interesting results. Try kneeling, or even lying down.

Bad weather photographs

You do not always need to wait for good weather before taking photos. In fact, overhead sunshine tends to give flat, dull pictures. Stormy clouds can be much more interesting than cloudless skies. Remember to protect your camera in extreme weather conditions to make sure it stays dry.

SPECIAL PHOTOGRAPHY

Most cameras and lenses are designed for general photography. However, there are some types of camera that take photographs in unusual formats or in special conditions. For example, you can use certain cameras to take really wide panoramic views, or to shoot scenes entirely underwater. It is also possible to take pictures inside the human body with an attachment called an endoscope. There are also some unusual types of film. Some produce odd colours or shades in your photographs. Another type of film records technical information about each shot, while self-processing film does not have to be developed.

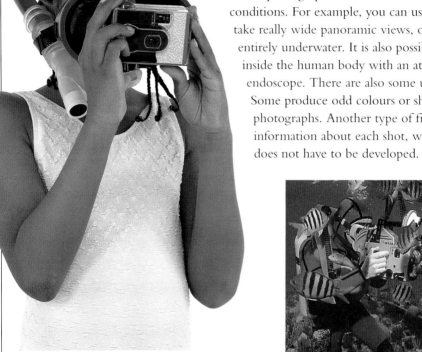

Disposable underwater cameras can take photographs while completely submerged. The camera's body is recycled after the film is processed.

Underwater SLRs

Divers take photographs underwater with special SLR cameras that are waterproof even when they are many metres down. They can also withstand the high pressure of being in deep water. Special housings are available for many cameras to enable land cameras to be used underwater or in adverse conditions such as during a cave diving or pot-holing expedition.

If you want to photograph anything deep down in the sea, you need to use extremely bright lights.

Spacious photographs

Panoramic cameras can take very wide photographs, which are good for shots of large groups of people or landscapes. Many compact cameras take pictures that are called panoramic, but they actually only appear to be so. They are no wider than a standard frame, just shorter, to help you compose your shot.

FACT BOX

• Certain cameras are able to decide themselves whether a scene is a portrait, a landscape, or an action shot, and adjust the aperture and shutter to suit the photograph.

• APS film is similar to 35mm film. It records information, such as the exposure settings and frame size, on a special magnetic layer and this is used during processing.

• You can buy disposable panoramic cameras.

Laser photographs

A hologram is a three-dimensional (3-D) picture that looks 3-D no matter what angle you look at it from. The picture changes as you move your head from side to side. However, holograms are not taken with a camera. Another kind of equipment is used to record how laser light bounces off the subject from different directions.

Advanced systems

Many new compact cameras (and some SLRs) work according to the APS, or the Advanced Photographic System. They allow you to set the frame size for each shot individually and even to swap film rolls midway without damage.

AMAZING EFFECTS

Discover how to take stereo photos and how to get an amazing three-dimensional effect from them. It is easier than you might think, and you can do it with the most basic compact camera. Simply take two photos of the same scene from different angles. When they have been developed, place them side by side to see the three-dimensional effect for yourself. The effect works because, like many animals, humans have binocular vision. This means that the two different views from our two eyes overlap. In the overlapping area, our eyes see slightly different views, which makes things appear in three dimensions. Once you have tried this experiment, read on to find out how to construct a grand panoramic picture by taking a series of photos of the same scene.

Place your stereo pair of photographs side by side to view them.

The diagram on the right shows how the stereo effect is created – because our two eyes see slightly different views.

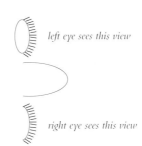

left eye sees this view

right eye sees this view

the actual 3-D box you are looking at

MAKE YOUR MODEL COME ALIVE

M A T E R I A L S

You will need: camera, model.

1 Choose a simple object such as this model of a dinosaur. Holding the camera very steady, take a picture. Try to include a bit of space around your subject.

2 Take a step about 20cm to your left, and take another photo. Try taking more pairs of photographs, using different distances between the two photographs.

PROJECT

3 Put your pictures down side by side on a flat surface. Stand over them and place your index finger between the two. With your eyes directly above the photos, look down at the finger and slowly raise it towards your nose, keeping it in focus. The two images you see below should merge into one 3-D image.

Make a panorama

Choose a good general landscape scene, with no close-up objects in it. Now, using a camera lens set at 35 or 50mm, take a series of photographs that overlap slightly. Start by looking towards your left and move your head slightly round to the right for each of the following shots. When your prints are developed, lay them out in the right order to recreate all of your scene. When you are happy with the arrangement, tape them together carefully.

This completed panorama (above) works well because it is a simple, open scene. If it had been filled with small objects, then the effect might not have been as good. If you want people in your scene, try to keep them away from areas that will overlap in the finished panorama. On the other hand, you could ask a friend to move into different parts of the scene for each different shot and produce a picture with multiple images of him or her.

MOVING PICTURES

Acine camera is used to take moving pictures. It takes a whole series of photographs in quick succession (usually about 25 every second), on a very long roll of film. Any moving object appears in a slightly different position in each frame. When the photographs are displayed quickly, one after the other, the movement in the original scene appears to be recreated. The films are usually transparency, or positive rather than negative. The films are put into a projector to be shown. Today, cine cameras are used mainly for professional movie-making. Home cine cameras used to be very popular, but today they have been replaced by video cameras.

Moving pictures rely on the fact that we have persistence of vision. This means our eyes remember a picture for a split second. To see how this works, look at a scene and close your eyes quickly.

  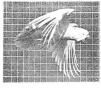

Recording motion

The early movie cameras grew out of experiments to record and study animal motion rather than for entertainment. This sequence *(left)* was taken by British photographer Eadweard Muybridge (1830–1904). He had first come up with the idea of moving pictures in 1877 after taking a series of photographs of a horse running, using 24 different cameras. Muybridge produced hundreds of images recording the complex movements of animals and human which were too quick for the unaided human eye to follow. Artists used his pictures as reference for their paintings.

Cine film

This is just like the rolls of film you put in a stills, or ordinary, camera. In fact, 35mm film was originally made for cine cameras. The image in each frame of the film is slightly different to the one before.

Electronic images

Unlike the film used in cine cameras, camcorders such as this one use video tape which has a magnetic coating. The camera translates pictures into an electronic signal which is recorded on the tape. This camcorder's small screen lets the user see the pictures as they are being taken. The pictures can later be played back on a video player using a television screen.

Inside a cine camera

A cine camera has similar parts to a stills camera – a lens, shutter and aperture. It also has some extra parts for taking photos in quick succession. The film is wound on, ready for the next frame, while the shutter is closed. The shutter speed is always the same and the exposure is controlled just by the aperture.

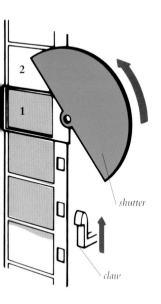

shutter

claw

shutter open, first frame exposed

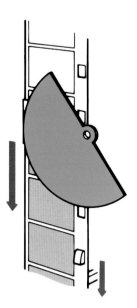

shutter closed, claw pulls film down

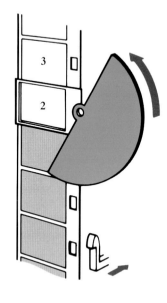

shutter open, second frame exposed

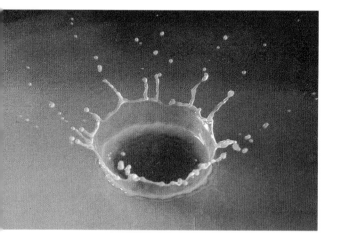

High-speed photos

This is a frame from a high-speed film. Some cine cameras can take hundreds, or even thousands, of photographs every second. When they are played back at normal speed, the action is slowed right down.

FACT BOX

• The world's fastest cine cameras are used by scientists. They can take 600 million frames every second.

• If you used a cine camera like this to film a bullet fired from a gun, the bullet would take 1,000 frames to move just one millimetre.

• Like normal camera film, cine camera film comes in different formats. Professionals on location shoots tend to use 16mm format.

• In an IMAX cinema, the screen is as high as seven elephants sitting on top of each other.

• On IMAX film, the frames are four times larger than 35mm film.

ANIMATION

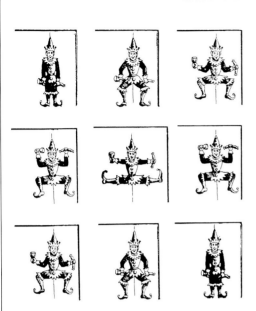

A nimation is making inanimate objects, or objects that cannot move by themselves, appear to move. Frames of the film are photographed one at a time with a special cine camera, although you can create animation using video cameras. Between each frame, the objects are moved slightly. Sometimes this is combined with camera movement or zoom effects. When the finished film is viewed, the objects seem to move. Some animated objects are models, which are photographed to make animated movies. Others are drawings, which are photographed to make cartoons. Modern cartoon animation is often done by computer, so the photography stage is not needed. Quite often only the main drawings are made by an artist and a computer plans the movements and frames using animation software.

Photo flick-book

The simplest way of making moving pictures is to put all the frames into a book and flick through the pages. In the early 1800s, flick books of photographs (called filoscopes) were used to entertain children as movies had not yet been invented. You can see some of the pages from an old filoscope above.

Turning marvel

A thaumotrope is a double-sided disc, often made of card, which has partial pictures on either side. When you spin the disc, the pictures appear to merge. So, if you had a bird on one side and a cage on the other, when the disc was spun you would see the bird in the cage. The name "thaumotrope" comes from the Greek words for marvel and turning.

This picture shows a scene from one of the popular Wallace and Gromit films, made by Aardman Animations Ltd. Model animation is a highly skilful and time-consuming job. The models must be moved very, very slightly between each frame. There are around 25 frames for every second of film.

FACT BOX

• A cine camera used for shooting cels is fixed so that it looks down on a flat baseboard. The cels for one frame are placed on the board and a photo is taken. Then the cels for the next frame are shot, and so on.

• Model animation is done with a camera, held firm on a rostrum, or platform, so that it does not shift between frames. However, it can be tilted, panned (moved to follow a moving object) and zoomed to create different effects.

• A 20-minute animated film uses between 15,000 and 30,000 frames.

This picture appears in the top right-hand corner of every other page in this section. Flick all the pages of the section quickly and watch the pictures. What can you see happening?

Enjoying animation

Producing animated children's films is big business. Many cartoons are made with the aid of computers. Some computer packages do all the time-consuming drawing and painting. They can also produce complex, three-dimensional characters, or add cartoon elements to film of real actors. In special effects scenes, real actors may be replaced by computer-generated images of themselves.

Cartoon cels

Until the 1980s, cartoons were made by photographing a series of drawings. The drawings were done on transparent plastic sheets called cels. Moving characters were drawn on one cel and the still background on another, to save drawing the background again and again for each frame. Once the cels were completed, they were photographed with a cine camera. When these were shown in rapid succession, a moving film appeared.

background cels

character cels (notice how each one is different either in expression or the clothing)

EASY ANIMATION

During the 1800s, there was a craze for optical toys, such as flick-books. Many of them created an illusion of movement by displaying a sequence of pictures in quick succession. At first, the pictures were hand-drawn. Later, photos taken by early movie cameras were used as well. Here, you can find out how to make a toy called a phenakistoscope, and how to use it to turn a series of pictures into animation. Our toy is slightly different from the Victorian one on the right, as it has slots cut around the edges, rather than in the centre.

A phenakistoscope (above) was an early device used to view moving pictures in a mirror. It held a set of images that were all slightly different. When you spun the disc, you saw an action sequence through the slots.

A series of simple drawings work best. This strip of images is for a zoetrope.

You will need: thick, dark-coloured card, sharp pencil, ruler, scissors, paper, dark felt-tip marker, tape, camera, models.

MAKE YOUR OWN PHENAKISTOSCOPE

1 On a piece of thick card, draw a circle measuring 26cm across. Divide it into eight equal segments. At the end of each segment line, draw slots 4cm long and 5mm wide.

2 Now cut out your disc, and the evenly spaced slots around the outside of it. Make sure that the slots are no wider than 5mm. These will be your viewing holes.

3 On pieces of light-coloured paper, draw a series of eight pictures. These should form a sequence of movements. Make sure that your drawings are fairly simple and clear, and that they are drawn with clean, strong lines.

4 Attach the little drawings to the disc by taping them just under the slots. You may need to cut them to fit, but make sure the picture is centred below the slot. Push a pencil through the centre of the card disc to make a handle.

5 Stand in front of a mirror. Hold the disc vertically, with the pictures toward the mirror. Spin the disc and look through the slots. You should see an animated loop of action in the mirror.

Once you have mastered the technique of making a photo phenakistoscope, you can get more adventurous with your subjects and story lines. Try adding more models or props, for example putting hats on the models.

PHOTO PHENAKISTOSCOPE

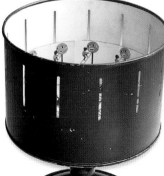

1 Now try a model animation. Take eight photographs of a model from the same position (use a tripod if you can). Move the model(s) slightly each time. The models should take up the middle third of the photograph frame.

2 Cut your photos to size and stick them to the phenakistoscope, one under each slot. Your phenakistoscope will work better if the photos have a dark frame, or you can just cover the edges roughly with a black felt-tip marker pen.

A zoetrope
This zoetrope from the 1860s was used to display long strips of drawings showing simple action sequences. They were placed inside a cylinder that could be rotated by hand. The moving pictures were then viewed through the vertical slots cut in the cylinder.

CAMERAS IN SCIENCE

Some advanced microscopes (above) *can take very detailed close-up photos. You can also do the same thing with a normal microscope, by fitting an SLR camera to it. You remove the SLR's lens and the microscope acts as a close-up lens for the camera.*

Most of us use our cameras for recording holidays and special occasions, or for taking pictures of our friends. Photography is also extremely important in science and technology. For example, it is used for recording images that have been made by scientific instruments, so that they can be studied later. It is also used to record experiments that happen too fast for the human eye to see, and for analyzing experimental results. In many modern scientific instruments, electronic cameras have taken the place of film cameras. Their images can be transferred easily to computers for analysis.

Microscope photographs
A photograph that is taken with a microscope is called a photomicrograph. This one is a close-up of the red blood cells in our blood.

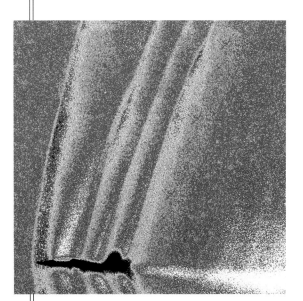

Recording speed on camera
This type of photograph is known as a schlieren photograph. It shows the shock waves around a T-38 aircraft flying at great speed – 1.1 times the speed of sound, or Mach 1.1. The waves appear as red and green diagonal lines in the photograph. It enables scientists to see that the main shock waves come from the nose and tail of the plane. Smaller shock waves come from the engine inlets and wings. The yellow stream behind the aircraft is caused by the exhaust of the jet engine.

Photographing heat
All objects give off heat rays called infra-red rays. Hotter objects give off stronger rays. A special type of film called infrared film is sensitive to heat rays rather than light rays. Hot and cold objects show up in different colours or shades.

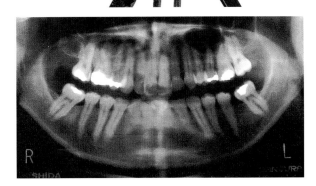

When you are taking photos of the sky with a telescope using long exposures, the telescope often has to move slowly across the sky. This is to prevent the stars from becoming streaks on your prints. This happens because the Earth and stars are slowly moving. It is like taking a picture of a traffic light from a moving car. The lights would appear streaked.

Capturing the stars

Just as a camera can be added to a microscope to take close-up pictures, one can also be added to a telescope. The telescope acts like a very powerful telephoto lens for the camera. (A telephoto lens makes distant objects seem much closer.) Light from the stars is very weak, and so long exposures are needed.

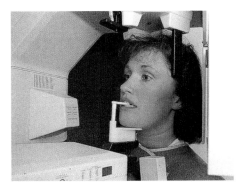

Where more X-rays reach the film, through soft parts of the body, the film turns a darker tone when it is developed. Bones and teeth show up white.

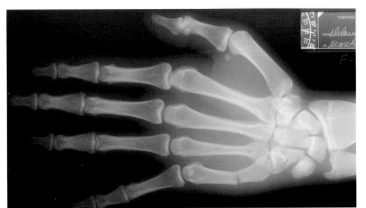

Taking X-ray pictures

X-rays are used to photograph inside bodies. Unlike light rays, X-rays can pass though the soft parts of your body – skin and muscle. X-ray film is simply processed to produce negatives not prints. X-rays help dentists or doctors to find out all kinds of things about the body. The picture on the left shows the hand of a boxer with a fractured finger caused through punching. Other kinds of X-ray technology are used to scan for faults in the structure of buildings or aircraft, enabling repairs to take place before a part fails or causes an accident.

CAMERAS AND COMPUTERS

Photographs are often used in computer applications. For example, a multimedia CD-ROM about nature might contain thousands of photographs of animals and plants. Photographs stored and displayed by computer are called digital images because they consist of a long series of numbers as opposed to being a physical print on paper. Digital images are either prints that have been scanned into a computer to turn them into digital form, or images that have been photographed with a digital, filmless, camera. Digital images can be copied over and over again, without any loss in quality. This means that they can be sent easily from one computer to another – over the Internet, for example.

Just like ordinary cameras, digital cameras come as compacts and SLRs. They have a lens and shutter, but, in the space where the film would normally be, they have a light-sensitive microchip. This means that the photographs are stored in the camera's memory.

FACT BOX
• The highest resolution digital cameras divide a picture into a grid about 7,000 pixels (dots) wide and 5,000 pixels deep.

• Many digital pictures use 24-bit colour. This means that each pixel can be any one of 16,771,216 different colours.

Video phone
The digital video camera on top of this computer *(above)* takes pictures that are sent down the telephone line and appear on another computer's screen. This lets the people at both computers see each other.

Floppy disk camera
The digital camera on the right uses a normal floppy disk which can be placed directly into a computer. The pictures can then be worked upon using computer software.

Pixel pictures

A digital image is made up of pixels, or dots. A number represents the colour of each tiny dot. High-resolution (sharper) images divide the picture into a greater number of smaller dots than low-resolution ones, but they take up more computer memory.

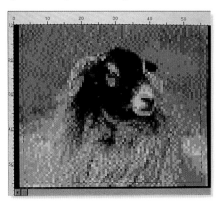

Retouching

Once a photo is digitized, it can be altered in any way by the computer. For example, colours can be changed or another photo can be added in. A polar bear could be put in a desert! It is much easier than trying the same thing with normal photography.

Morphing

Many films and television programmes make use of computer-manipulated photographs and film images to create stunning special effects. Morphing, for example, is where a person or object changes into something or someone else slowly, on screen. To achieve this, the computer software gradually merges two totally different images together.

This shows a digitized picture on a computer screen before it has been manipulated.

Here is the same picture after it has been manipulated by computer. Can you see how it has changed?

PART FOUR

COMPUTERS

The explosion of computer technology towards
the end of the 1900s transformed people's lives.
Complex, repetitive tasks that previously took
hours or days could suddenly be accomplished in
minutes, or even seconds. Early computers took
up entire rooms, while today's computers, with
far more power, fit on a person's lap. At home and
at work, the worlds of e-mail and the Internet have
opened ways of communicating ideas and of
buying goods of every kind at a speed that would
have been thought impossible only fifty years ago.

AUTHOR
Stephen Bennington
CONSULTANT
Paul Fisher

COMPUTER BASICS

THOUSANDS of everyday tasks are now much easier to do thanks to the development of computers. Many activities, such as writing, drawing, playing music, sending messages, playing games, looking up information and even shopping, are regularly done using these powerful machines. Living in today's computer age means that everyone has access to the technology – in offices, schools, shops and at home. Indeed, computers are such an integral part of modern society that it is hard to imagine how humans once coped without them.

monitor

Some people believe that computers can think like people. In fact, they can only use information that is put into them. The most important job computers do is to process such information much more quickly and accurately than a person could. Performing complex calculations, checking for spelling mistakes in a story or copying pictures from one place to another, for example, are done much faster using a computer. Essentially, computers are just tools like washing machines or cars. They are used in many different ways to do an enormous range of interesting and useful tasks.

Disks and data
Data (information) can be stored on disks outside the main part of the computer. The disk can be in the form of a CD (compact disc), DVD (digital versatile disc), Zip disk or floppy disk. These are placed in different slots, called drives, in the computer to allow new data to be put in and recorded data to be taken out.

Processing power
The computer's brain, where data is handled and rearranged, is called the processor. This is a complicated electronic circuit board, which contains smaller electronic circuits called silicon chips. These chips are the powerhouses of all computers. They contain other electronic circuits that are so small that they can only be seen under a microscope.

hard drive

Storage system

The hard drive is the computer's storage unit where all the data it needs is kept. It consists of a set of spinning disks and a moving arm that reads what is stored there. We cannot see the hard drive because it needs to be enclosed in a box to keep it free from dirt.

speaker

Play the game

A joystick, gamepad or steering wheel are sometimes needed to play computer games. They are easier to use than a mouse for this purpose and they make the game feel more real. For instance, using a steering wheel to play a driving game makes it feel as if you are really driving.

Sound it out

Most computers have a built-in speaker, but external speakers add to the quality of the sound. External speakers come in a range of shapes and sizes and have to be able to generate all kinds of sounds, from CD-quality stereo to movie soundtracks.

Mouse clicks

The mouse is used to control the pointer, or cursor, on the screen. The pointer moves according to the direction the mouse moves. You press part of the mouse to do a range of tasks, such as moving objects. Pressing the mouse is called clicking.

keyboard   *mouse*   *mouse mat*

Hard copy

A printer translates what you see on screen, such as pages of text or pictures, on to paper. Modern inkjet colour printers can produce photographic-quality prints, but black-and-white laser printers are most commonly used in offices.

Scan it in

A scanner turns ordinary pictures on paper, such as photos from a book, into a form that the computer can read. The scanner analyzes the image and sends the data to the computer in a form that it can read.

ALL TALK

EVERY subject uses a set of words and phrases, called jargon, to describe things that have not existed before. This is certainly true when you start exploring the world of computers. Computer jargon is usually made up of either new scientific terms, such as 'computer', or existing words that have been given a new meaning, such as 'mouse'. They can also be words made from the first letters of phrases, such as 'PC', which stands for Personal Computer. These are called acronyms.

One of the main reasons people have difficulty with learning a new subject, or even give the subject up, is because they come across a lot of new and confusing words that they do not fully understand. If you are not sure what a word means then you will probably find it in the Glossary at the end of this book. If not, then you are bound to find it in an up-to-date dictionary. Knowing what computer jargon means when you see and hear it is very important. Remember that everyone is in the same position when they learn about a new subject. You will gradually pick up what each new word means as you read and learn more about it. The boxes on the opposite page will start you off with some essential computer jargon.

HARDWARE WWW NETIQUETTE INTERNET SOFTWARE ICON

What does it mean?
Sometimes people find themselves feeling puzzled, confused or even bored when they try to learn about computers. These feelings often come from not fully understanding the many new and sometimes strange words that are associated with the subject.

Speaking the language
Lots of unusual words and phrases are used to describe computers. For example, the piece of equipment above is called a monitor, and it displays computer data on a screen much like a television. The monitor above shows a CD-ROM. Do you know what CD-ROM stands for?

SOME FIRST JARGON WORDS

• **Hardware** – Equipment, such as the processor, monitor, keyboard, scanner and mouse, that makes up your computer system.

• **Home page** – An introductory page on a web site, which contains links to other pages.

• **Icon** – A small picture that you can click on with the mouse to make the computer do something.

• **Internet** – A worldwide computer network, through which computers can communicate with each other.

• **Netiquette** – A code of good conduct and manners, developed by Internet users, which suggests acceptable and unacceptable ways of behaving on the Internet.

• **Software** – A set of coded instructions, called an application, that tells your computer what to do.

• **Web site** – A computer document written in HTML (see right), which is linked to other computer documents.

EASY ACRONYMS

Here are some common acronyms that you will come across regularly.

• **CD-ROM** (**C**ompact **D**isc **R**ead-**O**nly **M**emory) – A disk similar to an audio CD, which contains information that can only be read by the computer.

• **CPU** (**C**entral **P**rocessing **U**nit) – The brain of the computer, which contains the processing chips and circuit boards.

• **HTML** (**H**yper**T**ext **M**ark-up **L**anguage) – A computer code that is added to word-processed documents to turn them into web pages.

• **ISP** (**I**nternet **S**ervice **P**rovider) – The companies through which Internet connection is made.

• **Modem** (**MO**dulator/ **DEM**odulator) – A device that allows computer information to be sent down a telephone line.

• **RAM** (**R**andom **A**ccess **M**emory) – Computer memory that holds information temporarily until the computer is switched off.

• **URL** (**U**niform **R**esource **L**ocator) – The address of a site on the Internet that is specific to one web page.

• **WWW** (**W**orld **W**ide **W**eb) – A huge collection of information that is available on the Internet. The information is comprised of web sites, which are made up of lots of web pages.

INTERNET

A worldwide computer network, through which computers communicate with each other.

A helping hand

There are many ways to find out about computers and the jargon that comes with using them. Your family and friends may be able to help, or you could join a computer club and meet lots of other like-minded people who are trying to find out about computers. You could even use the Internet to try and answer your questions.

HISTORY OF COMPUTERS

Blaise Pascal's calculator
In 1642, the French mathematician Blaise Pascal invented the first automatic calculator. The device added and subtracted by means of a set of wheels linked by gears. The first wheel represented the numbers 0 to 9, the second wheel represented 10s, the third stood for 100s, and so on. When the first wheel was turned ten notches, a gear moved the second wheel forward a notch and so on.

THE idea of using machines to do automated tasks and calculations is not a new one. The first calculating machine was developed in the 1600s and used moving parts such as wheels, cogs and gears to do mathematical tasks. The first big step towards developing an automatic computing machine came about in 1801 Joseph-Marie Jacquard, a French weaver, invented a weaving machine that was controlled by a series of punched cards. Where there were holes, the needles rose and met the thread, but where there were no holes, the needles were blocked. This was the first time that stored information had been used to work a machine.

Early in the 1900s, electronic devices began to replace mechanical (hand-operated) machines. These computers filled an entire room, yet they could only perform simple calculations. In later years, two main inventions – the transistor in the 1950s and the silicon chip in the 1970s – allowed the modern computer to develop. Both of these devices control tiny electrical currents that give computers instructions. Today, computers can be made to fit in the palm of your hand.

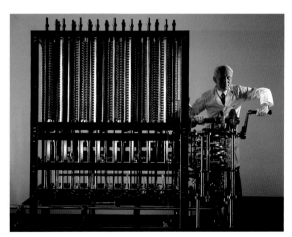

Mechanical mathematics
In 1835, British mathematician Charles Babbage invented a mechanical calculating machine called the Analytical Engine. When performing calculations, the machine stored completed sets of punched cards that were reusable. The Analytical Engine had all the elements of a modern computer – storage, memory, a system for moving between the two and an input device. The people who used his machines were called 'computers'.

The first programmer
Ada, Countess of Lovelace, was the daughter of the English poet Lord Byron and probably the world's first computer programmer. Between 1833 and 1843, she became interested in the work of fellow mathematician Charles Babbage. She created a punchcard program that was used to record the data for Babbage's Analytical Engine.

Controlling the current
Nowadays, computers work by electrical currents that flow through circuits. The current is controlled by devices called transistors. These are found on a wafer-thin piece of silicon called a chip. Some chips are no larger than a fingernail and contain millions of transistors. These are known as integrated circuits (ICs).

Code cracker

During World War II, British mathematician Alan Mathison Turing developed the first fully electronic calculating device. It was called Colossus because of its huge size. This machine was equipped with over 1,500 vacuum tubes that were used to control thousands of electrical currents. Colossus was designed to decipher a German communications code called Enigma. The machine was successful and helped Britain and its allies win World War II (1939–1945). Colossus can still be seen at the Bletchley Park Museum in the UK, the site where the code-cracking operation took place.

Two-room calculator

In 1943, ENIAC (Electronic Numerical Integrator and Computer) was constructed by Presper Eckert, John Atansoff and John Mauchly at the University of Pennsylvania in the USA. This early computer was enormous, filling two rooms and using as much electricity as ten family homes. It contained about 18,000 vacuum tubes, which acted as electronic switches and could perform hundreds of calculations every second. ENIAC was slow to program, however, because thousands of wires and connections had to be changed by hand.

COMPUTER DEVELOPMENTS

Television link

British inventor Sir Clive Sinclair developed many personal computers, including the ZX80 in 1980. This used a normal television as a monitor.

All in one

The Commodore 8032-SK was launched in 1980 and was the first computer to have a built-in monitor to display information.

BBC Model B

The BBC Model B was launched in 1981 by British computer firm Acorn to accompany the British Broadcasting Company (BBC) computer literacy program.

Laptop

International Business Machines Corporation (IBM) was instrumental in the development of a portable computer, called a laptop, in the early 1990s.

iMac

The iMac, developed by Apple Computers, Inc., revolutionized the design of desktop computers when it appeared on the market in the late 1990s.

iBook

Apple introduced the iBook in 1999. As powerful as a desktop iMac, this portable model also comes in a variety of bright, attractive colours.

Palm Pilot

A hand-held, pocket-size computer appeared in the late 90s. Not only does it feature an electronic pen for writing directly on the screen, it can also connect to the Internet.

BREAKING THE CODE

COMPUTERS are digital machines, which means they work by using a sequence of alternating numbers. The word 'digit' actually means a counting finger, but it is used in computing to mean every single number between 0 and 9.

The number code that computers use is called binary code, which means it is made up of just two digits – 0 and 1 (binary means two). Combinations of 0 and 1 can be used to represent any kind of information, for example, the letters of the alphabet. The theory behind this binary code is essentially the same as the one that Joseph-Marie Jacquard used for the punched cards that worked his weaving looms. Jacquard's punched cards were used to represent two kinds of information – a hole (1 in binary code) or no hole (0 in binary code).

Coded messages

This device, called the Enigma machine, was used by German forces during World War II (1939–1945). Uncoded messages were typed into the keyboard, and the machine then converted the message into a complex coded form. So complex was Enigma that a single letter could be represented by several different coded characters.

	BINARY CODE				
A	01000001	N	01001110	0	00110000
B	01000010	O	01001111	1	00110001
C	01000011	P	01010000	2	00110010
D	01000100	Q	01010001	3	00110011
E	01000101	R	01010010	4	00110100
F	01000110	S	01010011	5	00110101
G	01000111	T	01010100	6	00110110
H	01001000	U	01010101	7	00110111
I	01001001	V	01010110	8	00111000
J	01001010	W	01010111	9	00111001
K	01001011	X	01011000	10	00111010
L	01001100	Y	01011001		
M	01001101	Z	01011010		

Zeros and ones

Binary code is the language that all computers use in their calculations. Computers understand the code in terms of an electrical current (flow of electricity). An electrical current being on or off is represented by 0 and 1. In computing, zeros are used to mean off and ones are used to mean on. In this way, binary code can be used to represent all kinds of different information on a computer. For example, it can be used to represent decimal numbers or the letters of the alphabet, as shown in the chart on the left. Computers recognize each numbe or letter as a group of eight binary digits. Combinations of binary digits represent different numbers or letters.

A STRING OF BITS

You will need: 16 small pieces of coloured paper, black marker, stencil, two 1m lengths of string, 16 clothes pegs.

1 Look at the binary code version of the alphabet on the opposite page. See how many 0s and 1s you need to represent the initials of your name. Use a black marker and a stencil to draw them on the paper.

2 Arrange the 0s and 1s in two rows, one for each initial of your name. Each piece of paper represents a bit. This is the smallest amount of digital information in a computer.

3 When you have finished, double-check with the chart opposite to make sure you have got the 0s and 1s in the right place. The group of eight bits that represents each letter of the alphabet is called a byte.

4 Take the two pieces of string and the clothes pegs. Peg each bit to the string in the correct order, putting your first initial letter on one piece of string and your second initial on the other piece. The example in the picture shows the binary code version of the letters P and C.

GETTING STUFF IN AND OUT

COMPUTERS can only work with the information that you put into them. The main way that you put information into a computer is by using a keyboard and a mouse. The mouse controls the cursor (a movable visible point) on the monitor and allows you to select different options. The keys on a keyboard have one or more characters printed on them, such as a letter or a number. When you press a key, the main character on the key will appear on the screen. Other keys on the keyboard are used to give the computer specific instructions. There are two main types of home computer – a PC (personal computer) and a Mac (Apple Macintosh – named after the company that developed it). Their keyboards are slightly different, but they do the same jobs.

You can see the work you have created as words, numbers or pictures on the computer's monitor. You can print it on paper, save it on the hard disk or save it to a removable disk at any time.

It is a good idea to save your work every few minutes so that it is firmly recorded. If anything should go wrong with the computer, the data that you have not saved will be lost and you will have to redo all the work you have done.

Using computer
When people use a computer, they are doing four different things:

1. Inputting data (information) using an input device.

2. Storing the data so that it can be reused (often called data storage).

3. Working with the data they put in (often called processing).

4. Retrieving and looking at the data using an output device.

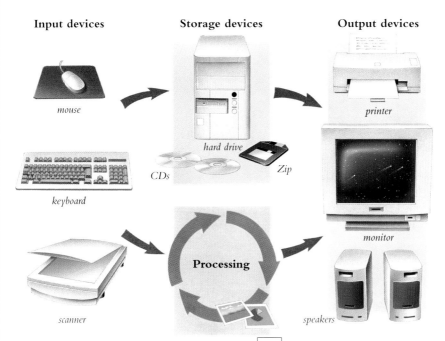

Input devices

mouse

keyboard

scanner

Storage devices

hard drive

CDs

Zip

Processing

Output devices

printer

monitor

speakers

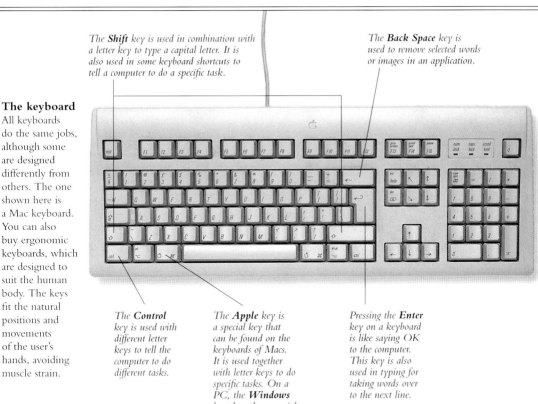

The **Shift** key is used in combination with a letter key to type a capital letter. It is also used in some keyboard shortcuts to tell a computer to do a specific task.

The **Back Space** key is used to remove selected words or images in an application.

The keyboard

All keyboards do the same jobs, although some are designed differently from others. The one shown here is a Mac keyboard. You can also buy ergonomic keyboards, which are designed to suit the human body. The keys fit the natural positions and movements of the user's hands, avoiding muscle strain.

The **Control** key is used with different letter keys to tell the computer to do different tasks.

The **Apple** key is a special key that can be found on the keyboards of Macs. It is used together with letter keys to do specific tasks. On a PC, the **Windows** key does the same job.

Pressing the **Enter** key on a keyboard is like saying OK to the computer. This key is also used in typing for taking words over to the next line.

Monitors

As you input information to the computer, the results of your actions appear on the screen of a monitor. The picture on the screen is made up of small dots of light called pixels. Some monitors can display more pixels than others, which produces a better-quality picture on screen. These monitors are said to have a high resolution.

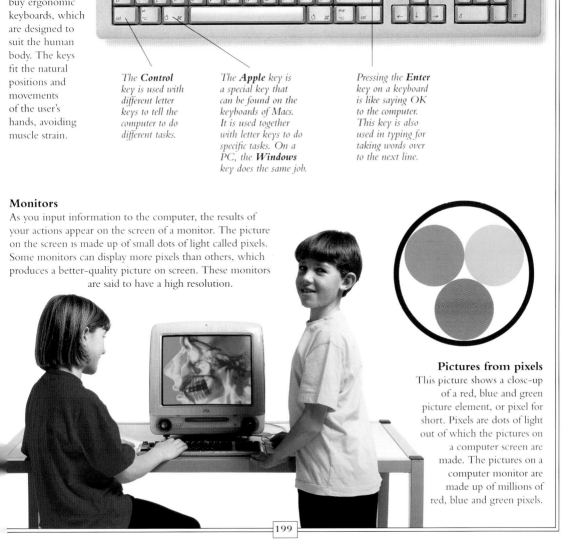

Pictures from pixels

This picture shows a close-up of a red, blue and green picture element, or pixel for short. Pixels are dots of light out of which the pictures on a computer screen are made. The pictures on a computer monitor are made up of millions of red, blue and green pixels.

STORING AND FINDING

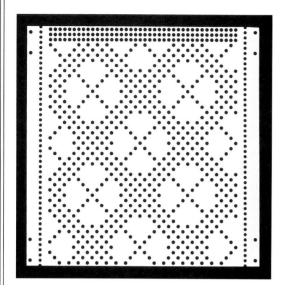

The first computer program

The punched cards that Joseph-Marie Jacquard used in 1801 to operate his weaving machine worked in exactly the same way as the electrical impulses in binary code. The needles could pass through a hole in the card to meet the thread and make a stitch (equivalent to the binary digit 1, or on), but they were blocked if there was no hole (equivalent to the binary digit 0, or off). In this way, different patterns of holes on the punched cards represented different patterns of woven cloth.

THE part of the computer that does all the calculations is called the microprocessor. It consists of millions of electronic switches, called transistors, and other electronic devices that are all built into a wafer-thin slice of a chemical element called silicon. Electricity passes through tiny lines of metal on the silicon chip. The transistors switch the electricity on and off. These on-and-off pulses of electricity represent the 0s and 1s of binary code, which the computer interprets to do different tasks.

Microprocessors control a number of other devices besides computers, including telephones, car engines and thermostats (heat-control devices) on washing machines.

Silicon chips control other devices in a computer such as memory chips. These store information that is needed by the microprocessor to run software such as a word-processing application. Other data is stored on various kinds of disks, including hard disks, floppy disks, Zip disks and CDs.

Ticker tape

Ticker tape was first used in the 1930s by the German scientist Konrad Zuse. Holes were punched in the tape in the same way as Jacquard's cards, but the tape was fed into the computer as a continuous strip. A hole was read as the binary digit 1. No hole was read as the binary digit 0. The smaller holes hold the tape in the machine.

Memory chips

There are two basic kinds of memory chips in a modern computer. RAM (random-access memory) chips remember information only when the computer is switched on. When you turn your computer off, everything on the RAM chip is erased. RAM chips provide the space your computer needs to run software. ROM (read-only memory) chips remember information permanently. They store essential data, such as the program that enables your computer to start up.

land pit

CD (Compact Disc)

Data is recorded on to a compact disc by a laser beam cutting into a thin metal layer under the plastic coating of the disk. The disk becomes covered with microscopic indentations (pits) and flat areas (lands), which are read by another laser in the computer. The pits are read as binary 1 and the lands as binary 0. Most CD-ROMs can store around 750MB of information.

Storing data

Magnetic disks, such as the computer's hard disk, floppy disks and Zip disks, store data arranged in a circular track. This is divided into sections, like pieces of pie, to make compartments. A device in the computer, called the read/write head, moves from one section to another to read or change the data. Hard disks have the largest storage capacity, and they are the most popular way of storing information.

FACT BOX

• The amount of digital information that the memory chips or storage disks can hold is measured in bits and bytes (words derived from **bi**nary dig**its**).

• A bit can be either a 0 or a 1. Computers read information as a sequence of eight bits of code, which is equivalent to a byte (an average-length word). A kilobyte (KB or K) is one thousand bytes. A megabyte (MB) is one million bytes. A gigabyte (GB) is one billion bytes.

• A modern hard disk can store well over 10 gigabytes, which is the equivalent of over 20 million paperback books. Hard disks are getting bigger all the time.

• Magnetic tape drives are another way of saving large files from your computer. The drive can be installed inside or outside a computer, and it has a large capacity – enough to hold all the data on a whole hard drive.

Floppy disk

These disks are made of thin magnetic plastic encased in a stiff plastic shell. The plastic inside the disk stores a pattern of 1s and 0s in the form of magnetic particles. Floppy disks can store up to 1.4MB of data, which is the same as three paperback books. Floppy disks are becoming less popular as a way of saving and sending information due to their small capacity.

Zip disk

Like floppy disks, Zip disks use magnetism to store data, but are able to hold about 80 times as much information. Although about the same size as a floppy disk, they hold between 100 and 250 MB of data (about the same as 80 floppy disks). Zip disks are a very useful way of storing large computer files, and many people use these disks to back up all the files on their computer's hard disk.

HARD DISK STORAGE

THE hard disk of a computer consists of a number of flat, circular plates. Each one of these plates is coated with microscopic magnetic particles. The hard disk also contains a controlling mechanism, called the read/write head, which is positioned slightly above the magnetic disks.

When storing information, a series of electrical pulses representing the data are sent through the read/write head on to the magnetic disks, which are spinning at very high speeds. The electricity magnetizes the magnetic particles on the disks, which then align to produce a record of the signal.

When reading information, the hard disk works in the opposite way. The magnetic particles create a small current, which is recognized by the read/write head, converted into an electrical current and then into binary code.

When you load new information on to the computer, it is stored in a section of one of the plates, depending on where there is free space. The computer then keeps a record of what is stored in each section. This project shows you how the magnetic disks in your computer's hard drive work.

STORING DATA ON A DISK

You will need: piece of white card, pair of compasses, pencil, scissors, ruler, red marker, plastic cup, reusable adhesive, paper clips, magnet, drawing pin.

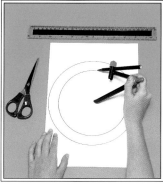

1 Draw a circle with a diameter of 20cm on the piece of white card. Draw three more circles inside, each with a diameter 2cm smaller than the one before. Cut out the largest circle.

Inside the drive

A typical hard drive consists of a stack of thin disks, called a platter. The upper surface of each disk is coated with tiny magnetic particles, and each disk has its own read/write head on a movable arm. When storing and reading information, the disks spin at very high speeds (up to 100 revolutions a second).

central point around which the disks spin

read/write heads

magnetic plates store information

hard drive inside the computer

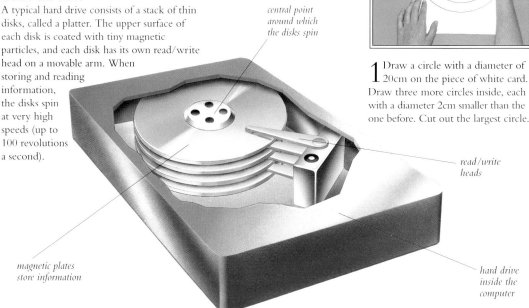

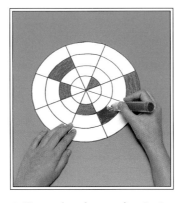

2 Position a ruler at the centre of the circle where the compass point has made a hole. Draw four lines through the middle to divide the circle into eight equal parts.

3 Use a red marker to colour in six or seven sections as shown above. Leave the remaining sections white. The white areas represent full disk space. Red areas are empty disk space.

4 Attach some reusable adhesive to the rim of a plastic cup. Then turn it upside down on a smooth surface. Press it down gently to make sure it is secure.

6 The paper clips will move around the disk surface of the disk, too, and will all line up in a section of the disk. This is what happens to the magnetic particles on a hard disk when an electric current is passed through them by the read/write head. In a computer, the way the magnetic particles line up is a record of the data stored on the hard disk.

5 Push the drawing pin through the middle of the coloured disk and into the base of the cup, making sure that the disk can move around the pin. Scatter some paper clips on the surface. Hold the magnet under the disk. Move it around the disk.

7 Remove the paper clips from the disk. Spin the disk clockwise with one hand and with a finger of the other touch areas of the disk. If you stop the disk on a white part you have found data. If you stop on a red section you have found empty disk space.

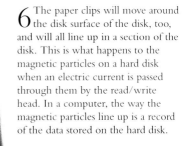

COMPUTER SOFTWARE

Linux
If you see this picture of a penguin when you are using a computer, then you know the computer is running an operating system called Linux.

The Mac start-up screen
If you see this picture when you start up a computer, then you know it is an Apple Macintosh computer running a version of the Mac operating system.

Mac OS
starting up

SOFTWARE is a means of carrying a series of instructions that controls what computers do. There are two different types – systems software and applications software.

The basic systems software that controls the computer and makes it possible for us to use it is called the OS, or operating system. It includes instructions that manage the computer's memory, organize files and control devices such as scanners, printers and external storage drives. The operating system you have will depend on the type of computer you have. The most common is Microsoft Windows, which is used to operate most PCs. Apple Macintosh computers work using the Mac OS. Linux is another operating system that will run on both Macs and PCs. The operating system runs in the background all the time that the computer is on.

Applications software includes programs that allow the computer to perform specific tasks. It runs on top of the operating system. Common applications software includes word-processing packages such as Microsoft Word, graphics applications such as Adobe Photoshop, and also games such as Tomb Raider.

Applications software
When you click on the Microsoft Word icon on your computer, a start-up screen appears on the monitor. Microsoft Word comes in many different languages so that people all over the world can use the application. The ones pictured are: Arabic (top left), German (bottom left), French (top right) and Spanish (bottom right). The start-up screen lets you interact with the computer. You can tell the computer what you want to do by clicking on various parts of the screen. Microsoft Word is an example of applications software, which is a set of instructions that allows you to carry out different tasks on your computer. Microsoft Word allows you to perform word-processing tasks such as writing a letter or a story.

The Mac desktop

When an Apple Macintosh computer is switched on, the Mac operating system will automatically boot up. The desktop then appears on the monitor. The desktop is the starting point for doing tasks on the computer, and there are a number of different options you can choose from. The white bar at the top of the desktop is called the Menu Bar. If you hold down the mouse button on one of the words in the Menu Bar, a drop-down menu appears. If you highlight View, for example, you can change the way your desktop appears on the screen.

Signpost icons

Each application software has a unique icon. When you double click on the icon with a mouse, the application opens so that you can use it. There are many different kinds of applications software. Word-processing software allows you to type and arrange text. Graphics software allows you to create images or manipulate old ones to improve them or turn them into a new picture. Internet browsers and e-mail software are essential if you want to use either facility. The icons above represent a range of different software.

Using icons

Simple pictures, called icons, appear on the desktop to represent different jobs that the computer can do. You click on them to access files or to perform tasks. Icons are easy to recognize and help you to work easily. For example, Folder icons are where you keep your work. You can name the different folders so that you can find different files easily. The Hard Disk icon represents the main disk drive built into the computer. It stores the Operating System software, applications software and your work. The Recycle Bin on a PC and the Wastebasket on a Mac are where you put the files you do not want any more before you delete them for good. As long as they stay in the Wastebasket, you can take them out again if you change your mind.

Drop-downs and pop-ups

Most software works using drop-down and pop-up menus. When you click with your mouse on a word on

the monitor screen, you often find that a menu either drops down or pops up on screen and offers you a number of choices. Move the cursor to the one you want to select and click on it to perform the task you want.

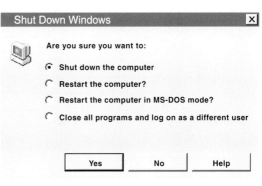

Dialogue boxes

When the computer needs to ask you a question, a window appears on the screen. If you are not sure what to do, there is a Help option, where you can look up information.

MOUSE CARE AND MOUSE MAT

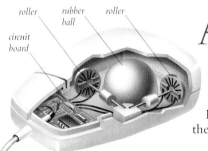

roller rubber roller
        ball
circuit
board

A MOUSE is a device that allows you to interact with your computer. It moves the cursor on the screen, so that you can select different options. A rubber ball inside the mouse rolls like a wheel so that the mouse can move over a special mouse mat. The ball then pushes against electrical contact points, which send signals to your computer. Unfortunately, the rubber ball picks up dirt from the mouse mat, which then sticks to the contact points. As more dirt accumulates, it becomes more difficult to move the cursor where you want it to go. The project on this page shows you how to clean your mouse.

Inside the mouse
Tiny circuits inside the mouse convert the movement of the rubber ball into electrical signals. The contact points are set on rollers in front of the mouse and to one side.

HOW TO CLEAN YOUR MOUSE

You will need:
methylated spirit, cotton wool buds.

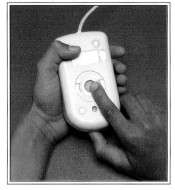

1 Hold the mouse upside down in one hand. Use the other hand to remove the cover around the ball. There are usually arrows on the mouse to show you how.

Mouse mats are made from a spongy material that provides a good surface for the mouse to move around on. There are lots of fun designs, but you can make your own one if you like. The project on the opposite page shows you how.

4 You can wipe the ball clean as well if you like. When it is clean, place the ball back inside the mouse. Reposition the cover. Now your mouse should work better.

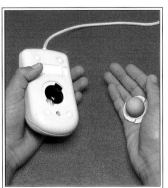

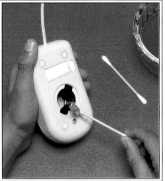

2 When the cover is loose, place the palm of your hand over the bottom of the mouse and turn it back the right way. The ball will fall out into your hand.

3 Moisten a cotton wool bud with methylated spirit and use it to clean the inside of the mouse. Most dirt sticks to the contact points, so be sure to clean these thoroughly.

PROJECT

MAKE A MOUSE MAT

You will need:
computer and printer, heat-transfer
printing paper (available from a computer store),
plain mouse mat, pencil, ruler, scissors, iron.

1 Open up a colourful picture file from the clip-art folder. Measure the mouse mat and adjust the height and width of the picture (using the Measurements tool bar) so that it will fit on the mat. The image will be reversed when it is on the mouse mat, so don't choose a picture that has any writing on it.

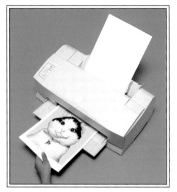

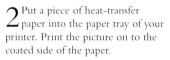

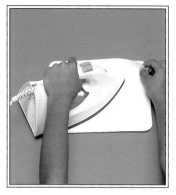

2 Put a piece of heat-transfer paper into the paper tray of your printer. Print the picture on to the coated side of the paper.

3 Place the mat over the printed picture and draw round the edge of the mat with a pencil. Carefully cut around the pencil marks.

4 Look at the instructions given with the heat-transfer paper and set an iron to the right temperature. Put the print face side down on the top side of the mat and iron over it.

6 It will take about 30 minutes for the mouse mat to cool before you can use it. The surface of mouse mats is designed to let the mouse run smoothly over them, but also to provide enough grip for the rubber ball to move. You could make a whole selection of mouse mats with different pictures on them – one for every day of the week.

5 While the transfer paper is still warm, carefully peel off the backing paper to reveal your image. Leave the mouse mat for a few minutes to cool.

WORKING WITH WORDS

WORD-PROCESSING applications are designed for working with text, such as a letter, and are widely used in offices and homes. They allow you to edit (change) the words you write at any time and even add pictures, too. If you want, you can stop your work for a while, store it on the computer's hard disk and return to finish it later. The final document can be printed on paper.

Word-processing applications can do some amazing things. You can move words around, copy words from one document to another and change the size and style of the letters very easily. It is even possible to check your spelling and grammar. Before word-processing applications were invented, people could write letters and documents on a typewriter. However, the time and trouble saved by using word-processing applications means that typewriters are rarely used today.

Typewriter trouble
An old-fashioned typewriter from the late 1800s could produce quicker and neater text than handwriting. However, mistakes had to be erased or painted over. The typist also had only one choice of type size and style.

News reporters
It would be hard to find a modern office that does not use computers in some way. Most of the workers in this CNN newsroom use a computer to do their work. The reporters use a word-processing application to type their reports, which makes it very easy to change any mistakes, add extra text or check the spelling and grammar. The most common word-processing applications are Microsoft Word for PCs and AppleWorks for Macs.

Fun with fonts

A typeface, or font, is a style of lettering. There are hundreds of fonts, and each one has a name that was thought up by the person who designed it. Some are installed on your computer when you buy it. These are called the system fonts. Others can be bought on a disk and loaded on to the computer's hard drive. You can put different fonts in the same document by choosing from the menu bar.

Helvetica

Times

Giddyup

Chicago

Styling the type

Styling means changing the appearance of a font. Most fonts come in a set that contains a plain font and its alternatives. The alternatives are **bold**, which is a heavy type, *italic*, which is sloping, and ***bold italic***, which is both heavy and sloping. However, you can change the format of any font by checking a box in the tool bar. Here, you can underline fonts, outline them and even put shadows on them. You can also make the typeface a different colour if you want, although you will only be able to print this if you have a colour printer.

plain

bold

italic

underline

outline

Font size

You can choose how big your type appears by changing its point size. Points are measurement units that are smaller than millimetres. This is 11.5 point, but you can see some different sizes on the right.

14 point

24 point

44 point

64 point

selected text

Selecting text

To delete words, copy them, align them or style them to change their appearance, you first have to select the text. To do this, move your cursor to the beginning of the words you want to change. Click with your mouse. You will see the insertion point appear. Drag your mouse across the words. They will become highlighted with a colour. You can now edit them as you wish.

Text alignment

Words need to start and end somewhere specific to look neat on the page. Alignment makes words line up to the left or right margin or line up with the centre of the page. You can change the alignment of a selected paragraph or sentence by checking one of three boxes (right, left or centre) in the main tool bar.

You can also make the text spread out evenly between the left and the right margins, which is called justification. This paragraph is justified.

Alignment is making words line up to the left, centre or right of the page.

This text is aligned or ranged LEFT.

Alignment is making words line up to the left, centre or right.

This text is aligned CENTRE.

Alignment is making words line up to the left, centre or right.

This text is aligned or ranged RIGHT.

MY LETTERHEAD

Y OU can design a personal letterhead to use whenever you write a letter. As well as including your name and address, you can also add pictures. To design your letterhead, you will need word-processing application software such as AppleWorks or Microsoft Word, but any kind of word-processing software will do. You will also need a printer to print the finished design.

To illustrate the letterhead, you can use a photograph or a ready-made picture from a clip-art collection on disk. You can even draw and paint your own, using a graphics application if you have one. You will be amazed at the professional-looking results that can be achieved in a short space of time.

Your personal logo

Companies and organizations all over the world have their own logo (badge), which identifies them. The logo might include a picture, a name designed in a certain typeface, and a colour. You could design your own logo for your letterhead, using some of these ideas.

Clip art

Ready-made images that come on disks are known as clip art. The different language versions shown in this picture of Microsoft Word clip art are: Hebrew (top left), German (bottom left), French (top right) and Spanish (bottom right). You can buy clip-art disks but some come free with computer magazines. Most office software includes clip-art collections. You can also download images from Internet sites to build up your own collection. Images are usually arranged into categories, such as animals or sports. To illustrate a word-processing document, you need to import the picture file from where it is stored, such as your computer's hard disk or a CD-ROM.

MAKE YOUR OWN LETTERHEAD

You will need:
computer with a word-processing application, printer, paper.

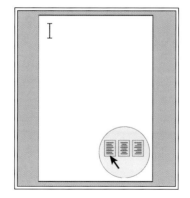

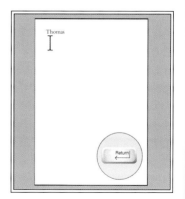

1 Open a new document. Set the size of your paper to A4. Click on the page and look for the insertion point. This is where your writing will appear when you start to type.

2 Type in your name. Press the Return key when you want to go to a new line. You can choose a different font and change its size and colour if you like.

3 When you have finished typing your address, place the insertion point where you want the picture to be. Drop in the picture file using the appropriate command on your computer.

5 When you have finished writing your first letter, save it under a different name, such as 'Letter 1'. This means you can keep the original version of your letterhead to use again. Finally print a copy of your letter from your printer.

4 Try arranging the words and pictures in different ways. When you are happy with your design, save the document as 'My letterhead' in your documents folder.

HOME OFFICE

MANY people keep records of useful information on their computer. They might list people's names and telephone numbers or record what needs to be done each day, just like a computerized diary. Office software, such as Microsoft Office, can be used for this purpose. As its name suggests, office software is mostly used by businesses, but it can be used by anyone.

For instance, you may want to store the names and addresses of all your closest friends. You would use a database package to do this. Databases allow you to store lots of information, which can be easily accessed and updated. Libraries use databases to store information about all the books they have. Information about your allowance can be recorded by using a spreadsheet package, which can perform all kinds of automatic calculations. Spreadsheets can add and subtract, converting pounds to dollars, for example, with the data they contain. You can also plot graphs and charts to show the information in a visual way.

Organizing your life
Some computers have an appointments diary, or personal organizer, as part of the office software. Some organizers can even remind you that you have an appointment by sounding an alarm.

Address book
Databases are used to keep records of data such as names, addresses, telephone numbers and e-mail addresses. They help you find and use the stored information easily. Databases can sort the information in different ways, such as in alphabetical or numerical order. Most office software contains a database application.

NAME	ADDRESS	PHONE	E-MAIL
Lucy	4, Big Street	134 0846	lucy@
James	23, Long Road	758 0367	james@
Poppy	14, London Way	100 3899	poppy@

CANTEEN FOOD	January	February	March	Total of types
Pizzas	220	360	209	789
Pasta	170	238	273	681
Burgers	186	92	156	434
Fish	26	15	29	70
Total meals a month	602	705	667	

Counting and calculating
A spreadsheet is a display of numerical information that does automatic calculations. A spreadsheet is made up of lots of little boxes called cells. The size of the cells can be changed to fit the information – either words or numbers – entered. Spreadsheet software can work out calculations on numbers contained in the spreadsheet. For example, each column can be added up. If you change one number, the total appears automatically at the bottom of the column. In this way, people can easily keep up-to-date records of their finances.

Comparing information

Sometimes it is useful to show numerical information visually to help you understand it more easily. Many spreadsheet applications can automatically draw pie charts or graphs to represent information in an accessible way. The pie chart on the right shows how much of each kind of food is being eaten during school mealtimes. The total number of meals is represented by the circle. Each section, or pie, represents the different sorts of meals that are being eaten. From the chart, it is possible to see in an instant that pizzas are the most popular food by far and that fish is chosen the least. You can also see that about a quarter of the total number of meals eaten are burgers.

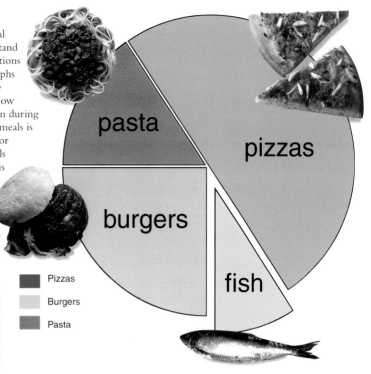

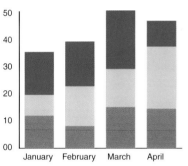

Column graphs

Spreadsheet packages can draw graphs to show how two different things, called variables, are related to one another. A common variable is time (days, weeks or months), which is always plotted horizontally, from left to right. Other variables, such as the type of food being eaten, can be plotted vertically from bottom to top. By reading the two sets of information on the graph above, you can see exactly how much of each kind of food was eaten in four given months of the year. There are two main types of graph – a column graph (above) and a line graph (above right). These graphs are two different ways of representing the same information.

Line graphs

As in the column graph, time is shown horizontally, and another variable, such as food being eaten, is show vertically. Each line represents one type of information, in this case pizzas or pasta. It is easy to see that more pizzas are being eaten than pasta in every month.

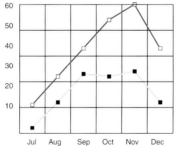

timetable	9.00	10.00	11.00	12.00	13.00	14.00	15.00
MONDAY	maths	games	science	lunch	computing	english	art
TUESDAY	music	english	maths	lunch	science	history	geography
WEDNESDAY	history	english	geography	lunch	english	games	games
THURSDAY	english	music	art	lunch	maths	geography	history
FRIDAY	science	computing	maths	lunch	music	art	art

Make a timetable

You could make your own chart to remind you of your daily schedule or important events. Using a spreadsheet package, make a chart for your school timetable. Type in the days in a vertical column on the left and the hours along the top line. Then fill in the corresponding activities.

213

DESKTOP PUBLISHING

DESKTOP publishing (DTP) is the term given to computer applications that allow words and images to be arranged together on a page. Most books and magazines are designed using desktop publishing software, because writing, typesetting (arranging words on a page) and illustration can all be done in one place and sometimes even by the same person. This has made the publishing process easier than ever before.

Nowadays, anyone with a computer and the necessary software can create their own magazine or newspaper. Each different part of the publication – the words, photographs and illustrations – is prepared separately. Then the software brings all the elements together. Desktop publishing software is fairly easy to use. Changes to the layout of a page, such as moving an illustration or inserting an extra paragraph into a story, can be done at any point during the process. Today, millions of books and magazines are created in such a way that they can even be published on the Internet.

From words to a page
Journalists and authors may make written notes or tape-record their work and then type it up using a word-processing application such as Microsoft Word. They can e-mail their work to the newspaper or publishing office where it can be worked on and made into pages.

Instant pictures
Digital cameras capture still images electronically and do not use photographic film. The photographs are stored on a disk and can be loaded directly on to a computer, missing out the expensive and time-consuming film-processing stage. The images can then be imported straight into the pages of the document.

Making the layout
All pages in newspapers, books and magazines are arranged on a basic grid like the one on the right, because it makes the pages neat and easy to read. The first stage in making a page is to design a blank grid or to use one that already exists. A grid shows the size of the page and the area in which the text and the pictures will fit. It might also show where the text and the pictures line up. Then the designer can start to work on each individual page. He or she will import (place) the pictures into boxes on the page where they look best.

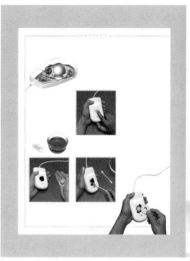

The publishing process

A book designer works on the illustrations before importing them into the pages. Before computers were invented, it took many different processes and many more people to arrive at a stage where a book or newspaper was finished. Today, the process is more straightforward and involves fewer people. This is especially important for newspapers, because they have to get the latest news to their readers as quickly as possible.

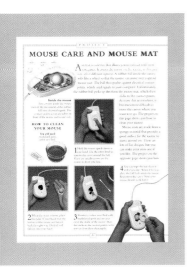

The finished page

The designer imports the text that goes with the pictures. He or she tries out different layouts until a good design has been found. The editor then checks the text and makes sure it matches the pictures, and that the blocks of text are not too long or too short. When the designer and the editor are both happy that the page is correct, it can go off to be printed and published. Desktop publishing applications make it easy to write, design and print your own pages, with a professional look. You can create posters, invitations or newsletters – any document that combines words and pictures.

FACT BOX

• Every publication, from a newspaper to a book, has a house style that distinguishes it from other publications.

• Desktop publishing applications can be used to set up a template in which the text and pictures follow a house style. The Fact Box you are reading now is written in a style that is the same throughout this book. Compare it with one on another page. You will see that the font is always the same size and the background is always the same colour.

• QuarkXPress is the most popular page-layout software. Other applications include InDEsign and Publisher.

DAILY NEWS

A LOT of thought goes into designing the pages of a book or newspaper. First, the contents of the page are carefully planned on paper. Then, the layout designer arranges the words and pictures using a professional page-layout application such as QuarkXPress. The good thing about using a computer to do this kind of work is that it can be changed with little effort. This project shows you how to make a magazine page using your own computer. If you do not have a page-layout package, word-processing applications, such as Microsoft Word or AppleWorks, can be used instead.

Type an article
The first step in making any publication is to decide what you want to write about. You could gather together some stories and poems from your friends, or you could type some articles about news and events. Arrange them into an order that would make sense if someone was reading them all together on a page.

Scan some pictures
You will also need some pictures for your publication. If you have a scanner, scan in all the pictures and save them in a separate folder. If you do not have one of your own, use the scanner at school. When you have scanned all the images, copy them onto a removable disk, take the disk home and copy all the files on to your hard drive.

EDITOR FOR A DAY

You will need: computer with a desktop publishing application or a word-processing application such as Microsoft Word, printer, paper.

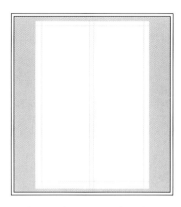

1 Collect all the items you want to put on your page. This will enable you to work out how much space you will need to fit all the words and pictures on to your page.

2 Open a document and set the document size to A4. Set a 2cm margin around the edge of your page. Position two guide lines in the centre of the page, about 1cm apart.

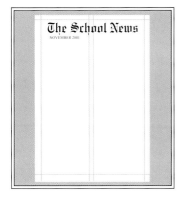

3 Make a text box at the top of the page. Type in a title. Increase the point size to make the words bigger. Make a smaller text box to add other header information.

4 Make another text box in the first column. Set the point size to 12 and type your story. You can resize the text box by dragging the corner points with the cursor.

5 Make a picture box and import your picture. You can resize the box by dragging the corner points to fit the column. Position the picture near the text box.

6 Add more pictures and words until the page is full. The boxes can be moved around or resized to fit everything on the page. If you have got too many things to fit on one page, make an extra page.

7 Once you are happy with the layout, print out as many copies as you need and give them to your family and friends.

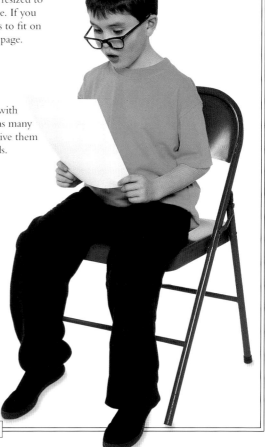

Pictures on screen
A layout designer in a newspaper office scans some images on to his computer. He will then use them to make up part of the article he is laying out on the page.

A SPLASH OF COLOUR

Angular Selection	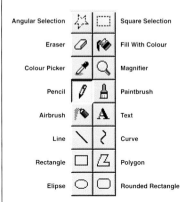	Square Selection
Eraser		Fill With Colour
Colour Picker		Magnifier
Pencil		Paintbrush
Airbrush		Text
Line		Curve
Rectangle		Polygon
Elipse		Rounded Rectangle

M ANY special visual effects are possible with computers that would be very difficult to do by hand. Graphics applications have the advantage that if mistakes are made, it is very easy to correct them. For example, all graphics applications have an Eraser tool, which can instantly remove something you don't like. As well as the normal drawing and painting tools, other tools can be used to create special effects. The Airbrush tool creates a fine spray effect to paint colours on your picture. There is a variety of backgrounds to give the final picture a different appearance. Most computers come with basic painting and drawing software. For a wide range of special finishing touches, such as gradient fills and airbrush effects, advanced software such as Painter and Microsoft Paint is available.

The tools palette
The Toolbar contains digital versions of real art tools such as a pencil, an airbrush and an eraser. Clicking on these icons will activate them. The Toolbar also gives you the option of drawing specific shapes, such as circles, and styles of lines. You can use a combination of all these effects on one illustration.

R	255%
G	0%
B	0%

Choosing colour
Painting software contains palettes of different colours from which you can select and mix. Each colour has a number equivalent on the Red–Green–Blue (RGB) scale. By typing in varying percentages of red, green and blue, you can mix different colours. You can save these numbers on the colour palette and use the same shade again.

Multiple techniques
Most painting software enables you to create many different effects. Some give brush strokes of varied thickness, and others create airbrush effects to add to your work. Try all the different tools. The four segments of this apple were drawn using (clockwise from top left): a coloured pencil, an airbrush, different brush strokes, chalk and wax crayon textures.

Brush strokes

Most applications provide a selection of different tools, such as brushes, pens, crayons and pencils, to choose from. You can experiment with crayon and chalk textures for graffiti styles, soft pencils and airbrushes for shading, washes for backgrounds and even watercolours and oil paint effects to recreate more classic works of art. You do not have to be a brilliant artist to draw and paint pictures on a computer, because the software is designed to be easy to use. Most of the effects can be created in just one click of a mouse.

Basic shapes

Basic shapes, such as circles and squares, can be made by selecting them from the Toolbar. Another tool, called the Polygon tool, lets you draw your own shapes. You can fill the shapes with colour.

Looking closer

When an image is magnified, you can see that it is made up of individual blocks of colour which, in turn, consist of thousands of tiny dots of light called pixels (short for picture elements). Just like words, pictures are stored in the computer as binary code.

Gradient fills

A gradient fill is a graduated blend between two or more colours or tints of the same colour. You can achieve smooth colour and tonal transitions when filling images with the Gradient tool.

Photo painting

Painting software allows you to work with photographs you may have already scanned and saved on your computer's hard disk. Draw in a hat, some glasses and a moustache to a picture of your face to make a fun picture.

COMPUTER GRAPHICS

ARTWORKS that are created using computer technology are called computer graphics. Graphics applications can be used to create new pictures or to change existing pictures, such as photographs, that are already stored as a picture file on a computer. Pictures are displayed on the screen as small dots of colour called pixels. The computer registers these tiny bits of information as binary code. Whenever you change a picture by moving it, cutting parts out or adding new parts, the computer makes a note of how the pixels have been changed and revises the binary code to record what you have done. Once people used to say that a camera never lies. Today, however, nearly all the photographs used in advertisements have been altered by computers in some way.

Computer graphics can range from simple photographic images to the complex and extremely realistic drawings used in virtual reality, the process by which a computer is used to create an artificial place that appears real, such as in a flight simulator.

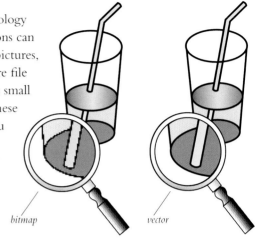

bitmap   *vector*

The make-up of an image
Computer graphics are either bitmap images or vector graphics. Photographs and painted effects are bitmaps. Each pixel that makes up a bitmap is given a specific colour and location by the computer. Vector graphics are used a lot for line drawings. In these, the computer records each shape and colour as a code. The difference is most apparent when the images are enlarged. Bitmaps develop jagged edges, but vector graphics stay smooth at any size.

Funny faces
Some weird and wonderful effects can be created by applying different filters to a photograph. A filter is a mathematical formula that the computer uses to distort a picture. Most computer graphics applications have filters built into them. Different filters move pixels around in different ways. Some filters do simple things such as sharpening or blurring an image. Others can distort a picture to add an unusual texture or make colour changes.

Coming to life

Animation is the process by which pictures are made to move about. Animation is done by putting together hundreds of pictures, each one showing a small change in movement. The pictures that make up an animation can either be flat (two-dimensional) or three-dimensional (appear to have depth). Before computers, animations were done by hand. Computers can fill in the gaps between movements and reduce the number of pictures that need to be drawn.

Clear or fuzzy?

The number of pixels that make up an image is known as the resolution, which is usually measured as the total number of pixels in a square inch. The more pixels, the clearer the image. For example, the two pictures above are the same, but the one on the left has a higher resolution.

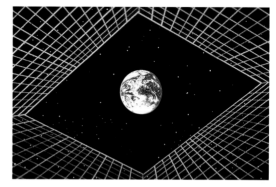

Creating the image

Three-dimensional graphics have to be modelled in the same way as sculptures. Firstly, a simple shape, called the wireframe, is made of lines. The wireframe above forms a tunnel looking down at Earth. It will be covered with texture and colour to give it a realistic appearance.

Altered images

Graphics software, such as Adobe Photoshop and Microsoft Paint, allow you to do amazing things with images. For example, you can copy parts of one photograph and put them on another to create an unusual or unreal image. In the picture on the left, the fish have been copied from one photograph and then positioned on the picture of Concorde flying in the sky. Using graphics software, you can also clean marks or scratches on a photographic image, change its size, brightness, resolution and colour and then print it out. Some graphics software allows you to select and remove areas of a picture or paint over them with other parts of the same image. So you could create a photograph of yourself in a famous city where really you have never been.

CREATE A PHOTO POSTER

CHANGING photographs is easy on a computer. You can erase parts that you do not want, paint in new areas, such as a background, or copy and move parts of the picture around. This project uses an application, such as Adobe Photoshop or Paint Shop Pro, which enables you to open picture files and then change them. Collect some photographs you find around the house, such as pictures of your family and friends. Even passport-size photographs will do. All the changes you make are done on a picture file on the computer, so you can be as experimental as you like without worrying about spoiling the original photograph. You will need to use a scanner unless you have your photos on a disk or stored in the computer already. A scanner transfers the photograph on to your computer as a picture file.

Caricatures
A caricature of the British pop group the Spice Girls has been drawn using computer graphics software. You could get together with some of your friends, take photos of each other and then scan them on to your computer's hard disk. Alter the photos using a graphics application such as Painter.

MAKING YOUR OWN PHOTO POSTER

You will need: *photographs, computer with a scanner, printer and a computer-graphics application.*

1 Collect some pictures of your friends. Use the scanner to transfer them on to your computer. Save each picture file in a new folder named 'Photos of my friends'.

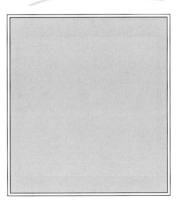

2 Start your graphics application. Open a new document and make a page 20cm wide and 20cm high. Fill it with a coloured background. Save the document as 'My friends'.

3 Open a picture file. Click on the picture and copy it. Click on your new document and paste the picture, dragging it into place with your mouse. Do the same with all the picture files.

4 Select the background colour from the colour palette. Select a brush and paint out the background behind the faces. Use a smaller brush around the edges of the picture.

5 Select the Text tool from the tools palette. Click where you want the words to start and type them in. Choose a bold typeface and a colour that shows up well on the background.

Computer art
There are lots of ways that people create art using computer technology. One of the most amazing effects can be produced by using fractals (short for fractal dimension). Fractals are complex shapes often found in nature. Computer programs create fractal images using complex mathematical formulae. By manipulating the formulae, artists can generate stunning and intricate patterns, such as this one on the right.

6 Once you are happy with your design, save the document on to your computer's hard disk. You can then print it out poster-size. Select the Print menu from the menu bar, adjust the printer setting to fit your poster on the paper and press Print.

GAME FOR A LAUGH

COMPUTER games are the second biggest use of computers after word-processing. The computers people use to play games come in different forms. The largest are arcade machines that have big screens, loud sound effects and special controls such as steering wheels and guns. However, you can play games at home on computers such as GameBoy, PlayStation, Nintendo 64, Dreamcast, or even on your desktop computer. The most popular computer games are probably the interactive games, in which the player can control what happens on screen.

Some games can be played using the mouse and keyboard. Other games use special devices, such as a joystick or gamepad, to control parts of the game. These allow easy and fast control of the graphics in action games, when you need to react quickly to what you see on screen. Today's computer games feature high-speed, colourful, three-dimensional graphics, as well as realistic visual and sound effects.

GameBoy

One of the most popular game computers is the hand-held GameBoy. The games are supplied on cartridges, which slot into the back of the GameBoy. There are hundreds of different games to choose from.

Sport for all
Today, you can play just about every type of sport on a computer. There are football, motor racing, and snowboarding games, to name but a few. Some sports games are called simulations, because they re-create the sport in lifelike way. In this skiing simulation, the player holds poles and stands on moving platforms, which simulate skis. The movements of his arms and legs are interpreted by sensors on the computer and then re-created on the computer screen.

Console computers
The PlayStation and Nintendo 64 are called console computers, which means they need to be connected to a television to display pictures. The game is controlled using a gamepad, which consists of two joysticks and lots of buttons. Console computers can now connect to the Internet so people from all over the world can play against each other.

Be a pilot

Simulation games let you imitate real-life situations that you control through the computer. In the flight simulator shown on the left, you can get an idea of what it is like to fly a civil aircraft to destinations all over the world. Others involve battles with military aircraft.

Rule the world

In strategy games, the player takes on the role of a government or ruler and must follow a set of objectives to create a successful city or civilization. Examples of strategy games include Alpha Centauri, Civilisation, Settlers, Sim City and Tiberian Sun. In Sim City, the player becomes the mayor of a futuristic city. The people who live there want it all – industry and clean air, convenient housing and open space, low taxes and low crime rates. Can you strike a balance and turn your city into a thriving metropolis? Other strategy games allow you to create people with different personalities. You can put them in houses and make them act out real-life situations.

Role playing

Forget what it is like to be human and become a fantasy character in a role-playing game such as Diablo II. You can immerse yourself in a world of intrigue and adventure set in a forgotten land. Role-playing games such as Diablo have attractive graphics and are very easy to use.

Spin and play

People watch while a girl spins around and upside down in an R-360 video game. The player is strapped into a small cockpit. She uses a joystick to control a jet fighter during a virtual dog-fight (fight between two planes). The cockpit is enclosed in a gyroscope, which allows the cockpit to spin around in any direction, simulating the movement of a real jet fighter.

DESIGNING GAMES

MANY people are involved in designing a computer game, and it is a very time-consuming process. Graphic designers come up with lifelike pictures of characters, and computer animators make characters and objects move in a realistic way. When all the parts of a game are finished, people called computer programmers write a list of instructions, called a program, which the computer uses to make all the different parts of the game work together so you can play it. It is very difficult to learn how to program modern computers to play games.

If you like playing games, here is a spot-the-difference game that you can make using your computer and play anywhere. It can be created just by using photographs or by painting and drawing your own picture.

Central character

Many games have a central character for the players to identify with. This is one of the characters from the game Crash Team Racing.

GAMING AROUND

You will need: *photographs, computer with a scanner, printer and a computer-graphics application.*

Playtime

A boy plays games on his computer. At the side of the keyboard, there is a selection of floppy disks from which he can download different games. More and more people have their own computers at home. Although computers are useful tools and are fun to play with, it is important not to spend all your spare time using your computer. You should do other things as well, such as playing outdoor sports, and talking or listening to music with your friends.

1 Choose some images to make into a picture. Before you begin, sketch out your picture as a guide. Scan each photograph and save them all on your computer's hard disk.

Computer chess
Chessmaster 7000 is a computerized version of the traditional board game chess. Instead of playing with another person, however, the computer is your opponent. Before you start, you select the level of difficulty to match the standard of your play.

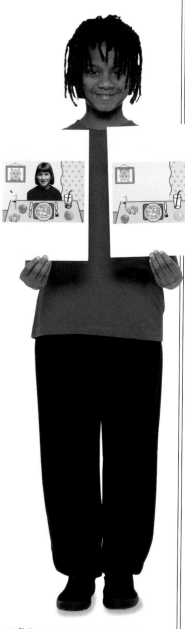

2 Open your graphics application. Then open a new document and save it as 'Picture 1'. Choose a background colour and draw in the main areas of your picture.

3 Open one of the photograph files you scanned. Copy and paste it on to the main picture. Do the same for all the photograph files. You can draw and paint images if you like.

4 When you have completed your picture, save it as 'Picture 1' again. Then select Save As from the File menu. Type 'Picture 2' and save a second copy of the same picture.

5 Now you can change things on Picture 2. Change the colour of something, change its size, move it to another place and remove or add things. Make around six changes.

6 Print out copies of both pictures, and ask a friend to spot the differences between the two. The more subtle you make the changes, the harder it will be for the person playing the game to spot them all. The person who spots all the differences quickest is the winner.

MULTIMEDIA

MULTIMEDIA means bringing together different kinds of communication (media) such as text, photographs, moving pictures and sounds. Encyclopedias, especially, can be great fun when they can let you hear the sound a bird makes or show you how a machine moves. Multimedia is used for teaching, games, giving information in public places, advertising and accessing reference material. The multimedia user is given control over the information, which means he or she can make choices about how they move through the work and can select what is presented to them. This way of working with the information is called interaction. Click with a mouse on a picture or highlighted words to jump to other pages or bring special effects into play such as animations, sound or a video clip. Multimedia is commonly found on the Internet and reference CD-ROMs such as Microsoft's *Encarta* encyclopedia.

Home library

Reference books, such as encyclopedias and atlases, work well when translated into multimedia because they can show much more than flat, still, visual information. Video clips can show how machines or animals move or what people and places look like. Added sounds can reproduce people's voices or allow the music of a singer or composer to be heard. Multimedia reference publications can also link similar articles together.

Showing the way

Museums, airports and other public places often have multimedia kiosks to give information to the public. They often use a technology called touch screen where viewers point to the item they want to know about with their finger instead of a mouse. Sensors detect changes in the electrical current on the screen, work out what area of the screen is being touched and then provide information related to the area of interest.

Learn a language

This boy is learning how to speak French on his home computer using a multimedia language package. Foreign language students can hear the language being spoken as well as having their own voice recorded and checked for the correct pronunciation. Interactive games and puzzles can test the student's understanding of a particular topic they have learned. Multimedia is an extremely useful tool in the classroom, because the students can work through the topic at their own speed. They can replay any information they are unsure about and can quickly cross-reference related areas by adding bookmarks and their own personal notes. Many school subjects are now being taught using multimedia CD packages.

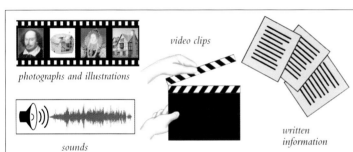

photographs and illustrations

video clips

sounds

written information

Making multimedia

There are many stages involved in making a multimedia product. First, how the product is going to look, what it will contain and how the parts will link together have to be worked out. When this has been decided, a team of researchers must find all the material, such as video clips, images, sounds and written information.

The final result

Once all the information has been gathered, the various media are linked using a special computer language. This is an electronic connection between media in the product, allowing the user to cross-reference between similar topics, pictures, animations or videos. At the same time, a team of software engineers will develop the 'run-time engine', a computer application that co-ordinates and runs all the elements of the product. Once everything is in place, the product is tested extensively to identify any problems that may have cropped up during the production process.

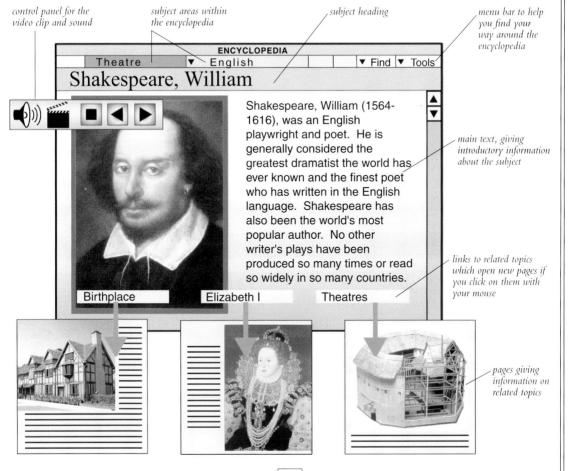

control panel for the video clip and sound

subject areas within the encyclopedia

subject heading

menu bar to help you find your way around the encyclopedia

ENCYCLOPEDIA

Theatre ▼ English ▼ Find ▼ Tools

Shakespeare, William

Shakespeare, William (1564-1616), was an English playwright and poet. He is generally considered the greatest dramatist the world has ever known and the finest poet who has written in the English language. Shakespeare has also been the world's most popular author. No other writer's plays have been produced so many times or read so widely in so many countries.

main text, giving introductory information about the subject

links to related topics which open new pages if you click on them with your mouse

Birthplace

Elizabeth I

Theatres

pages giving information on related topics

VIRTUAL REALITY

COMPUTERS can create an artificial place and situation that looks very real indeed. The virtual world is actually made up of many different three-dimensional graphics, which together, imitate the real world or create a very convincing one. The viewer can move around the virtual environment by using an input device such as a control pad, mouse or keyboard. As the viewer changes view or moves somewhere, the graphic on the screen changes to respond to the action of the viewer. There are two types of virtual reality (VR) – immersive and desktop. Immersive VR is extremely realistic and is most often used for arcade games and for scientific and business research. Desktop VR is less sophisticated and can be experienced on a home computer.

In another world
Immersive VR is so realistic that it makes viewers believe they are actually inside a different world. The user may have to wear a head-mounted display unit on his or her head. This is a helmet that has a computer screen inside. The screen displays the virtual environment. As the user's head turns, the display on the computer screen changes, just as in real life. The viewer can interact with the environment using a glove with sensors to detect hand movements.

Squash for one
A boy plays squash on a virtual reality court. As the ball comes towards him, he swings the racket. The computer senses his movements and plays the ball back to him. Virtual squash might be fun, but you would get more healthy exercise playing a real game of squash.

Drive safely
In this version of virtual reality, the image is projected on to a screen in front of the user. The screen fills the field of vision, so that the player actually feels as if he or she is driving along the road. Sensors attached to the car and to the driver's helmet detect the eye, arm and leg movements. This virtual reality situation is designed for developing a computerized warning system in cars that will alert the driver if he or she is about to do anything dangerous. Applications of this type are increasingly popular ways of training people in situations that would otherwise be too dangerous.

Virtual visitor

VR has been used to recreate the tomb of Nefertari, the wife of Pharaoh Ramses II of Egypt. The virtual visitor can walk through the burial chambers, which are decorated with murals and hieroglyphic writing. The viewer uses a trackball mouse to move around the burial chambers. This mouse has a rolling ball on top, which makes navigation smoother. Some even have an up and down facility so that the viewer can observe high and low viewpoints of his or her surroundings. This virtual reality is called desktop VR, because you can use a home computer to explore the environment. Although the effect is convincing, it is not as lifelike as immersive virtual reality. The controls available are less sophisticated, although headsets are now becoming available.

Fun and games

These people are playing a virtual reality game in an amusement park in the USA. The players are using their headsets to collect clues needed to solve a mystery in a virtual world. Games such as these allow players to interact with one another as they move around their environment.

Practice makes perfect

The cockpit of a flight simulator imitates all aspects of flight, including weather conditions and details of all the airports in the world. By imitating real flight, the pilot can make mistakes without putting real passengers in danger.

The future of virtual reality

The cybersphere is the next step in virtual reality technology. It allows the user to be totally immersed in a simulated world, not just via a headset. It is a large see-through ball made of interlocking plates and mounted on a cushion of air. Users can walk, run or jump, and a smaller ball connected to the large one detects these movements. In the future, this technology could be used in the military to train soldiers.

THE SOUND OF MUSIC

RECORDING and playing sounds and music is another job that a computer can do. You can play audio CDs or write, record and mix your own music. The sound that we hear – for example, from a musical instrument – travels to our ears through the air in waves, called sound waves. Computers can convert sound waves to electrical signals. These are subsequently converted into binary code, so that the computer can recognize them. When a microphone picks up sound waves, it passes them to an analogue-to-digital converter. This device converts sound waves to digital signs. The opposite conversion takes place when the computer plays music.

Sound files take up a lot of the computer's memory, but new technology, such as the MP3 system, can reduce the size of the files while keeping the quality of the sound. There are hundreds of web sites on the Internet where you can download MP3 files of your favourite music and store it on your own CDs. In the future, most of our music may come from the Internet in this way. In this project, you can find out how to make your own CD covers for music that you download.

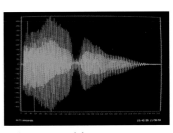

Voice recognition
Talking to a computer is not as strange as it might seem. Software can now analyze a person's voice patterns, making it possible to give a computer instructions without ever touching it. This software is very useful for people with disabilities.

MAKE A CD COVER

You will need: a selection of images, computer with a computer-graphics application, printer, scissors, CD box.

Sound studio
Digital sound recording has practically replaced analogue (tape) recording because the sound quality is so much better. Computers have made the job a whole lot easier, too. Applications called sequencers record tracks (different parts of a piece of music, such as guitar or drums). The sequencer records short sequences of the sound the instruments are producing at regular intervals. These are then translated into binary code so they can be stored in the computer.

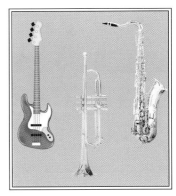

1 Choose all the images you would like to use on your CD cover. Place them all in their own folder on your computer so that you will be able to find them easily.

2 Using your graphics application, draw a box that measures 12cm x 12cm. Use the ruler guides to help you get the right size. Start to create a design using the painting tools.

3 Bring in photographic images if you want to use them. Open the photo first, select it and then use Copy and Paste to transfer it to your design. Add some text for the title.

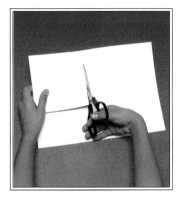

4 When you are happy with your design save it on your computer's hard disk. Print the final design out at 100 per cent. Carefully cut out your print.

5 Slide the print into the CD box lid. You can also take out the removable plastic disc holder and make another design for the back and spine of the CD box.

Music maker
Some music software can actually make the sounds of musical instruments. It also writes out the music as the notes are being played. The computer then records the sound and stores it so it can be played again.

6 If you have a CD writer and regularly download music from the Internet, you will not have a cover to make your CD stand out. It is easy to make your own covers using existing pictures and photos. Look in your clip-art folder to see if there are any images you can use. You can even draw and paint your own designs.

THE INTERNET AND E-MAIL

THE Internet is a global network that allows computers to exchange information. The first computer networks were developed in the 1960s, but the rapid explosion of the 1990s resulted from the rapid growth of personal computing and the improvement of the modem (modulator/demodulator). The Internet has many applications. Perhaps the most popular is electronic mail, or e-mail for short. Using e-mail, messages can be delivered to a computer user on the other side of the world in a matter of minutes. However, the most impressive application of the Internet is the World Wide Web (www). This allows a user to set up a computer document called a web page, look up other web pages, search for data using a search engine and download the latest software.

Sky high
Communications satellites are just one part of a vast system that enables data to be transmitted all over the world by the Internet.

Traffic jams
A computer graphic represents Internet traffic throughout the world. Each coloured line represents the Internet traffic from a different country. For example, the USA is pink and the UK is dark blue. Internet traffic is set to increase as more and more people connect to the Internet.

Around the globe
Most people use the Internet to send and receive useful data but some send unpleasant things, such as computer viruses. It is difficult to monitor what is being sent on the Internet, because a huge amount of data is sent all over the world each day.

mary@bigworld.com

What's in an address?
All e-mail addresses contain the @ symbol, which means 'at'. The part before the @ is called the user name, in this case 'Mary'. The part after the @ is called the domain name, which is the place where the user can be found. In this case, the domain name is 'bigworld'. The domain name is often followed by a code that tells you what type of site it is. For example, 'com' means it is a commercial site. Many addresses also contain a code for the country, such as uk for the United Kingdom, fr for France and au for Australia.

Mailing electronic messages

E-mail software allows you to send and receive e-mails, write and edit messages and store e-mail addresses in a contacts folder. To use e-mail on your own computer, you must be connected to the Internet, and a company known as an Internet Service Provider (ISP) allows you to do this. You also have to install a browser (software that lets you look at the Internet) on your computer. Alternatively, you can use a service provided by an e-mail portal company, such as Hotmail and Yahoo! This service allows you to send and access your mail from any computer connected to the Internet.

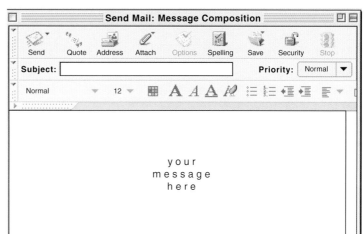

Internet browsers

Two well-known browsers are Internet Explorer and Netscape Navigator. Both have an e-mail facility built into them. When you start up your e-mail software, which is called logging on, messages that have been sent to you show up automatically on the screen.

Smileys

These little pictures are made up from combinations of keyboard punctuation marks, such as semi-colons, colons, dashes and brackets. Smileys are used by people in their e-mails to describe an expression or emotion that they want to communicate to the reader. They are used to represent faces. Look at them sideways to see the face. Here are some well-known smileys. Maybe you can think of some new ones.

:-)	happy	;-)	wink
:-(	sad	:-o	surprised
:-x	not speaking	/-o	bored
O:-)	angel	:-/	confused
;-(	crying	]:-[	angry
:-P	tongue out	:-D	laughing
:-*	clowning around		

Tea and Internet

Internet cafés, or cybercafés, allow people who do not have a computer of their own to access the Internet. You can surf the Internet and look at different web sites while you have a cup of coffee or some lunch. Cybercafés are also ideal for people who travel a lot or are on holiday. However, they may become less popular when pocket-size personal computers that can connect to the Internet become available.

SEND AN E-POSTCARD

Have you ever missed an important birthday and found yourself rushing to catch the post? This will never happen again if you use an e-postcard. You can choose, write and send a card at any time of the day and all without leaving your comfort of your home. Electronic postcards, or e-postcards, are picture postcards that can be sent over the Internet from your computer in minutes. To receive an e-postcard, you must have an e-mail address. You can even send one to yourself. There are many web sites on the Internet that offer this as a free service. A good one can be found at http://www.apple.com/icards, which is part of the Apple Computer web site. Other e-postcard web sites include http://www.greetings.yahoo.com and http://www.egreetings.com.

Snail mail

Traditional mail sent across great distances is normally transported by plane. Even so, it can take a week for letters to reach Europe from North America. Traditional mail is nicknamed snail mail by Internet users, because it is so slow compared to e-mail.

POST AN E-CARD

You will need: *computer connected to the Internet, your friend's e-mail address.*

1 Open your Internet browser and connect to the Internet. Type in one of the addresses shown above to access the e-postcard web site. A page then shows you all the different cards.

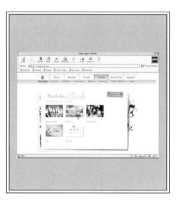

2 Select a category by clicking on it. A new page opens, which will contain a selection of different cards in the category you chose. Click on the one you like.

3 Another page opens, which displays a larger version of the picture to let you see it better. If you are happy with it, click on the icon that says 'Edit This Card'.

4 Choose a typeface that will suit your greetings card. When you have chosen a suitable typeface, type your message in the box at the bottom of the screen.

5 Fill in your name and e-mail address and your friend's name and e-mail address in the spaces provided so that the computer will know where to send the card.

6 The computer then combines your message with the e-postcard and sends it to your friend. The computer will tell you if there has been a problem with the system and the card hasn't been delivered.

7 If you like, you can print off any e-postcards that you receive and keep them just like birthday cards and Christmas cards. Collect as many different e-postcards as you can.

An e-journey

Whenever you send an e-mail, it travels down a telephone line to your ISP. Here, e-mails are sorted according to their destination and then sent by satellite to the recipient's ISP. It is then sent back down a telephone wire to the recipient of the e-mail. E-mails can arrive in minutes, but sometimes they are sent in batches and can take a few hours to reach their destination.

THE WORLD WIDE WEB

THE World Wide Web (www) has created huge interest in the Internet, because it makes it possible to access information from all over the world. The Internet and the www are not the same thing. The www is just a way of finding information on the Internet. The www is made up of millions of web sites about almost anything you can think of. Many organizations, colleges and schools have web sites, and there are a million others made by people just like you. You need an Internet browser to display web pages for you.

Web sites are much like a magazine. There is always a first page, similar to a magazine cover, which is called the home page. This displays a list of the web site's contents and allows you to explore your way around the web site.

Worldwide success
In 1990, an Englishman called Tim Berners-Lee developed the World Wide Web at the European Laboratory for Particle Physics in Switzerland (also known as CERN). He wrote the original HTML (Hypertext Mark-up Language) code. This enables web pages to be viewed on a computer. Today, the www is the most popular way of accessing information on the Internet, and it is used by millions of people throughout the world.

Web site addresses
Web addresses always start with http:// (hypertext transfer protocol), which is the way your computer reads web pages. Then comes www, followed by the domain name, which tells you where the web site can be found.

http://www.apple.com

YAHOOLIGANS!®

the Web Guide for Kids

Arts & Entertainment

Around the World

Computers & Games

Web sites
When you open a web site, the first page you will see is the home page. A home page such as Yahooligans! has a list of the site's contents, which will to help you to navigate your way around the web site. Yahooligans! is a site that acts as an Internet guide for young people. You can find all kinds of subjects, varying from information on arts and entertainment to computers and games. With a home computer and Internet access it is possible to answer such questions as 'What is the capital of Peru?' or 'Who was the first person in space?' in just a few minutes. There are web sites devoted to information on any subject you can think of, as well as commercial sites, which seem destined to change forever the way we do business.

Search engines

Many people find that the Internet is one of the best ways to find out information. Unfortunately, searching the Internet for specific information can be difficult, because there are so many web sites that you might have to search through. In this situation, a search engine may be a handy tool. Yahoo! is just one of many search engines on the Internet. Simply type in your question in the text box on screen, and let Yahoo! do the work for you. Yahoo! also presents information in organized categories, such as science and sports, to make searching for information even easier. Just click on the category link and pick one of the sites. Despite their name, search engines are not really engines at all. They are a piece of automated software that search web sites, making a note of the essential information such as the site title, address and often the first line of text on the web site. This information is stored on a huge database, which can be accessed by the Internet user.

Servers

All the web pages on the www are stored on large, powerful computers known as servers. The picture to the right shows the main server room for the www in Geneva, Switzerland. Servers belong to the many different Internet Service Providers (ISPs). When a user types in the unique address of a web site using an Internet browser, the browser links to the server where the web site is stored and sends a GET command. It then tells the server to send all of the information needed to reconstruct the web pages on your own computer.

Web games

There are many Net game web sites, and some allow you to download games on to your computer and play with people from all around the world. Some games need special software called a plug-in, which may make the graphics of the game look much more realistic. You can download plug-ins free from games web sites.

WEB CULTURE

MUSEUMS house some of the world's finest collections of antiquities and art, but their one disadvantage is that they are spread out all over the world, so it is difficult to get to all of them. Thanks to the World Wide Web, however, you can see museums such as the Metropolitan Museum of Art in New York on your computer screen. Most museums have their own web sites, which include pictures of the galleries and the exhibits they contain. Some web sites allow you to take a 'virtual tour' of the galleries, and you can zoom in to take a closer look at the exhibits. One of the most popular web sites of this type is that of the Louvre Museum in Paris, France (http://www.louvre.fr).

See Paris

When you visit the Louvre's web site, this is the image that you see. It is just as if you are visiting for real. In the 1990s, large parts of the Louvre were reconstructed to make the museum more accessible to visitors. The ground level entrance to the museum was relocated to the central courtyard, called the Cour Napoléon, and was crowned by a steel-and-glass pyramid designed by US architect I. M. Pei.

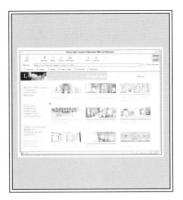

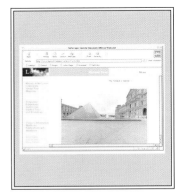

1 Open your Internet browser and connect to the Internet. Type in the web site address of the Louvre (http://www.louvre.fr). Click on the words 'Discover Our Virtual Tour'.

2 A new page offers you choices of different areas of the museum that you might want to visit. Choose 'Architectural Views' to see the huge glass pyramid.

3 You need to download Quick-Time to view the pictures. Type http://www.quicktime.com. Follow the instructions. Then click on the icon next to 'Pyramid at daytime 1'.

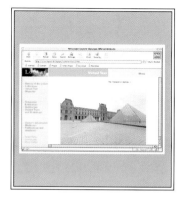

4 When the picture appears, look at the buildings by holding the mouse button down and dragging it over the picture. The picture moves to show you different views.

5 You can see the courtyard and the pyramid from different sides, as if you were walking round it. If you can't go to Paris to see it for yourself, this is the next best thing!

6 Return to the main menu and click on 'Paintings Galleries'. See the *Mona Lisa* by Leonardo da Vinci in the *Salle des Etats*. Move around and zoom in and out using the mouse.

7 The Egyptian Antiquities Galleries are also good to look at. Again, use your mouse to move around the gallery and look at the exhibits close up.

8 You can also browse round a 'virtual shop', which sells cards, posters and books about some of the things you have seen in the museum.

London museums online

The Victoria and Albert Museum in London in the UK is the world's largest museum of decorative arts, containing over 140 galleries of photography, sculpture, fashion, furniture and painting. Many of the works of art can be viewed online, through the museum's web site. Access the web site by typing in www.vam.ac.uk. This takes you to the museum's home page. You can then choose to explore one of the galleries by pressing your mouse on the 'Explorer' box. Not only will you be able to look at the works of art on the web site, but you can also find more information about them. Other web pages contain pictures of the museum's galleries, and you can also access the museum shop and buy reproductions of some of the pieces of art.

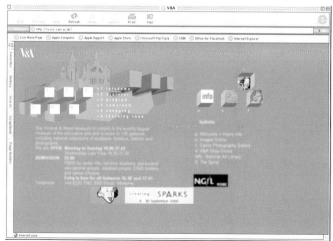

COMPUTERS IN EVERYDAY LIFE

COMPUTERS are used in all areas of our lives. They are found in shops, libraries, offices and in our homes. Most simple electronic machines, such as washing machines, microwave ovens and telephones, contain some kind of computer technology. Even a digital watch contains microchips. Some people worry that we are becoming too dependent on computer technology. Most, though, admit that computers make many things a lot easier and faster. It is amazing to think that computers were almost unheard of only 50 years ago. Today, almost everyone's lives are affected by computers in some form or another.

Bar codes

Many libraries use bar-code scanners that electronically scan bar codes printed on all their books. Bar codes consist of a number of parallel lines and spaces, which the reader scans and feeds back to the library's main computer. The bar code represents lots of data about the book, for example, its author, publisher and when it was published. This computer keeps a record of all this data. The computer also records who has borrowed the book and when they borrowed it, so the library staff will know when the books are due to be returned.

Computer-aided clothing

A clothing production designer uses computer-aided design (CAD) software to transfer the paper patterns seen at the lower left of the picture on to the computer screen. The shapes, or 'nest', of patterns together form a single garment. CAD helps the production designer to check the different sizes and shapes of clothing before they are manufactured. CAD is used in many areas of industry. Systems generally consist of a computer with one or more work stations, featuring video monitors and interactive graphics-input devices.

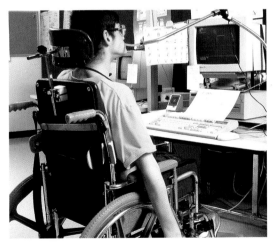

Computers and disabled people

This man is unable to use his arms, but he can still operate a computer by using a mouthpiece. Computers have made the lives of disabled people much easier than before. For example, the homes of people who have difficulty moving around can be set up so that many tasks, such as turning on a light switch, can be done using their computer.

Tracking flights
The air traffic control tower at Los Angeles Airport in the USA uses an array of computerized equipment to keep track of the positions of hundreds of aircraft. Air traffic is increasing every day. The technology used by air traffic controllers and pilots to avoid collisions and bad weather has had to become more sophisticated.

Medicine
A doctor uses a digital camera to photograph a man's eye for keeping with his medical records. The resulting image is displayed on the computer screen and is kept for analysis by other doctors. Specialist doctors who may live far away can be consulted. This enables instant response and saves on travel costs.

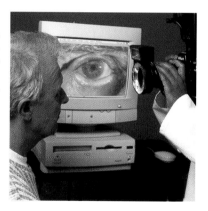

Computer banking
Plastic bank cards are used to obtain cash from ATMs (automated teller machines or cash machines). Credit and debit cards, often called electronic money or plastic money, are also used to pay for goods without using real money. People can even access their bank accounts on the Internet to transfer money between accounts and pay bills.

Growth of the Internet
Today, over 50 million people around the world own a personal computer. Soon, using the Internet will become as common as using the telephone. Even those people who do not have their own computer, or who are travelling, can find one to use. Many libraries have computers that can be used for free. Internet cafés, where you pay to connect to the Internet, are opening up all over the world. Today, you do not even have to own a computer to use the World Wide Web. Televisions and telephones have already been developed that connect to the Internet.

HEALTH AND ORGANIZATION

IT is essential to organize the space around your computer so you can use it properly. Keep all your papers in files and make sure your desk is tidy so you can use your keyboard easily and see the screen clearly to prevent muscle and eye strain. The project on the opposite page shows you how to make some files to help keep your work tidy.

Store your floppy disks and CDs in their covers when you are not using them to keep them clean and safe from scratches. The disks can also be affected by magnets, so do not put them on objects such as speakers, which have magnets in them. Positioning your computer is also important. If there is too much light shining on the screen, the glare will make it hard to see what you are doing.

Sitting positi
You mus
comfortably w
using a compu
Adjust the hei
of your sea
look dow
the screen
always keep y
back straight. T
regular brea
you are usir
computer f
long ti

Eye strain
Staring at a computer screen for long periods of time is not good for you, because it will cause you to strain your eyes. Here are some eye exercises you can do to help prevent eye strain.

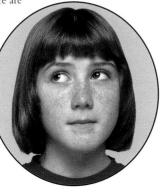

1 Keeping your head still, first move your eyes so that they are looking at the top right corner of the room.

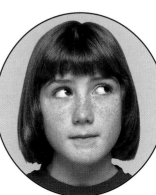

2 Relax them for a moment. Then move your eyes to look at the top left corner of the room.

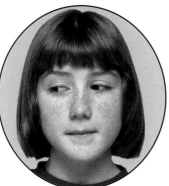

3 Relax again. Now move your eyes to look at the bottom right corner of the room.

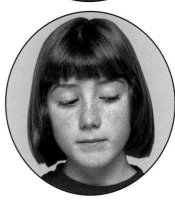

4 Relax once more. Finally, move your eyes to look at the bottom left corner of the room.

MAKING YOUR OWN FOLDERS

You will need:
one large piece and some small pieces of coloured paper, black marker pen.

1 Take the large piece of paper. Fold it in half and flatten the crease. Make sure the corners meet. Fold the other pieces of coloured paper in the same way.

2 You will end up with one large folder and four smaller ones. Draw a symbol on each folder to show what will be kept in it. You could either copy those above, or design your own.

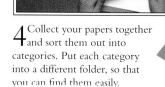

3 For instance, you could draw an envelope on your letters folder, a paint palette for your paintings and drawings, a CD for your music homework, or a book for your essays

4 Collect your papers together and sort them out into categories. Put each category into a different folder, so that you can find them easily.

5 Now put each small folder in the large one. This system of keeping things in folders is the one used by most computers. The large folder represents your computer's hard disk. The smaller folders represent the individual folders for different subjects.

6 To make a new folder on your computer, go to File in the menu bar and select New Folder if you are using a Mac or Folder if you are using a PC. A new folder will be created with the name bar highlighted ready for you to type in its name. Your work will be organized, so that you can find it easily.

CHANGING LIFESTYLES

COMPUTERS are becoming smaller, faster and more powerful all the time. Microprocessors have developed very rapidly in the last ten years, and it looks as if they will continue to do so. Data storage is improving all the time. In a few years, huge amounts of data will be stored on tiny pocket-size computers. Computers will become so small that they will be incorporated into the clothes that we wear. In fact, they have changed human life so much in recent years that it is difficult to imagine how they will be used in the future.

Growth of the Internet
Televisions and telephones that connect to the Internet are already in production. This is a WAP (wireless application protocol) phone, which means the user can access the Internet without connecting to a normal telephone line.

Computer glasses
This man is wearing an i-glass. It is a head-mounted display unit that links up to a tiny personal computer. Information is displayed as three-dimensional images on a colour monitor in front of the man's eyes. Sound is heard through earphones. Data is inputted into the computer using a hand-held keyboard, a microphone or cameras attached to the man's clothing. This is truly mobile computing.

Computerized clothing
These futuristic outfits were designed by a team of fashion designers and computer scientists. The red outfit has a solar panel in the hat, which powers a mobile telephone. The chest brooch contains a device to stop the woman getting lost, while the kneepads light up so that she can see where she is walking in the dark. The silver outfit can receive e-mail, which is played through earphones or projected on to the glasses.

Wrist camera

The world's first mini digital wrist camera, the Casio WQV-1, was launched in January 2000. The camera can store up to 100 images, which can be viewed on the watch's screen. The images can then be stored, deleted or downloaded on to a PC for editing and archiving using the latest infra-red technology.

FOODSTORE.COM

SEARCH

bananas

DEPARTMENTS

bread and cakes

breakfast cereals

canned goods

dairy

delicatessen

fruit & vegetables

jams and preserves

pasta and grains

ADD TO BASKET?

apples, cooking

bananas

grapes, seedless

oranges

pineapple

Internet shopping

Foodstore.com, shown above, is a fictional web site, but from the picture you can imagine just how easy it is to shop online. Just type in what you want to buy, and add it to your shopping basket. When paying for products on the Internet, you type your credit card details in to a secure form. This is checked by the Internet retailer, who will then arrange for the goods to be delivered to your door.

New working lifestyles

Once it was thought that people who worked together had to be in the same place. Today, the Internet allows people from all over the world to work together. By using video conferencing, they can see each other on their computer monitors, and they can also have a live conversation.

Movies on a disc

Sony's new Digital Versatile Disc (DVD) player allows you to watch the latest feature films on a disc the size of a conventional CD. DVDs may contain a combination of video, audio and computer data, but the advantage lies in the fact that they can hold up to seven times as much data as a typical CD.

GLOSSARY

A

aperture A hole behind the lens which can be adjusted to let more or less light on to the film.

application Computer software designed for a specific type of activity, such as word-processing or graphics.

APS (Advanced Photographic System) camera Camera that allows you to change the format for individual shots.

artificial Not achieved by natural means.

astrology The belief that human lives are affected by the ways in which the planets and stars behave.

auger A large tool shaped like a corkscrew, for boring holes in the ground.

autofocus A feature on a camera which automatically adjusts the lens position to make sure a scene is in focus.

axle A bar which joins wheels together. Axles turn on bearings.

B

belt drive A device that uses a belt to transfer a drive from one pulley to another. Many sewing machines have belt drives.

bevelled gears Gears with teeth set at an angle.

bifocal Having two points of focus.

binary code The digital code computers use, made up of two numbers, '0' and '1'.

bionic machine A machine that acts like a living thing.

bit The smallest amount of computer information such as a 0 or 1 in binary code.

bitmap An image that is built out of tiny dots of different colour and tone. They can be edited dot by dot.

block and tackle A device that uses two sets of pulley blocks to help raise very heavy weights.

browser A piece of software such as Netscape Navigator and Internet Explorer, that finds and displays web pages.

byte One letter or number in binary code. A byte is 8 bits.

C

camera obscura A darkened box or room in which images of outside objects are projected.

capstan wheel A revolving barrel in which the effort is applied by pushing against long horizontal levers.

CD-ROM (compact disc read-only memory) A disk similar to an audio CD that stores data that can only be read.

cellular Things built out of single units (cells) joined together to make a whole.

chain drive A device that uses a chain to transfer a drive from one gear wheel to another.

chemical A pure substance present in the Earth that can be formed by or react to other substances.

compressed air Air that has been squashed into a smaller volume than usual.

construction machine A machine, such as a digger, used on building sites.

converging (or convex) lens A lens that curves outwards, like a magnifying glass.

CPU (central processing unit) The 'brain' of the computer, which contains the processing chips and electronic circuits.

crankshaft An axle that has parts of it bent at right angles so that the up-and-down motion is turned into circular motion.

D

data Pieces of information.

database An organized store of information.

depth of field The distance in focus between the nearest and farthest parts of a scene.

desktop publishing (DTP) Creating printed material using a desktop computer and page-layout software.

desktop The main interface of the operating system that is shown on the screen after start up and before any programs are running.

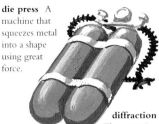

die press A machine that squeezes metal into a shape using great force.

diffraction The scattering of light rays.

diffuser A filter than can be attached to a camera to soften light from a flash.

digital Any device that utilizes binary code is described as being digital. All computers are digital.

digital camera A camera that takes electronic images which are downloaded on to a computer to be viewed.

disk drive The device that holds, reads and writes on to a disk.

diverging lens Lens that causes light rays to spread outwards.

document An electronic file.

downloading Copying files from the Internet to your computer's hard disk.

draughtsman A person who makes drawings for specific purposes such as building a new house.

driveshaft The bar that is turned by an engine to drive wheels.

drug A substance used for fighting illness.

E

effort The force applied to a lever or other simple machine to move a load.

electricity The form of energy produced by the movement of electrons (charged particles) in atoms.

electron A tiny part of an atom that has an electric charge.

electronic circuit A circuit that consists of transistors.

e-mail (electronic mail) A way of sending messages from one computer to another using the Internet.

endoscope A camera attachment that goes inside the body to take pictures of internal organs relaying the images to a computer screen.

engine A device that provides turning power.

exposure time The time it takes for the camera to take a picture.

exposures Photographs on a film.

F

fax machine A machine that can send and receive words and pictures that have been changed into electrical messages.

file A document in digital form that is stored either on the computer's hard disk or on an external disk.

fill-in flash Using the flash to light up certain areas of your phototgraph, but leaving natural light in the background.

filter Transparent material fitted to a lens that alters the colour of the light or the way the light rays pass through it. Also a special effect that can be applied to a graphics image, such as a texture.

first-class lever A simple lever such as a see-saw, in which the pivot is between the two ends.

fish-eye lens A very wide-angle lens that collects light from 180 degrees. The centre of the scene looks much bigger.

flash A bulb attached to the camera that provides a quick burst of light so that a picture can be taken in darkness.

fleece The coat hair of animals that is spun into yarn and woven into cloth.

floppy disk A portable data-storage disk. Floppies only hold about 1.4MB of data and are useful for storing text files.

focal length The distance between the centre of a lens and the focal point – the point where light rays come together.

focal plane The area at the back of a camera where the exposed film is held flat.

focus A camera is in focus when the light rays from an object meet on the focal plane to form a sharp image of the scene.

folder A storage place for computer files. Folders can store anything from applications to your personal work.

force A push or a pull which results in an object moving faster or slower.

format The size and shape of a print and the way it can be viewed.

frame The area seen through the viewfinder of a camera.

G

gear A wheel that has teeth that mesh with another gearwheel's teeth.

gearbox A set of gearwheels of different sizes that can turn wheels at different speeds and with different mechanical advantages.

germ A micro-organism that, once it is inside the human body, can cause illness.

gigabyte One billion (a thousand million) bytes or characters.

gravity The pulling force between all masses.

groove A channel cut in a pulley wheel to keep a belt drive in place.

H

hard disk A computer's main storage disk, which holds the operating system and application files.

hardware Equipment that makes up a computer – disk drives, processor, monitor, keyboard, mouse etc.

hertz The name for the frequency of an electromagnetic wave.

home page An introductory page that contains links to other pages on a web site.

HTML (hypertext mark-up language) The computer code that makes text and graphics appear on a web site in an interactive way.

HTTP (hypertext transfer protocol) The language computers use to transfer web pages over the Internet.

hydraulics The use of water or other liquids to move pistons and other devices.

hydroelectric power Electricity generated by turbines that are driven by the force of falling water.

I

icon A tiny picture on which you click to make your computer do a task. Icons also tell you that your computer is busy.

inclined plane A slope up which heavy objects can be moved more easily than by raising them vertically.

infection An attack on cells in the body by germs that cause people to fall ill.

internal combustion engine A motor that burns petrol or diesel in cylinders to supply hot gases to push pistons.

Internet A worldwide computer network that is made up of many smaller networks of computers that can all communicate with each other.

inventor A person who finds a new way to make human knowledge useful in people's everyday lives.

ISO (International Standards Organisation) rating International rating system for film which tells you their speed.

ISP (Internet Service Provider) One of the companies through which Internet connection is made.

K

keystone The central stone in the arch of a bridge or curved part of a building.

kilobyte 1,000 characters or bytes.

L

laptop A portable computer that is powered by a rechargeable battery.

laser A device that produces an intense beam of light.

latent image Invisible image made by light hitting the silver crystals in the film.

lathe A machine that spins an object against a cutting tool.

layout The way text and pictures are arranged on a page.
leaf shutter A camera shutter that is made up of a number of plates that overlap and retract to open.

lens A transparent material curved on one or both sides. It bends rays of light and directs them on to the film.
lever A long bar that is used against a pivot to help move a heavy object.
light spectrum The colours that light can be split into.
load The weight moved by a lever or other machine.

M

macro lens A close-up lens with a very short focal length.
magnet A piece of iron or other material that attracts other pieces of iron.
mass The amount of material in an object. Mass is measured in kilograms.
mechanical advantage The number of times by which the load is greater than the effort.
megabyte (MB) One million characters or bytes.
microchip A device with thousands of electronic circuits on one silicon sliver.
micromachine A very small machine.
micro-processor A single chip containing all the elements of a computer's CPU.
microwaves Radio waves, often used to cook food quickly.

mill To grind or cut metal, stone, wood, grain etc using a machine with a turning motion.
modem (modulator/ demodulator) A device that allows computer data to be sent down a telephone line.
monitor A screen used to display the computer's visual output.
monochrome Black-and-white film or photographic paper, it shows colours as shades of black /grey.
mortar A mixture, usually of sand, cement and water, which is used in building to fix bricks or blocks of stone firmly together.
mould A kind of fungus in the form of a woolly growth that is often found on food.
mouse A computer input device that translates its movements into the movement of the cursor on the screen. It received its name because it is roughly mouse-size and has a 'tail' wire that links the device to the computer.
multimedia A combination of text, graphics, sound, animation and video.

N

nanotechnology The study of how to make and use micromachines and other very tiny devices.
negative The photographic image on the developed film from which photographic prints are made. The colours in a negative are reversed, so that dark areas appear to be light and light areas appear to be dark.
neon A gas found in the air that glows when it has an electric current passed through it.
Nobel Prize Prizes that are awarded each year to eminent world scientists, writers and peacemakers.
nut A piece of metal, usually hexagonal, that fits on to a screw.

O

organism An animal, plant or fungus.
OS (operating system) The main piece of software that is needed by all computers to allow them to function properly.
over-exposure A photograph that looks washed out as too much light from the subject has hit the film.

P

panning Moving a camera to follow a moving subject.
pendulum A swinging mass hanging from a thread or bar. Pendulums were used in old-fashioned clocks to help keep regular time.
piston A disc or cylinder that fits snugly inside another cylinder, but is still able to move up and down.
pivot The point about which a lever turns.
pixels Tiny dots that make up a digital image.
plastic A durable, synthetic material that is easily moulded or shaped.
plough A large blade used in farming that cuts through soil and turns it over.
pneumatics The use of air or other gases to move pistons and other devices.
Polaroid camera A type of camera that can take and develop individual prints immediately as it has developing chemicals inside.
positive A print or slide showing a photographic image with colours or tones which are the same as in the original scene.
power station A group of buildings that house powerful machines which convert energy from fuels like coal into electric power.
primary colours There are three primary colours – red, blue and green or cyan, magenta and yellow. When these colours are mixed together, they make any other colour.
prism Specially shaped glass used to split white light into the spectrum, or to reflect and light rays away from their normal path.

pulley A wheel over which a rope or chain can be slung to help move heavy objects.

pylon A tall structure of metal struts designed to carry electric power lines high above the ground.

R

RAM (random access memory) Computer memory that holds data temporarily until the computer is switched off.

ratchet A device that allows movement in one direction only.

reflectors A sheet of reflecting material or umbrella used to light a subject.

refraction The bending of light rays.

reservoir Resources, such as water, that are frequently stored to use in times of scarcity.

resolution The number of shades of colour a computer monitor can display.

reversal film or slide film A film that when developed gives a positive image, known as a transparency.

ROM (read-only memory) Computer memory that holds information permanently.

rotor A device that rotates on its axis.

S

scaffold A skeleton structure made out of poles put up to help in erecting or repairing a building.

scanner A device used to scan data.

screw A spiral thread on a metal bar that can be used to join objects or raise a load.

screw jack A device that uses a screw to help raise a weight from below.

second–class lever A lever, such as a wheelbarrow, in which the pivot is at the end of the bar.

sewage Human and animal waste mixed with water.

shutter Camera mechanism, which controls the amount of time light is allowed to fall on to the lens.

silicon A non-metal which as an oxide forms quartz.

silicon chip A small piece of silicon on which are etched thousands of tiny electrical circuits.

SLR (Single Lens Reflex) A design of camera that allows you to see exactly what the lens sees.

software Applications that enable computers to carry out specific tasks.

spoke A piece of metal that joins the rim of a wheel to the hub.

steel A hard, long-lasting metal made by blowing pure oxygen into molten iron.

stills photography Photography showing a single image (as opposed to photography taking moving images with a cine camera).

synthetic An artificially produced version of a natural substance.

T

telegraph A device that receives messages sent as electrical impulses.

telephoto lens A lens which takes a close-up picture of a distant scene.

third–class lever A lever in which the effort is applied between the pivot and the load.

tooth The part of a gear wheel that fits into a chain in a chain drive.

transistor A miniature device which amplifies or switches electric signals.

treadmill A wheel that can be turned by an animal or a person walking on the inner rim of the wheel.

tungsten film Film designed to be used inside. It reproduces light from a lamp or indoor light as if it was white so the pictures do not look yellowy.

turbine A machine in which angled blades turn water or air to create power.

type The metal letter shapes used until the late 1970s to print books.

U

under–exposure A photograph that looks dark because not enough light rays from the subject are hitting the film.

URL (uniform resource locator) The address of a web site on the Internet.

V

valve A device that allows liquids or gases to flow in one direction only.

viewfinder The window you look through to see what will be in your photograph.

virtual reality (VR) The process by which computers are used to create an artificial place that looks real.

volt A way of measuring the strength of an electric current.

W

web page A computer document written in HTML and linked to other web pages.

web site A collection of web pages.

wide-angle lens Lens with an angle of view that is wider than normal for the human eye.

winch A wheel on which rope is wound at the top of a framework, in order to lift heavy weights.

WWW (World Wide Web) A huge collection of information that is available on the Internet.

X

X-ray A kind of electromagnetic wave that passes through the body and is picked up on specially prepared film.

X-ray photographs Pictures taken of the inside of our bodies, used to show broken bones.

Z

Zip disk A portable data storage disk that comes in two storage sizes – 100MB and 250MB.

zoom lens A lens with a variable focal length, which is altered to get close to a subject.

INDEX

A

address books, computers 212, 234
air pumps 104, 106–7
air traffic control 243
aircraft 10–11, 60–1, 70, 112–13, 124
alchemy 48
anaesthetics 25
Analytical Engine 121, 194
androids 125
animal power 101, 116, 119
animation 180–3, 221
aperture 150–5
Appert, Nicolas 21
AppleMac 195, 198, 204–5
applications 204–5
APS 145, 153, 175
Archimedes 93, 118
Arkwright, Richard 19
Atansoff, John 195
ATMs 243
augers 86, 117–18
autofocus cameras 138–9, 172–3
axes 71, 86, 98
axles 72, 80–3, 90, 108, 112

B

Babbage, Charles 62, 121, 194
back lighting 153, 166, 168
Baird, John Logie 44
balance scale 74, 78–9
baling machines 117
bar codes 242
batteries 26, 102
Bell, Alexander Graham 11, 34
belt drives 94–7
Benz, Karl 59
Berliner, Emile 35
Berners-Lee, Tim 238
Bessemer, Sir Henry 48
bicycles 95, 112
binary code 196–7, 200, 220, 232
binoculars 39
bits, binary code 197, 201
black-and-white film 142–4, 156, 170
block and tackle 90–3
body parts 72, 76–7
bolts 86–7
books 214, 228
bottle openers 87, 108
Bramah, Joseph 16
bread 20, 22
bridges 14–15
bronze 48
browsers 235
Brueghel the Elder, Pieter 114
Brunel, Isambard Kingdom 103
building machines 71, 90, 114–15
buildings 12–16
bytes, binary code 197, 201

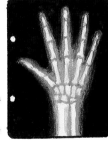

C

calculators 62–3, 66, 70–1, 194
camera obscura 134–5
cameras 42–3, 129–87
cans 108, 110
capstan wheels 82–3
cars 70–1, 81, 102–3, 112–13, 122–5, 200
cartoons 180–1
cassettes, film 132, 144
CDs 35, 190, 200–1, 232–3
CD-ROMs 192–3, 228
chain drives 94–5
chemistry 23, 48, 50–1, 142
chisels 86, 114
cine cameras 178–81
cinema 42–3
circuits 103, 120, 126
clocks 52–5, 95
close-up shots 133, 162–3, 165
clothes 10, 17–19, 66, 246
codes, computers 196–7
Colossus 195
colour 170–1, 186, 218–19
colour film 142–5, 157
communications 30–7
compacts 132–3, 148, 161–2, 164
compasses 56
compressors 105
computer-aided design 242
computers 62–7, 70–1, 120, 189–247
control discs 126–127
cooking 20–1
corkscrews 87
cranes 71, 84, 91–92, 106, 114–115
crystals, film 142–4
cybercafés 235, 243
cybersphere, virtual reality 231

D

Daguerre, Louis 42
dental drills 104
depth of field, photography 150–1, 154, 172
desktop publishing (DTP) 214–17
developing film 142–3, 146, 156
die presses 122
Diesel, Rudolf 58
diggers 71, 86, 104–5, 114
digital cameras 35, 47, 186, 214
disabled people, computer aids 242
disks, computer 190, 200, 202–3
disposable cameras 132, 141, 174–5
dogs, robotic 124
domestic machines 70, 108–11
drills 104–5, 116, 123
drives, computer 190
driving force 87
DVDs 190, 247

E

e-mails 120, 205, 234–7
Eckert, Presper 195
Edison, Thomas 26, 34, 42
effort 76–8
Einthoven, Willem 25

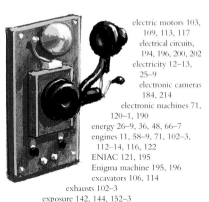

electric motors 103, 109, 113, 117
electrical circuits, 194, 196, 200, 202
electricity 12–13, 25–9
electronic cameras 184, 214
electronic machines 71, 120–1, 190
energy 26–9, 36, 48, 66–7
engines 11, 58–9, 71, 102–3, 112–14, 116, 122
ENIAC 121, 195
Enigma machine 195, 196
excavators 106, 114
exhausts 102–3
exposure 142, 144, 152–3

F

f-numbers 150–1
fabrics 18–19
Faraday, Michael 13, 26, 42
fax machines 46
fermentation 22–3
film 131–2, 142–5, 156, 172, 178–9
filters 145, 170–1, 220
fire-fighting 106–7
fish-eye lenses 160
fishing rods 76–7
fixer 143, 146, 156
flash, photography 131, 166–9
Fleming, Alexander 23–4
flight 60–1
floppy disks 190, 200–1, 244
focal length 150–1, 160–5
focal plane 138, 148, 154–5, 160
focus138–9, 150–1, 172–3
folders 245
fonts, typefaces 209
food 20–2
force measurers 88–9
Ford, Henry 59
fork-lift trucks 105
formats, film 144–5
Fox Talbot, William 157
frame filters 171
Franklin, Benjamin 38
front lighting 166
future machines 124–5

G

Galileo Galilei 38–9, 54
games, computer 224–7, 231, 224, 239
gas 12, 21, 27, 102
gears 94–7, 108, 112–13
Goodyear, Charles 49
graphics, computers 205, 218–23, 228–30
Gutenberg, Johannes 30

H

hairdryers 109
hammers 70, 76–7
hard disks, computers 191, 198, 200–3

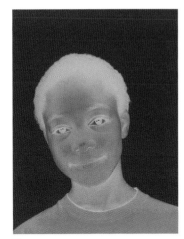

ACKNOWLEDGEMENTS

The publishers would like to thank the following children, and their parents, for modelling in this book:

Nana Addae, Rees Arnott-Davis, Emily Askew, Sara Barnes, Emma Beardmore, Daniel Bill, Maria Bloodworth, Anum Butt, David Callega, Jessica Castaneda, Liliana Conceicia, Gary Cooper, Diane Cuffe, Sheree Cunningham-Kelly, Joe Davies, Aaron Dumetz, Louisa El-Jonsafi, Laurence de Freitas, Alistair Fulton, Ricky Edward Garrett, Anton Goldbourne, Eleshia Henry, Sung-Kiet Hoang, Sasha Howarth, Sarah Ann Kenna, Lee Knight, Shadae Lawrence, Jon Leming, Alex Lindblom-Smith, Sophie Lindblom-Smith, Laura Masters, Jessica Moxley, Aidan Mulcahy, Fiona Mulcahy, Seán Mulcahy, Robert Nunez, Ifunanya Obi, Joshua Parris, Kim Peterson, Emily Preddie, Elen Rhys, Jamie Rosso, Paul Snow, Kisanet Tesfay, Nicola Twiner and Joe Westbrook.

PICTURE CREDITS

b= bottom, t= top, c= centre, l= left, r= right

INVENTIONS AND DISCOVERIES

Advertising Archives: 43br; Ancient Art and Architecture Ltd: 16tl, 48tr; Barnaby's Picture Library: 24br; BBC Photographic Library: 45tl; Bridgeman Art Library: 20tl, 48bl, 54tl; Paul Brierley: 49tr; Contour Colour Ltd: 10br; Corbis Images: 11br, 12tr, 12bl, 17r, 18tl, 19bl, 19br, 27br, 31bl, 48br, 52bl, 56br, 57cr, 59tr, 60tr, 60cr, 61c, 62tr, 63br; E. T. Archive: 9cr, 12br, 16bl, 18bl, 20bl, 30tr, 31br, 35tl, 49tl, 54tl, 57tr, 58bl; Mary Evans Picture Library: 33bl, 38tr, 39tl; G. D. A. Ltd: 21cr; Hoover European Appliance Group: 17c; Hulton Getty Picture Library: 42bl, 43t, 49b, 59c, 61t; Mercedes-Benz: 59b; National Maritime Museum: 53tr, 56bl, 57t; Peter Newark's American Pictures: 58br; Oxford Scientific Picture Library: 13tl; Panasonic: 45br; Ann Ronan Picture Library: Endpaper, 11bl, 21t, 26tl, 26bl, 26br, 27tl, 30br, 31tl, 34tl, 41b; Science and Society Picture Library: 7, 8, 9tr, 10bl, 13tr, 14tr, 16br, 17l, 18br, 19tl, 19tr, 20br, 21cl, 23b, 24tl, 25tl, 27tr, 34bl, 35bl, 38bl, 38br, 39c, 39br, 40tl, 42tl, 42br, 43cr, 44tr, 44br, 52br, 53c, 53bl, 53br, 56tl, 58tr, 59tl, 60cl, 62bl, 62br; Science Photo Library: 9bl, 25tl, 25bl, 25br, 27bl, 63cl, 63cl, 66tr, 66bl, 66br, 67tl, 67tr, 67br; Spectrum Colour Library: 22tl, 46tr; Tony Stone Images: 28tr, 50tr; T. R. H. Pictures:

9bc, 57b, 61bl, 61br; Zefa Pictures: 21b, 45bl.

MACHINES

Ancient Egypt Picture Library: 84tr, 84b; Bruce Coleman Ltd: 98bl, 98br, 99tl; /M Borchi 81tr; /G Clyde 91c; /Gryniewicz 122bl; /J Jurka 77c; /H Lange 71tr; /N McAllister 81cl; /HP Merton 123bl; Ecoscene: 98c, 115bl; /N Hawkes 85bl, 114bl; /W Lawler 86cl; /M Maidment 117tl; /Towse 118tr; E. T. Archive: 81tl, 90b, 112tr, 114tr, 119bl, 121t; Mary Evans Picture Library: 95br, 98tr; Holt Studios: /I Belcher 116bl; /A Burridge 88c, 119br; /N Cattlin 114br, 116br, 116tr, 117tr; /J Hall 86c; /W Harinck 115tr; /P McCullagh 73bl; /P Peacock 122tl; /I Spence 91bl, 117c; ICCE: /M Boulton 71bl; Image Bank: 85tr; Powerstock: /Alex Bartel 99bl; Quadrant: 74br, 81bl, 81c, 85tl, 90bl, 91bl, 103tr, 105c, 107bc, 113br, 115c; Planet Earth Pictures: 71bl, 85br; Science Photo Library: 124cl, 127c; /M Bond 94c, 113t; /M Fielding 71t; /V Fleming 95br; /P Fletcher 102tr; /Food & Drug Administration 122b; /A Hart-Davis 91tr; /S Horrel 99br; /M Kage 124bl; /J King-Holmes 104tr; /S Ogden 125bl; /A Pasieka 96c; /Rosenfield Images Ltd 123br; /V Steger 122c, 124cr, 125cl; /US Department of Energy 126tr; Science Museum/Science & Society Picture Library: 80br, 95bl, 102bl, 103c, 109tr, 113c, 120br, 120bl; Tony Stone Images: 105tl; /Agri Press 78bl; /W Bilenduke 106c; /S Egan 71c; /B Lewis 117br; /P McArthur 109bl; /A Meshkinger 109c; /C Thatcher 109tl; /T Vine 92c; Superstock: 70tr, 71tl, 72br, 92tr, 99c, 115br; Zefa Pictures 105br.

CAMERAS

The Publishers would like to thank Keith Johnson and Pelling Ltd for the loan of props.
Aardman Animations Ltd: 180br; Allsport: 149tr; Mary Evans Picture library: 130bl, 178c; Galaxy Picture Library: 185tr; Tim Grabham: 181br; Nigel Cattlin/Holt studios international: 163d, u, 179bl, 184bt, 187tl; Robin Kerrod: 185tl;

Microscopix: 184c; Laurence Gould/Oxford Scientific Films: 174r; Scott Camazine: 185b; Chris Oxlade: 173tr; Papilio Photographic: 178bl, 187bl, br, c; The Projection Box: 180tl, 182tr; Science Photo Library: Phillipe Plailly 175bl; Sinclair Stammers 184tl; Francoise Sauze 185cl; George Bernard: 185cr; L Weinstein, NASA: 184bl; Science and Society Photo Library: 135c, 149tr, 159tr, 180br, 183br; Sony: 178br; Tony Stone Images: 181cr; Lucy Tizard: 168tl; Zefa Pictures: 131bl, br, 160bl, 173bl, 174bl, 175t.

COMPUTERS

Air France: 197cl; Heather Angel: 216b; Austin J. Brown: 237bl, 238t; Bruce Coleman Ltd: 219; /Jane Burton: 216t; /John Cancalosi: 218; /Michael Kline: 205bl; /Gordon Langsbury: 211bl; /Hans Reinhard: 197t; /Kim Taylor: 210b, 211t, 217tr; Liz Eddison: 231tr; /Royal Aeronautical Society: 234br; Mary Evans Picture Library: 246tl, c; Mansell Collection: 246b, 237tl; Nature Photographers Ltd/Roger Tidman: 193t; Papillo Photographic: 190tr, 214bl, bc, br, 215tl; Popperfoto: 239b; Quadrant: 191t, 193br, 200tl, 220br, 221bl, br, 223tr, 227c, b, 231bl, 235tl, b, 236t, 237t, br, 238br, 239c; /Paul Bowen Photography: 231tl; /Flight International: 207br; /Flight/Wagner: 223tr; /Peter R. Foster: 235tr; /Erik Simonsen: 197cr, 239t; Rolls-Royce plc: 230br; Spacecharts: 190tr, 242t, 243tl, c, br, 244t; /NASA: 242b, 243tr; Trip: 238bl; /T. Legate: 198br; /T. Malcolm: 220t; /R. Marsh: 201bl; /Picturesque/Bill Terry: 197b; /P. Ridley: 203t; /J. Ringland: 208br; /C. Smedley: 226bl; /Streano/Havens: 227t; /TH-Foto Werbung: 202t; /Derek Thomas: 207bl; Zefa Pictures: 191bl, 193bl, 196cr, 201tl, tr, br, 203br, 207tr, 214tl, 215tr, 217tr, b, 222, 226br, 230t, 231br, 234bl, 240t, 241bl, 247b; /J. Sedlmeier: 247tr.

This edition is published by Lorenz Books

Lorenz Books is an imprint of Anness Publishing Ltd
Hermes House, 88–89 Blackfriars Road, London SE1 8HA
tel. 020 7401 2077; fax 020 7633 9499
www.lorenzbooks.com; info@anness.com

This edition distributed in the UK by The Manning Partnership Ltd, 6 The Old Dairy, Melcombe
Road, Bath BA2 3LR; tel. 01225 478 444; fax 01225 478 440; sales@manning-partnership.co.uk

This edition distributed in the USA and Canada by National Book Network, 4501 Forbes
Boulevard, Suite 200, Lanham, MD 20706;
tel. 301 459 3366; fax 301 429 5746; www.nbnbooks.com

This edition distributed in Australia by Pan Macmillan Australia, Level 18, St Martins Tower,
31 Market St, Sydney, NSW 2000;
tel. 1300 135 113; fax 1300 135 103; customer.service@macmillan.com.au

This edition distributed in New Zealand by David Bateman Ltd,
30 Tarndale Grove, Off Bush Road, Albany, Auckland;
tel. (09) 415 7664; fax (09) 415 8892

Publisher: Joanna Lorenz
Managing Editor, Children's Books: Gilly Cameron Cooper
Project Editors: Jenni Davidson, Joy Wotton
Additional Design: Roger McWilliam, Michael Morey
Illustrators: Stephen Bennington, Peter Bull, Richard Hawke, Nick Hawken, Caroline Reeves,
Guy Smith, Clive Spong, Linden Artists
Photographer: John Freeman
Stylists: Marion Elliot, Melanie Williams
Designers: Caroline Grimshaw, Mike Leaman, Joyce Mason, Caroline Reeves, Ann Samuel,
Miranda Snow
Production Controller: Wendy Lawson

1 3 5 7 9 10 8 6 4 2

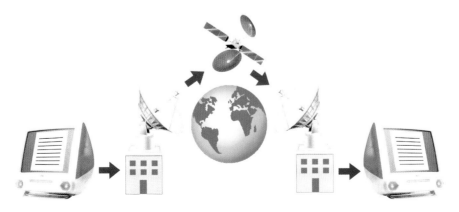

NOTES

N OTES

NOTES

NOTES

NOTES

NOTES

Notes

NOTES